JUSTICE
★and★
DISSENT

*Ready-to-Use Materials
for Recreating Five
Great Trials
in American History*

GARY PARKER SCHOALES

**THE CENTER FOR APPLIED
RESEARCH IN EDUCATION**
West Nyack, New York 10994

©1995 by

THE CENTER FOR APPLIED
RESEARCH IN EDUCATION

West Nyack, New York

10 9 8 7 6 5 4 3 2

Library of Congress Cataloging-in-Publication Data

Schoales, Gary Parker.
  Justice and dissent: ready-to-use materials for recreating five great trials in
American history / Gary Parker Schoales: illustrated by Virginia Schoales and
Dover Publications, Inc.
    p. cm.
  Includes bibliographical references.
  ISBN 0-87628-752-6
  1. Law—Study and teaching (Secondary)—United States—Handbooks, manuals,
etc. 2. Trials—Study and teaching (Secondary)—United States—Handbooks, man-
uals, etc. I. Title.
KF283.S34   1994
347.73'7'071273—dc20
[347.3077071273]   94-28394
                                                                       CIP

ISBN 0-87628-752-6

THE CENTER FOR APPLIED
RESEARCH IN EDUCATION
BUSINESS & PROFESSIONAL DIVISION
A division of Simon & Schuster
West Nyack, New York 10995

Printed in the United States of America

DEDICATION

for Ginger

ABOUT THE AUTHOR

Gary Parker Schoales received his B.A. degree in American History from The College of William and Mary, and his M.A. degree in History and Education from Boston College.

For more than twenty years, Mr. Schoales has had a variety of national and international experiences in the education field. He has taught at Arlington and Brookline high schools in Massachusetts, the Copenhagen International School in Denmark, the Anglo-American School of Moscow in the former Soviet Union, and the American Overseas School of Rome in Italy. He is currently employed by Georgetown Day School in Washington, D.C.

He has made numerous presentations for the European Council of International Schools and the National Council for the Social Studies on topics related to active-learning strategies, including two recent workshops given in Birmingham, England and Rome, Italy entitled "The Student's Court: Conducting a Historical Simulation Trial in Your Classroom."

Mr. Schoales has also been involved with curriculum-development projects for the state of New York, the Arlington (Massachusetts) Public Schools, the Anglo-American School of Moscow, and the National Council for the Social Studies in cooperation with the Government of Greece. These projects involved extensive travel in India, the People's Republic of China, the former Yugoslavia, Greece, and the former Soviet Union. In addition, Mr. Schoales is the co-author of *Boston During the Colonial Period* (Cambridge, MA: Abt Associates, 1979).

ABOUT THIS RESOURCE

Justice and Dissent provides teachers and students with extensive resource materials and clear directions so that together they can recreate five of the most exciting and controversial trials in U.S. history: The Salem Witch Trials of 1692; Rex vs. Captain Preston, et. al. (the Boston Massacre); the Trial of Simeon Bushnell (violation of the Fugitive Slave Law of 1850); the Trial of Captain Wirz (Andersonville prison camp commander during the Civil War); and the Trial of Julius and Ethel Rosenberg and Morton Sobell (conspiracy to commit espionage during wartime). Taken together they provide an in-depth historical look at American law and how it reflected and shaped the events of the times. Each trial relies heavily on contrasting primary source information to ensure historical accuracy and to promote controversy.

These trials can be used in a variety of settings including American history, law, citizenship and drama classes, and typically appeal to students with a wide range of interests and abilities. Additionally, they provide a valuable resource for teachers needing materials not available in traditional textbooks to buttress lessons related to Colonial American History, the American Revolution, Slavery, the Civil War, Reconstruction, and the Cold War.

These trials are adaptable to a wide variety of class sizes, subject matter, and behavioral objectives. All five trials can accommodate more than thirty students or as few as fifteen. Each trial includes background information about the case, individual role sheets for each character including judge(s), defendant(s), court officials(s), members of the jury, and witnesses.

Additional features include primary source documents, illustrations, exhibits, a glossary of legal terms, a chronology, an evaluation check list, discussion questions, and a suggested bibliography for further research. There is even a subpoena form for formally enlisting the help of individuals outside the classroom.

Each trial has been thoroughly tested with a variety of students over the author's twenty years of teaching. The trials contain sufficient historical data to conduct the trial without further research, yet they are flexible enough to allow students and teachers the option for further inquiry. Each trial can be completed in a few days or more than a week, depending on the teacher's objectives. Within obvious historical limitations (for example, there were no attorneys in the Salem trials), they all follow a nearly identical format.

Recreating a historical trial can be one of the most dynamic, exciting and memorable experiences a student can have in school. A trial contains all of the necessary ingredients to introduce students to the concept of historical inquiry in the context of an active-learning environment. It challenges students to gather information, form hypotheses, and then subjects these hypotheses to critical examination. It introduces and reinforces many important skills including: public speaking, careful listening, working in groups, critical thinking, clear writing, organizing information logically, using body language with speaking, employing visual aids when presenting, evaluating evidence, recognizing the use and limitations of primary sources, and learning to identify underlying assumptions, values, biases and stereotypes.

Finally, students need to see themselves as active participants in the learning process. They need to develop awareness of how people in the past created, reacted, and adjusted to conflict and change. They need to learn empathy, the capacity to appreciate what it is like to be in someone else's position. They need to attend to the opinion of others and accept the value and importance of asking questions. And they need to develop the confidence and willingness to develop and defend moral positions that may even put them at odds with the majority.

Gary Parker Schoales

WHY RECREATE HISTORICAL TRIALS?

"Faithfulness to the truth of history involves far more than research, however patient and scrupulous, into special facts. Such facts may be detailed with the most minute exactness and yet the narrative, taken as a whole, may be unmeaning or untrue. The narrator must seek to imbue himself with the life and spirit of the time. He must study events in their bearings near and remote, in the character, habits, and manners of those who took part in them. He must be, as it were, a sharer or spectator of the action he describes."

—Francis Parkman
Autobiography

"Truth is the secret of eloquence and of virtue, the basis of moral authority; it is the highest summit of art and life."

—Henri-Frederic Amiel

A quest for the truth and justice is what these pivotal American trials are all about. They seek to make students confront the age-old questions that writers from Herodotus to Tuchman have asked about historical events: What was the temper of the times? What exactly took place? Why did it occur? Who was right? Often these questions are masked in legal rhetoric and verbiage, but the answers nearly always bring us a deeper understanding of our history. These trials mirror the issues and values of the age, and from their reflection we can see the earliest Puritan settlers confronting deep-rooted religious fears of the devil and witchcraft; the perceived tyranny of an English army of occupation; the division of a young nation over perpetual human bondage; the struggle of America to mend the wounds of its great Civil War; and the fear and hysteria unleashed by the atomic bomb and the threat of world-wide communism.

In 1692 the court of "Oyer and Terminer" began meeting to "hear and decide" the allegations of witchcraft raised by a group of adolescent girls against several women in the small Puritan community of Salem Village. Within months Puritan jails throughout New England were swollen with accused witches and wizards as the hunt for more of the "devil's agents" spun out of control. Individuals with names like Sarah Good, Rebecca Nurse and Giles Corey were accused, tried and eventually executed on evidence that today would be totally inadmissible in court. The accused had no legal council and could do little more than confess to witchcraft, or deny their guilt and be hanged.

On a cold March day in 1770 five Bostonians, part of a crowd of colonists harassing a British sentry, fell dead before the smoking muskets of a squad of "redcoats" and their Irish captain, Thomas Preston. The soldiers were indicted for premeditated murder and later tried in a Boston court, with defense council that included two of Boston's leading Patriot lawyers: John Adams and Josiah Quincy. The soldiers claimed their lives were threatened by a dangerous mob throwing ice and wielding clubs, and they only fired their Brown Bess muskets on hearing a command "fire" from Captain Preston. Patriotic views were captured shortly after by a vivid print drawn by silversmith Paul Revere. It shows Captain Preston, sword uplifted, ordering his men to fire, at point-blank range, into an unarmed group of citizens, some of whom lie bleeding on the street.

In March of 1859 thirty-seven black and white residents of the quiet college town of Oberlin, Ohio were indicted by a Federal grand jury for violating the Fugitive Slave Law of 1850. Slavecatchers had snatched one of their black residents, an escaped slave from a Kentucky farm, and were attempting to bring him back to his master. Nearly all the male citizens went to the neighboring town of Wellington to rescue him, and he was forcefully taken from his abductors. Simeon Bushnell was the first of the thirty-seven so-called "Oberlin Rescuers" to be tried. It was alleged that he drove the get-away buggy that eventually helped the fugitive ex-slave "John" reach freedom in Canada.

In 1865 Union soldiers liberated Camp Sumter in Andersonville, Georgia and revealed the shocking conditions of the prison camp. A vengeful Northern public, still reeling from the assassination of President Lincoln, demanded prompt justice. Although conditions in many Union camps were similar in brutality and deprivation, they could not compare with the nearly 13,000 deaths at Andersonville. The prison camp commander, Captain Henry Wirz, was placed on trial before a special military commission and accused of "war crimes" including premeditated murder, conspiracy to commit murder, and willfully allowing the horrible conditions to exist in Camp Sumter. As Telford Taylor, one of the primary Nuremberg prosecutors, aptly pointed out, from a factual standpoint, that the concentration camp cases of the WWII era were a throwback to the Andersonville case of the Civil War period.

In 1951 Julius and Ethel Rosenberg and Morton Sobell were indicted for espionage. It was alleged by the prosecution that they represented the iceberg tip of an enormous Communist conspiracy that had directly led to the explosion of a Russian atomic bomb. The Rosenbergs were only "discovered" as accused spies through the confession of Ethel's brother, an admitted spy, David Greenglass. The *Columbia Law Review* called their trial the "outstanding political trial of this generation."

These five trials are linked by enduring similarities: The rigidity of law versus the perceived need for exceptional individual morality; the complexities of defining crimes committed during war; the difficulties of defending oneself against charges of conspiracy; blatantly prejudicial courts; civilian versus military justice; questionable witnesses and illegal evidence; and the role of individuals outside the defined parameters of the legal system.

Both the Salem trials and the trial of Ethel and Julius Rosenberg and Morton Sobell were "witch hunts." The atmosphere surrounding the trials was one of hysteria and fear. People were not sure who was going to be accused next. In the Salem trials close relatives accused each other of witchcraft. Immediate neighbors pointed accusing fingers at people they had known all their lives. In the Rosenberg trial, David Greenglass, the major prosecution witness, testified against his own sister, Ethel Rosenberg. The accused were considered guilty by the legal establishment, and there was great pressure on them to reveal the names of others involved in the conspiracy. In both trials, confessing guilt and revealing names was a means of escaping the death penalty. The accused witches in Salem, like Tituba, who confessed were not executed, while those who maintained innocence were sent to the gallows. Similarly, the Rosenbergs steadfastly denied guilt to their death in the electric chair, even when privately assured that a confession would result in a lesser penalty. Those who admitted spying for the Soviets—Klaus Fuchs, Harry Gold and David Greenglass—received jail sentences.

Allegations and charges of "conspiracy" were echoed in all the courtrooms, not just by the Salem magistrates in 1692 or in 1951 by Judge Kaufman in the Rosenberg trial. In 1770, many Bostonians felt that the redcoat soldiers stationed in Boston prior to the so-called "Boston Massacre" were involved in a conspiracy to murder innocent citizens. In contrast, Captain Preston and his men firmly believed Patriot leaders had deliberately provoked the incident on March 5, 1770. In 1859 prosecution attorneys painted Simeon Bushnell and the rest of the so-called "Oberlin Rescuers" as obvious willing tools in an anti-slavery "conspiracy" designed to undermine the effectiveness of the Fugitive Slave Law of 1850. Six years later, in 1865, after the Civil War had finally ended the question of slavery, Captain Wirz was formally charged with "conspiring" with other Confederate officers, including his immediate superior, General Winder, to destroy the lives of Union prisoners-of-war.

The trial of the British soldiers involved in the "Boston Massacre," Simeon Bushnell and the violation of the Fugitive Slave Law of 1850, and Captain Wirz's administration of the prison camp at Andersonville dramatically spotlight the immutable question: When is an individual obliged to obey laws that he knows are illegal, illogical, or morally repugnant? In 1858 Simeon Bushnell clearly believed that the Fugitive Slave Law of 1850 was morally wrong, and he was obligated to follow a Biblically inspired "Higher Law" when it came to resistance to the institution of slavery. Similarly, Colonel William Peters, an officer in the Confederate Army during the Civil War, refused a direct order to burn the town of Chambersburg, Pennsylvania. He believed it was an illegal order that he was morally obligated to disobey. He was relieved of his command, placed under arrest, but he was never brought before a court martial. In contrast, Captain Wirz maintained throughout his trial that it was his duty to follow—without question—the orders of his superiors regarding the care and detention of Union prisoners-of-war, even when it was obvious that thousands of men in his care were dying from disease, poor sanitation, and ill treatment. Earlier, in 1770, the defense of "following orders" was used by the British soldiers accused in the "Boston Massacre." They all swore that they only fired into the largely unarmed crowd after hearing and obeying what they believed was an order to "fire" from their commanding officer, Captain Preston.

Despite claims of objectivity, Judge Kaufman intervened several times during the Rosenberg trial and asked the defendants direct questions about their Communist associations. Julius and Ethel Rosenberg were repeatedly forced into using their fifth amendment rights saying, "I refuse to answer on the grounds that it might tend to incriminate me." The magistrates in the Salem trial, in a like manner, allowed all kinds of malicious gossip to be accepted as evidence and frequently goaded witnesses into prejudicial testimony. In at least one case, that of the aged Rebecca Nurse, the magistrates were not satisfied with an innocent verdict. The case was reconsidered, a guilty verdict was pronounced and the woman was eventually hanged. Judge Willson, a known Democrat, delivered introductory and closing remarks to the jury in Bushnell's trial that were clearly biased. Additionally, it was revealed during the trial that Charles Allen, one of the jurors, was an officer of the court—a deputy marshal. The judge overruled the defense objection and a jury of twelve citizens, all Democrats, were empanelled. In the trial of Captain Wirz, it is hard today to give full credence to a military tribunal of senior Union officers trying a defeated Confederate captain for complacency in the death of nearly 13,000 Federal prisoners-of-war. Only in Captain Preston's murder trial (and that of his men) did the court go out of its way to see that the defendants received an impartial trial and they were nearly all acquitted (two soldiers were convicted of the lesser charge of manslaughter).

Individuals outside the formal legal system played significant and influential parts in the process. Puritan ministers like Cotton Mather were obsessed with the devil and used their pulpits to fan the witchcraft firestorm. In 1770 Patriot leaders like Samuel Adams and Paul Revere turned the killings on King Street, and the subsequent trial of the soldiers involved, into an unparalleled piece of propaganda against British oppression. In 1859 President Buchanan was determined not to let abolishionists destroy the fragile compromise holding the Union together. Federal laws had to be obeyed, however objectionable they might be to individual citizens like Simeon Bushnell. Similarly, President Johnson (himself a Southerner) could not afford to show any leniency to a lowly captain in the Confederate Army—especially one accused of conspiracy in the death of thousands of Union soldiers. In 1951 the Rosenbergs and Sobell were faced with Senator Joe McCarthy and other "red scare" advocates constantly reminding the American public of a Communist "plot" to destroy the United States and the need to uncover Soviet agents involved in espionage.

Finally, these trials are designed to challenge learners to struggle with the same milieu and evidence that the real historical characters encountered at the time of the trial. Whether the defendants were found "guilty" or "not guilty" is really secondary to the process of the trial itself, and the historical and moral questions raised by that litigation. These trials force students and their teachers to face these dilemmas and, often, themselves.

ACKNOWLEDGMENTS

I would like to thank a number of people for their assistance and encouragement in this project, including Richard W. Hoover, political officer for the U.S. State Department, who provided me with many important books from his extensive library. To Frances Traher who gave me access to the letters and papers of her great-grandfather, a prisoner-of-war in Andersonville. To my wife who supported me throughout this project. And finally, to the hundreds of students from the Brookline, Hull, and Arlington Public Schools in Massachusetts, the Copenhagen International Junior School, the Anglo-American School of Moscow, and the American Overseas School of Rome who recreated these trials with enthusiasm over a period of twenty years and provided me with the most exciting, rewarding, and professionally satisfying experiences in my teaching career.

CONTENTS

SECTION ONE

PRELIMINARY MATERIALS FOR TEACHERS AND STUDENTS

TEACHER'S GUIDE

"Without sympathy and imagination the historian can copy figures from a tax roll forever—or count them by computer as they do nowadays—but he will never know or be able to portray the people who paid the taxes."

—Barbara Tuchman
Practicing History

TECHNIQUES FOR ORGANIZING AND CONDUCTING EACH TRIAL

1. Be well-organized from the beginning; then you can improvise as needed.

2. Try to match roles to student personalities and academic strengths. For student-attorneys, it is particularly important that you select students who are well-organized and not afraid to speak in front of the class.

3. In trials that require only one judge, it is better if you play that role. Students are not used to being the authority figure in the classroom and have great difficulty keeping "order in the court."

4. The students playing the parts of attorneys have the most difficult roles and need additional time to prepare. Prior to beginning the trial, they should be given a week or more to get ready.

5. You can limit the length of the trial by setting time limits for opening remarks, direct testimony, cross-examination, closing remarks and jury deliberation. You can pressure a jury into a verdict by reading them the "Riot Act" which essentially orders them to make a quick decision or "face the consequences."

6. You can also limit the length of the trial by omitting roles.

7. Be prepared to expect the unexpected. Four-day trials often go a fifth day when something unexpected happens. Preset time limits frequently break down under the heat of examination.

8. Make signs or labels to put on the desks or tables indicating where the various trial participants are to sit.

9. Have witnesses write their names on the chalkboard before giving testimony.

10. There is a form for the magistrates, military commission, or jury. Urge them to keep a record of "memorable" pieces of evidence.

11. It is unwise to allow students to switch roles except under special circumstances.

12. As in real trials, often the most difficult questions that student-witnesses face come from cross-examination. They can't fully prepare for these questions. They should be prepared, however, when confronted with a difficult question, to say "I don't know," "I don't remember," or make up an answer that would be a "reasonable conclusion" based on their understanding of the facts. Tell students that outright lying should be discouraged. As Marcus Fabius Quintilianus said in A.D. 35, "A liar should have a good memory."

13. Encourage students to do additional research and make costumes. It will only add to the realism of the experience, and give you a further measure of evaluation.

14. Use the subpoenas to involve members of the school community outside your classroom. For example, students really enjoy having their school principal "subpoenaed" to serve on the jury or act as a witness.

15. In the trials that involve juries, to insure some degree of fairness, it is best if they come from another class.

16. Secretly "prime" a student to do something "unexpected," like yelling "liar" at a testifying witness. Then he or she can be "escorted" out of the courtroom by the bailiff. It will keep the students on the edge of their seats for the rest of the trial—wondering what will happen next.

ORGANIZING AND CONDUCTING EACH TRIAL

PRETRIAL PREPARATION

STEP 1

Thoroughly familiarize yourself with the case and decide: (a) when you want to begin the trial and (b) how long you want the trial to last (see the section on suggested ways of determining length). It is wise at this time to advise other members of the school staff when and where this activity will be taking place. You may need to "recruit" additional students and teachers for the trial; members of another class, unfamiliar with the case, make excellent juries and additional witnesses. There are "subpoena" forms provided in the "Additional Information" section of each trial, should you want to "formalize" the process.

STEP 2

Duplicate all materials needed for the trial including background information, role sheets, the section "Student Guide to Simulation Trials," and any additional information for the student-attorneys, witnesses, jury, and judges.

STEP 3

Use the "master role sheet" to assign each student a role. It is recommended that a teacher play the role of one of the magistrates in the Salem trial, General Wallace on the military commission in Wirz's trial, or the judge in the other trials. However, there is a section in the "Student's Guide" covering the responsibilities of the judge.

STEP 4

The most difficult role(s) in recreating a trial are for the student attorney(s) and the magistrates in the Salem trial. You should have them read the sections in the "Student's Guide" dealing with those roles several days before you plan to start the activity, and then meet with them privately to discuss any questions about their task. For the student attorneys, stress the importance of forming a consistent "theory of the case" and using the "direct testimony" of their witnesses to prove it.

STEP 5

Make a packet of information for each student in the trial that includes the background information, his or her individual role sheet, the section in the "student's guide" dealing with his or her role, and any other additional information you want students to have including further historical data, exhibits, and books.

BEGINNING EACH TRIAL*

STEP 1

Set up the classroom to look like the courtroom using the diagram provided in the trial's "Additional Information" section as a model.

STEP 2

Make signs or labels for the courtroom indicating where each student should sit depending on his or her assigned role. Have students sit in their "role position" and distribute the packets of information.

STEP 3

Explain that you are going to recreate a historic American trial and that they have been assigned various roles. Discuss what attorneys, witnesses, judges, clerks, jurors, and court officials do in a trial. In the Salem and Wirz trials review the special nature of the trial format. Explain how you plan to evaluate their performance in this activity. (See the section on evaluation.)

STEP 4

Read the background information aloud in class and answer any questions students might have about the case. Explain that the trial will begin on such and such day and time and that they will have one, two, or three class periods to prepare. You can recommend additional research that can include general familiarization with the period and time. For some roles it will be extremely difficult to find additional information, so students should not be pressured to do the impossible.

STEP 5

The various groups (defense, prosecution, judge(s), and jury**) should be separated to prepare for the first day of the trial. It is recommended that they work in different rooms, but if that is impossible stress the need for confidentiality. Obviously, if one side knows what the other is planning, it is a great advantage.

---

*It will normally take at least two days to complete the pretrial preparation.

**Particular care should be taken to make sure that members of the jury, the magistrates in the Salem trial, and the members of the military commission in the Wirz trial are not "influenced" by either side. They can be assigned a research project in the school library related to the overall "conditions of the time," but not the specifics of the case.

STEP 6

Circulate among the groups to answer questions and give advice. The student-attorneys should explain their theory of the case to the witnesses. Each witness should carefully study his or her role and prepare to answer questions about their knowledge of the case. The student-attorneys and his or her witnesses should develop questions that they will be asked when giving their testimony.

THE TRIAL*

DAY ONE

STEP 1:

Students are in their courtroom positions. It is effective to have the magistrates, military commission, or judge enter the room at the start of each session. The entire court should "rise" when they enter the room.

STEP 2:

The charges are read, the defendants make their plea, and the prosecution and defense make opening remarks. (In the Salem trial Cotton Mather and one of the magistrates should make an opening remark to the court.)

STEP 3:

The prosecution begins its case. Preset time limits for direct testimony and cross-examination should be enforced by the judge or clerk depending on the number of witnesses. (In the Salem trial the magistrates will begin their questioning with the accused witch Tituba and then begin questioning the afflicted girls.)

DAY TWO

STEP 1:

The prosecution concludes its case and the defense begins its case. Preset time limits for direct testimony and cross-examination should be enforced by the judge or clerk depending on the number of witnesses. (In the Salem trial the magistrates will continue their questioning with the afflicted girls and the witnesses against the accused witches.)

DAY THREE

STEP 1:

The defense concludes its case. (In the Salem trial the accused witches will be questioned.)

*Based on a four-day (50-minute class period) trial. However, the entire trial could be conducted in one four-hour span of time.

STEP 2:

If time permits rebuttal witnesses may be called. (In the Salem trial the afflicted girls or witnesses may be recalled.)

DAY FOUR***

STEP 1:

Prosecution and defense make closing remarks. (In the Salem trial Cotton Mather and one of the magistrates should make a closing statement.)

STEP 2:

Magistrates, military commission, or jury members deliberate and reach a verdict.

STEP 3:

The sentence is delivered. The trial ends.

STEP 4:

Aftermath and discussion questions.

***This may take two days if the magistrates, military commission, or jury members take a long time deliberating a verdict.

STUDENT EVALUATION

Students will naturally view "winning" as the most important measure of success. The prosecution will expect positive evaluations to emerge from convictions. The defense will view acquittals as a sure sign of high grades. It is important that <u>from the beginning</u> you encourage them to try and win the case, but you must tell them that winning alone <u>will not</u> determine success in your evaluation. In short, it is not whether you win or not, but how you play the game.

Some possible ways of evaluating student performance include:

1. How well have they prepared for their role? Have they obviously done additional research? Did they make a costume?

2. How effective were they working with their group (defense, prosecution, jury, magistrates, judge)? Were they an effective member of the pretrial planning sessions?

3. How well did they actually "do" their role during the simulation? Often students who are "quiet" in class perform unexpectedly well as witnesses in a trial.

4. Have each student write an analysis of the events and outcome of the trial from the perspective of his or her role.

5. How well did they contribute to the post-trial discussion questions?

6. Have each student write the answer to one or more of the discussion questions included in the "Additional Information" section of the trial.

SUGGESTED WAYS TO DETERMINE TRIAL LENGTH

FOR A LONG TRIAL

1. Allow three or more days to prepare for the trial.

2. Include all roles possible (including optional roles).

3. Allow the jury to be impaneled. The student attorney(s) and judge(s) can ask questions and disqualify certain proposed members.

4. Do not set any time limits on opening or closing remarks, direct testimony, or cross-examination.

5. Allow prosecution and defense to recall witnesses.

6. Have students research and create additional roles (there were, for example, 135 witnesses for the prosecution in Wirz's trial).

FOR AN AVERAGE-LENGTH TRIAL

1. Allow two days for pretrial preparation.

2. Exclude some or all of the optional roles. In the Salem and Preston trials eliminate some of the defendants.

3. Set time limits to opening and closing remarks (maximum of five minutes), direct testimony (two minutes) and cross-examination (one minute).

4. Set a time limit to jury deliberation. If the jury cannot reach a verdict by consensus, then it has to be "majority rule" (or permit a "hung jury").

FOR A SHORT TRIAL

1. Allow only one day for pretrial preparation.

2. Omit selected roles and all optional roles.

3. Set strict time limits to opening and closing remarks, direct testimony and cross-examination.

4. Set a maximum number of questions that each witness can answer.

5. Only allow one defendant.

6. Do not have a jury. Have the judge(s) decide the case.

GENERAL BIBLIOGRAPHY

Bailey, Thomas. *The American Pageant*. Lexington, MA.: D.C. Heath & Co., 1983.

Black, Henry Campbell. *Black's Law Dictionary*. Minneapolis: West Publishing Co., 1968.

Byrne, Edward M. *Military Law*. Annapolis, MD: Naval Institute Press, 1976.

Commager, Henry Steele (ed.). *Documents of American History, Vols. 1 & 2*. NY: Appleton-Century-Crofts, 1968.

Current, Richard N. *American History: A Survey*. NY: Knopf, 1983.

Dimona, Joseph. *Great Court Martial Cases*. NY: Grosset & Dunlap, 1972.

Doyle, William. *The Oxford History of the American Revolution*. London: Oxford University Press, 1990.

Fenstrom, Peter G. *The American Law Dictionary*. Los Angeles: ABC-CLIO, Inc., 1991.

Friedman, Lawrence M. *A History of American Law*. NY: Simon and Schuster, Inc., 1985.

Gifis, Steven. *Law Dictionary*. NY: Barron's, 1984.

Guinther, John. *The Jury in America*. NY: Facts on File Publication, 1988.

Mauet, Thomas A. *Fundamentals of Trial Techniques*. Boston: Little, Brown & Co., 1988.

Marszalek, John F. *Court-Martial: A Black Man in America*. Boston: Charles Scribner's Sons, 1972.

Ulmer, S. Sidney. *Military Justice and the Right to Counsel*. Lexington: University of Kentucky, 1970.

Wellman, Francis L. *The Art of Cross-Examination*. NY: Barnes & Noble, 1936

STUDENT GUIDE

"Eternal vigilance is the price of freedom."

—Lord Acton

"A liar should have a good memory."

—Marcus Fabius Quintilianus

13

 # HOW TO BE AN EFFECTIVE JUDGE

In order to do an effective job as a judge in recreating a historical trial, you will have to learn many of the skills and techniques actually employed by modern trial judges. It will not be a simple task and will require considerable study. Most judges have spent many years practicing law before they were able to "sit on the bench" and preside over a trial. The following information will give you some practical suggestions about how to make your historical trial a worthwhile learning experience, and it will help you overcome some of the difficulties experienced by novice judges.

BEFORE THE START OF THE TRIAL

You must carefully study the meaning of the law(s) that will apply in the coming trial. If the defendant is charged with premeditated murder, you must understand what that means and how it differs, for example, from manslaughter. Later, it will be your job to explain the law to the jury. They must fully understand the law, too, in order to render a just verdict.

You must carefully review all the various motions and objections that may be raised during the trial by the prosecution and defense attorneys. Reading the section "For the Student-Attorneys" will give you a clear idea of how they should be operating.

Common objections raised by attorneys during questioning include:

1. *Objection, Your Honor, IRRELEVANT TESTIMONY:* The witness is being asked a question that calls for an answer which has nothing to do with the alleged crime.

2. *Objection, Your Honor, BADGERING THE WITNESS:* The attorney is deliberately harassing, annoying, provoking, or otherwise exhibiting hostile behavior toward a witness.

3. *Objection, Your Honor, LACKS EXPERTISE or NOT QUALIFIED:* The witness is not qualified to answer a question. An auto mechanic would not, for example, be able to testify to the exact cause of death in a murder case.

4. *Objection, Your Honor, COACHING or LEADING THE WITNESS:* It is objectionable to ask leading questions to a witness under direct testimony. It is permitted, however, under cross-examination to ask leading questions like: "Isn't it true, Mr. Smith, that you were in the mob on the evening of the murder?"

5. *Objection, Your Honor, CALLS FOR A CONCLUSION:* It is objectionable to ask a witness to make a conclusion while giving testimony. Conclusions are for the jury after hearing all the evidence.

6. *Objection, Your Honor, HEARSAY EVIDENCE:* It is normally objectionable for a witness to testify about something he or she heard secondhand. If, for example, a witness's statement as to what he or she heard another person say is elicited to prove the truth of what that other person said, it is hearsay; if, however, it is elicited to merely show that the words were spoken, it is not hearsay. The witness's answer will be admissible only to show that the other person spoke certain words and not to show the truth of what the other person said.

You must be prepared to rule on these objections saying either:

HOW TO BE AN EFFECTIVE JUDGE, continued

1. OBJECTION OVERRULED: The objection raised by the attorney is not valid and the trial may proceed.

2. OBJECTION SUSTAINED: The objection raised by the attorney is valid and the jury should disregard the question and/or answer. You may ask the attorney to either "rephrase his question" or "proceed with a different line of questioning." You may also explain why you either "overruled" or "sustained" an objection, but according to the law, it is not necessary.

DURING THE TRIAL

It will be your responsibility to organize and run the trial from start to finish. When you enter the court, the clerk will say "all rise" until you are seated.

Your first job will be to "charge" the jury. This means that you must:

1. Explain the crime(s) involved and the law(s) that apply in this case.

2. Explain the meaning of "burden of proof." In criminal cases the burden of proof is on the prosecution. It must show that the person(s) are guilty "beyond a reasonable doubt" or the jury must find them "not guilty." (A jury never declares a person "innocent"; therefore, individuals on the jury can <u>believe</u> the person is guilty and still have "reasonable doubt" because of the evidence.)

After you have "charged the jury" proceed with the trial according to the "Trial Procedure" section of the simulation. Normally this will call for having the clerk read the charges against the defendants, having them make a "plea" (guilty or not guilty), opening remarks by the prosecution and defense attorneys, direct testimony and cross-examination of prosecution and defense witnesses, closing remarks, jury deliberation, verdict, and sentence. You should be prepared during this time to rule on objections (quick responses of "Overruled!" or "Sustained!" have the most impact—so stay alert!), receive evidence including exhibits (the clerk will assist you in this task), and deal sensibly with any problems that may arise.

Finally, use a gavel or something similar to maintain "order in the court." Don't let the attorneys argue with each other (or for that matter, anyone else). For example, if there is a problem or controversy over a ruling or evidence, call the attorneys to "the bench" and quietly explain your decision. You may even call a "recess" if a brief period of time is needed either to restore order in the court or consider points of law. Remember, you are the supreme authority in the court and anyone who does not conform to courtroom behavior can be held in *CONTEMPT OF COURT,* which is anything that obstructs or interferes with the orderly administration of justice.

HOW TO BE AN EFFECTIVE STUDENT-ATTORNEY

In order to do an effective job as a student-attorney in a historical trial, you will have to learn many of the skills and techniques actually employed by modern trial lawyers. It will not be a simple task and will require considerable study. The following information will give you practical suggestions about how to make your historical trial a worthwhile learning experience, and will help you overcome some of the difficulties experienced by novice attorneys.

PRETRIAL PREPARATION

You must develop a theory about what happened in the case <u>before the trial</u>. A theory of the case is merely your views on all the evidence that will be presented at the trial. If you do not have a crystal-clear picture about what happened, you will never be able to convince a student jury.

Once you have developed your theory of the case, you must begin <u>organizing</u> your witnesses and their evidence. First, each of your witnesses needs to be fully prepared for <u>direct testimony</u>. You must go over their testimony carefully and make sure that what they intend to say on the witness stand is consistent with your theory of the case. One of the best ways to prepare witnesses is to have them use their role sheet (and any other additional information) to write out what they intend to say. Then you can review their account of what happened and make suggestions for any necessary changes. You should prepare questions that you intend to ask your witnesses to help them relate their information about the case. Go over their testimony <u>repeatedly</u> to make sure you know exactly how they are going to answer your questions. However, remember that the witnesses are playing historical roles and they must be consistent with their identity.

Second, you must prepare your witnesses for <u>cross-examination</u>. Try to think of questions that the opposing attorney might ask. Advise the witness to pay close attention to the lawyer's questions and answer only the question. Caution your witnesses to never volunteer information under cross-examination.

Prepare cross-examination questions for the opposition witnesses. Try to discover what testimony they are likely to give that will appear believable. What testimony will they likely give that will conflict with what your witnesses intend to say? What testimony will damage your exhibits?

Finally, always remember that the lawyers are on trial, too. The judge and jury are evaluating your performance and polite conduct will work in your favor. Show respect to the judge and always assume an intelligent jury. Student-jurors have demonstrated time and again that favorable impressions are created by attorneys who act and look well prepared and knowledgeable, have good speaking ability, respect their witnesses, and show a dedication and concern for their clients.

OPENING REMARKS

Your opening remarks to the jury may be the most important part of the trial. The jury will be students like yourself and their first impression may determine how they picture the entire trial. It is important that you appear knowledgeable and confident from the beginning.

HOW TO BE AN EFFECTIVE STUDENT-ATTORNEY, continued

Perhaps the most common mistake that student-attorneys make in their opening remarks is that they fail to clearly state the facts of the case. Clearly outline your theory of the case using basic English. If you use long complex sentences and elaborate vocabulary, the student-jury will probably either fail to understand what you are saying or, even worse, think you are a pretentious snob and not care what you are saying.

It is improper for you in your opening remarks to directly state your personal opinions about the facts or the believability of a witness. Phrases like "I believe," "I think," or "We believe that" are objectionable by the opposition and should be eliminated from your trial vocabulary.

Nothing is more damaging to your case than to overstate the facts in your opening remarks. Keep things simple and let the jury find out later that you have plenty of evidence to prove what you are saying is true. Always try to "personalize" the individuals on your side of the case by referring to them by their names. Always refer to your opponents in a "depersonalized" way using such terms as "the plaintiff," "the defendant," "this witch," "the other side," "this enemy officer," or other such references.

Student-lawyers who can give opening remarks without notes have a decided advantage over their opponent. You will appear intelligent, organized, and much more confident. If you cannot memorize the entire speech, use index cards with notes. Never read your speech to the court. The jury will either not pay attention or fall asleep.

You should always conclude your opening speech by simply and directly telling the jury that the facts will support your case and asking for a favorable verdict.

DIRECT EXAMINATION OF WITNESSES

You will win the trial for your side primarily on the strength of the direct testimony of your witnesses, not on clever cross-examination of the opposition. The purpose of a direct examination is to get the witness—in a clear and logical fashion—to make a believable statement that the jury will remember. Inexperienced student-attorneys make two basic mistakes: They have their witnesses give too much unimportant information, and they spend too little time on the most crucial aspects of their testimony.

It is best to reveal any weakness in your case during the direct examination. Don't wait and hope the other side will not discover it. They undoubtedly will and then it will appear to the jury that you have been trying to hide certain facts. When you do show a weakness, it is best to "bury" it in the middle of a direct testimony. Jury members nearly always recall best what they hear first and last. The weakness will have less impact when freely given after the witness, hopefully, has made a good impression on the jury. A modern survey of juries has shown that 95% were most impressed with the testimony of "expert witnesses."

Students often find testifying in a simulation trial an unnerving experience. They are playing an unfamiliar "role" with lots of missing background. A student-witness will often "forget" an important part of his or her testimony. Don't panic! Think of questions that you can ask to help "refresh" the witness's memory. You may also have the witness refer to previously signed statements, exhibits, and other court documents. Remember, however, under direct examination you are not permitted to ask the witness "leading" questions.

18

HOW TO BE AN EFFECTIVE STUDENT-ATTORNEY, continued

Each witness you present must conform to your theory of the case. You must decide <u>when</u> each witness should appear in the trial so that the jury gets a clear logical view of the facts. It is usually wise to begin and end your case with your best witnesses. The jury will remember best the beginning and end of your case.

Finally, if one of your witnesses says something unexpectedly bad, <u>do not react to it</u>! Immediately go to another question and try to get the jury's mind off the negative point.

EXHIBITS

An exhibit is anything that you can introduce as evidence other than oral testimony. Exhibits can be powerful evidence and they often make a memorable and lasting impression on the jury. In order for an exhibit such as a letter, photograph, drawing, weapon, or document to be received as evidence, you must follow the following procedure:

1. Present the exhibit to the judge or clerk and have it assigned an exhibit identification letter or number <u>before</u> you plan to use it in the trial. You must also show the exhibit to the opposing attorney <u>before</u> you use it in court.

2. The exhibit must be introduced as evidence <u>while you are questioning a witness</u>. The witness must have some knowledge of the exhibit and be able to testify to its relevancy. The <u>most effective</u> method of introducing an exhibit is to literally hand the exhibit to the witness and then move to one side so the jury can see the witness with the exhibit. Never block the jury's view of the witness and make sure that they hear and see what the witness does with the exhibit.

3. After the witness has testified about the exhibit, you must ask permission of the court to have the exhibit entered into the record as evidence.

4. Finally, you must make the exhibit available to the jury. If you are showing a document that can be photocopied, it would be acceptable to have a copy made for the jury, opposing lawyers, and the court records.

Every exhibit you plan to introduce as evidence must meet three basic requirements:

1. It must be an exhibit given to you by the teacher at the beginning of the trial (marked "EXHIBIT" on the upper right-hand side of the paper).

2. It must be relevant to the trial.

3. The witness must be competent to evaluate the exhibit.

CROSS-EXAMINATION

There are two basic reasons to cross-examine a witness. First, to try and get the witness to agree with those facts that support your case rather than your opponents. Second, to discredit the opposing witnesses' direct testimony.

Use the following suggestions for effective cross-examination:

1. Focus your questioning on no more than two or three points that support your theory of the case.

19

HOW TO BE AN EFFECTIVE STUDENT-ATTORNEY, continued

2. Know the likely answer to your questions. But, listen closely to the answers. Witnesses sometimes give unexpectedly good responses, and you may miss something important by not paying attention.

3. Never argue with the witness. It is improper and will definitely hurt your case.

4. Never let the witness explain an answer. Keep the witness under control by asking a lot of "yes" and "no" questions. You are permitted to ask leading questions on cross-examination. A leading question is one that suggests the answer.

5. Make a statement of fact and have the witness agree to it.

6. Be a good actor. Every effective cross-examiner will get damaging answers to questions. When this happens simply go on as if nothing happened and perhaps the jury will conclude that the answer was not important.

7. Since the jury will be comprised of fellow students, it is often not wise to totally discredit their honesty and integrity. Instead, try to point out that something might have altered their perception, memory, or ability to communicate.

8. Juries love to see a witness get "caught" changing his or her story. Look for those opportunities.

9. If a witness constantly answers "I don't know" or "I don't recall" to your questions, don't worry; they are making a terrible impression on the jury.

10. If you get a witness who refuses to stop talking and wants to argue everything, cut him or her off by asking another question. You may also ask the judge to advise the witness to answer only the question asked.

OBJECTIONS

Be constantly on guard while the opposing attorney is questioning a witness—especially during cross-examination. If you have an objection, stand up and say "Objection, Your Honor, the counsel for the defense (or prosecution) is... (state your objection)...," then wait quietly for the judge to either say "Objection sustained" (it is a valid objection) or "Objection overruled" (your objection is not valid). You may ask the judge to explain the ruling, but he or she is not obligated to do so. Never argue with the judge! Common objections you may raise include:

1. *Objection, Your Honor, IRRELEVANT TESTIMONY:* The witness is being asked a question that calls for an answer that has nothing to do with the alleged crime.

2. *Objection, Your Honor, BADGERING THE WITNESS:* The attorney is deliberately harassing, annoying, provoking, or otherwise exhibiting hostile behavior toward a witness.

3. *Objection, Your Honor, LACKS EXPERTISE or NOT QUALIFIED:* The witness is not qualified to answer a question. An auto mechanic would not, for example, be able to testify to the exact cause of death in a murder case.

HOW TO BE AN EFFECTIVE STUDENT-ATTORNEY, continued

4. *Objection, Your Honor, COACHING or LEADING THE WITNESS:* It is objectionable to ask leading questions to a witness under <u>direct testimony</u>. It is permitted, however, under <u>cross-examination</u> to ask leading questions like: "Isn't it true, Mr. Smith, that you were in the mob on the evening of the murder?"

5. *Objection, Your Honor, CALLS FOR A CONCLUSION:* It is objectionable to ask a witness to make a conclusion while giving testimony. Conclusions are for the jury after hearing all the evidence.

6. *Objection, Your Honor, HEARSAY EVIDENCE:* It is normally objectionable for a witness to testify about something he or she heard second-hand. If, for example, a witness's statement as to what he or she heard another person say is elicited to prove the truth of what that other person said, it is hearsay; if, however, it is evoked to merely show that the words were spoken, it is not hearsay. The witness's answer will be admissible only to show that the other person spoke certain words and not to show the truth of what the other person said.

CLOSING ARGUMENTS

Closing arguments by the lawyers are the last opportunity to explain your theory of the case to the jury. Similar to your opening remarks, it is important that you write out your speech and practice saying it forcefully with a minimum of notes. If you can look the jury in the eyes while making your final remarks, they will be quite impressed. Effective closing arguments have two basic qualities: They simply state the facts proved by your witnesses, and they respect the jury's intelligence by avoiding arguments that were not proven by the trial.

In order to make an effective closing speech to the jury, you must argue the facts and avoid personal opinion. Refer to specific witnesses and refresh the jury's memory about the facts of your case. Remind the jury of your exhibits. In fact, you may save a key diagram or picture for the closing remarks so that it will have an immediate impact on the jury. Use analogies and stories to make your points, but keep them simple and short. While your closing arguments should concentrate on the positive, it is wise to confront any weaknesses in your case. The jury will appreciate your honesty and openness in facing problems in your case.

 **HOW TO BE AN EFFECTIVE WITNESS**

In order to do an effective job as a witness in a historical trial, you will have to learn as much as possible about the person you are portraying and the evidence you will be expected to give during the trial. It will not be a simple task and will require considerable study. It will be impossible, in many cases, to find out any more <u>specific</u> information about your character than what is given in the role sheet. However, the more you know about the historical period, the better you will be able to assume your role. First, you must decide what type of witness you are.

There are three basic "types" of witnesses: Witnesses who are directly testifying about what they saw, heard, or felt (this is the most common kind of witness in the simulation trials); character witnesses who are testifying about a person's good or bad personality; and expert witnesses who are considered by the court as "experts" in a particular field—for example, a medical doctor—and are testifying about a specific piece of evidence.

Second, you must carefully write out what you plan to say on the witness stand. Your attorney should assist you in this part of your preparation, so that what you plan to say conforms to his or her "theory of the case" or "what happened." Next you and your lawyer should frame a series of questions that you will be asked during "direct examination." These questions will help you relate what you have to say. Your testimony must be <u>memorized</u>. A witness is not allowed to refer to notes when giving testimony. You may, however, be asked to comment on a particular exhibit.

Third, you and your attorney should think of possible questions that you might be asked under cross-examination (then agree on what answer you will give). This is particularly difficult since you can never be completely sure what the other side is planning. If you don't know the answer to a question, it is often best to merely say: "I don't know." As the Roman statesman Marcus Fabius Quintilianus said: "A liar should have a good memory."

Finally, what you and the other witnesses say during the trial should determine the outcome. You are presenting the "evidence" to the jury, and it is from your "facts" they will determine a verdict of "guilty" or "not guilty." You will undoubtedly be considered by the jury as a "strong" witness if you speak clearly, know your part well, and appear confident.

HOW TO BE AN EFFECTIVE MEMBER OF THE JURY

In order to do an effective job as a member of the jury in a historical trial, you will have to strive to be as "objective" as possible. You are expected to be familiar with the "temper of the times", however you are not expected to know anything about what specifically happened. For example, you might know that both the North and the South kept thousands of prisoners-of-war during the American Civil War, but you don't know under what conditions they were detained. You might have heard that on March 6, 1770, five men were killed in Boston during a confrontation with British soldiers; however, you don't know any of the specific facts of what happened on the night of the shooting, March 5, 1770. You should not serve on the jury if you feel incapable of giving a fair verdict based on the evidence.

The judge will explain the charges against the defendants and the law that applies in the case. It is your task to decide the facts. The attorneys from both the defense and prosecution will explain the case from their point of view, but it is what the witnesses say—the evidence—that should determine your verdict. You must listen carefully to all the evidence presented by the witnesses, especially under direct examination. You must determine whether they are telling the truth, lying, or simply not contributing anything relevant to the case. A modern survey of juries has shown that 95% of them were most impressed with the testimony of so-called "expert witnesses."

When all the evidence has been presented the judge will ask you to "retire" to the jury chamber and consider a verdict. The judge should remind you at this time that the "burden of proof" is on the prosecution; a person is considered innocent until proven guilty "beyond a reasonable doubt." You should try to reach a vote of "guilty" or "not guilty" by consensus (everyone agrees). Remember, a jury never declares a person "innocent," only "guilty" or "not guilty." You may believe they are "guilty" but not think there is enough evidence to convict—in which case, you should find them "not guilty."

A "hung jury" is when you cannot reach an agreement by consensus. The judge may permit the trial to end this way, or may read you the "Riot Act" that essentially forces you to make a decision or face "serious consequences."

When you have decided on your verdict, you should return to the courtroom. The judge will either have you write the verdict on a piece of paper and give it to the clerk, or ask one of you to stand and announce the verdict (this may be a prior-appointed "jury foreman"). The jury's verdict is final. If a defendant is acquitted, he or she can never be retried for the same offense.

GLOSSARY

Accessory	One who aids or contributes in a secondary way or assists in or contributes to crime as a subordinate.
Accused	The person against whom a criminal proceeding is initiated.
Acquit	To set free or judicially discharge from accusation or suspicion of guilt.
Aid and abet	To actively, knowingly, intentionally, or purposefully encourage or assist another individual in the commission or attempted commission of a crime.
Burden of proof	The duty of a party to prove an allegation or accusation of guilt. A person is considered innocent until proven guilty "beyond a reason of doubt."
Conspiracy	A combination of two or more persons to commit a criminal or unlawful act, or to commit a lawful act by criminal or unlawful means.
Contempt of court	An act or omission tending to obstruct or interfere with the orderly administration of justice, or to impair the dignity of the court or respect for its authority. There are two kinds of contempt of court: <u>Direct contempt</u> which—openly and in the presence of the court—resists the power of the court and <u>constructive contempt</u> which results from matters outside the court, such as failure to obey the orders from the judge.
Cross-examination	The questioning of a witness by a lawyer other than the one who called the witness, concerning matters about which the witness has testified during direct testimony.
Cruel and unusual punishment	Such punishment as is found to be offensive to the ordinary person including beating, whipping and other forms of physical torture.
Expert witness	A witness having special knowledge of the subject about which he or she is to testify.
Hearsay rule	A rule that declares not admissible as evidence any statement other than that by a witness while testifying at the hearing and offered into evidence to prove the truth of the matter stated.
Leading question	A question posed by a trial lawyer that is ordinarily improper on direct examination because it suggests to the witness the answer he or she is to deliver, or in effect prompts the answer that is to be given irrespective of actual memory. Leading questions may be asked on cross-examination and when a witness is hostile to the party examining him or her.

GLOSSARY, continued

Manslaughter	An unlawful killing of another person <u>without</u> malice aforethought or premeditation.
Murder	The unlawful homicide or the killing of another person with malice aforethought or premeditation.
Objection	A procedure whereby an attorney asserts that a particular witness, a line of questioning, piece of evidence, or other matter is improper and should not be continued, and asks the court to rule on its impropriety or illegality.
Overrule	Applies to a court's denial of any motion or point raised to the court, such as "objection overruled."
Plaintiff	The one who initially brings a legal action and seeks remedy in a court of law. In criminal cases involving major crimes the plaintiff is normally the "state" or "the government."
Precedent	A previously decided case or point that is recognized as authority for the disposition or action in future cases.
Presumption	A rule of law that requires the assumption of a fact from another fact or set of facts.
Proof	The evidence that tends to establish the existence of a fact in issue.
Sustain	To support or approve. A judge may "sustain" an objection.

SECTION TWO

THE TRIALS

THE SALEM WITCH TRIALS OF 1692

BACKGROUND

"Execution of Witches in England," from *England's Grievance Discovered,* by Ralph Gardiner, London, 1655; reprint, 1796. Courtesy, Peabody & Essex Museum, Salem, MA.

"The wrongdoing of one generation lives into the successive ones."

—Nathaniel Hawthorne
The House of the Seven Gables

SALEM VILLAGE

The year 1692 was perhaps one of the most gloomy and depressing periods in the history of colonial America. It was a period of guilt, suspicion, conspiracy and hostility. The infant Puritan communities like Boston, Cambridge, and Salem were struggling to survive in the hostile New England environment. The tombstones in these early Puritan towns bear mute testimony to the high rate of mortality, especially among children. There were relentless conflicts between settlers and Native Americans with bloody massacres on both sides. Some of Salem Village's children were orphans of this conflict. It was a time in which religion was an important force in the everyday life of the people, and belief in God and his adversary, the Devil, was genuine. A leading Puritan minister said in a sermon that "no place...that I know of, has got such a spell upon it as will always keep the Devil out. The meetinghouse wherein we assemble for the worship of God, is filled with many holy people and many holy concerns continually; but, if our eyes were so refined as the servant of the prophet had his of old, I suppose we should see a throng of devils in this very place." It was in this atmosphere that the small Puritan town of Salem Village, less than ten miles from Boston, allowed a group of allegedly "afflicted" adolescent girls to control their lives, cause the execution of nearly thirty innocent people, and set a precedent for a series of political and criminal "witch hunts" that have marred our criminal justice system to this day.

The Salem Witch Trials of 1692-1693 originated with a West Indian slave named Tituba, a servant in the home of a leading Puritan minister, Reverend Samuel Parris. She began telling stories from her native Barbados of voodoo, magic, superstition, and fantasy to a group of impressionable young girls from Salem Village including Elizabeth Parris, Ann Putnam, Jr., Abigail Williams, Elizabeth Hubbard, and Mercy Lewis. Her bizarre tales perked the girls' imaginations. They began to have nightmares and hallucinations. They would suddenly drop to the floor writhing in agony. Dr. Griggs, the town physician, was called to examine them. He could find no physical explanation for their afflictions. He declared them "bewitched." The young girls were asked: "Who hurts you?" They named two Salem women, Sarah Good and Sarah Osborne. On March 1, 1692 Tituba, Sarah Good, and Sarah Osborne were arrested and the witch hunt began. The hysteria and accusations spread and soon hundreds of accused witches and wizards including Martha Corey and Rebecca Nurse—were in jail awaiting trial and possible execution.

A special court was set up in Salem to try the witch cases. It was called the Court of Oyer and Terminer. The terms "Oyer" and "Terminer" come from two words of French origin meaning "to hear" and "to decide." A Court of Oyer and Terminer, then, was one created especially to try cases involving a particular crime. The crime in Salem was witchcraft. In glaring contrast to our modern legal system, the accused were never allowed representation by a lawyer or other counsel. Since witchcraft was a capital offense, the sentence was always death.

Throughout 1692-1693 the Court met and tried the various individuals accused of witchcraft. The Court accepted as indication of guilt direct physical evidence that the accused had cast a spell, given an evil eye, referred to the Devil by name, or other observable evil actions. Witnesses came into the court and presented all kinds of malicious gossip against the accused and this was accepted as genuine evidence. The Court also accepted as proof of guilt "spectral evidence" in which the accused appeared as a "shape" of some sort (like a monster or distorted animal) and afflicted the unfortunate victim. This kind of evidence was particularly difficult to discredit since the accused would be said to have "afflicted" a person even when it could be proved that they had never had any real physical contact.

Evidence against the accused could even be established during the trial. When the accused glanced at the afflicted girls, they instantly succumbed to their afflictions including twisted necks, writhing contortions, and strange agonies. They would call out the names of their tormentors, swearing that the witches were sending their specter to attack them.

The Puritans believed the Bible gave clear instructions about how to deal with witches. It said: "Thou shalt not suffer a witch to live." Nevertheless, out of the hundreds of persons jailed during the witchcraft terror, not a single confessed witch was executed. In fact, many women who confessed to being witches were never even tried. Only those individuals who steadfastly refused to admit guilt were tried and executed. One man, Giles Corey, refused to even answer the Magistrates' questions. He was "pressed" to death with huge stones in an effort to get him to admit guilt. He refused. Many other unconfessed witches went to their deaths on Gallows Hill.

You will now have a chance to recreate the strange events of Salem Village in the spring of 1692. Remember, trust no one.

The House of the Seven Gables in Salem, MA. Nathaniel Hawthorne's grandfather changed the family name—adding a "w" to the name so as not to be confused with the Salem magistrate. Photo by author.

THE MAGISTRATES
COURT OFFICER AND CLERK
MINISTER

"The Trial of George Jacobs, August 5, 1692," by T.H. Matteson, 1855. Courtesy, Peabody & Essex Museum, Salem, MA.

"Woman! Woman! Repent!"

—Magistrate Danforth

JOHN HATHORNE
MAGISTRATE

You were born in Salem Village in 1641 the son of Major William Hathorne, one of the most powerful men in Puritan New England. You have rigid Puritan standards and support the death penalty for any kind of religious heresy or witchcraft.

At the trial you will serve as one of the magistrates or judges in the Court of Oyer and Terminer. It will be your job to act as both judge and jury during this trial. You will be responsible for the following:

1. Organizing and running the trial

2. Asking questions of the accused witches, the afflicted girls, and various witnesses

3. Considering the evidence

4. Deciding on a verdict and sentence*

QUESTIONS YOU SHOULD ASK

Questions to be directed to the afflicted girls

1. Who torments you?

2. How are you tormented?

3. Have you ever been visited by the "shape" or "spirit" of the accused witch? Explain.

Questions to be directed to the witnesses

1. Who are you accusing of witchcraft?

2. How do you know the accused witch?

3. What specific evidence do you have against the accused?

Questions to be directed to the accused witches

1. Have you tormented these afflicted girls or any of these witnesses?

2. Did you ever send your spirit or shape to torment these afflicted girls or witnesses?

3. Do you worship the Devil?

4. Are you in league with other witches?

5. Have you ever performed any evil acts? Explain.

6. Do you confess to witchcraft?

*If the accused witch is found guilty and refuses to confess, you must sentence her to death by hanging.

JONATHAN CORWIN
MAGISTRATE

You are 51 years old and your family is one of the most prominent and affluent in Salem. In 1676 you married Elizabeth Gibbs, a 31-year-old widow who had inherited a great fortune.

Like your colleague, Magistrate Hathorne, you believe in fundamental Puritanical standards and strict punishment for any discovered witches.

At the trial you will serve as one of the magistrates or judges in the Court of Oyer and Terminer. It will be your job to act as both judge and jury during this trial. You will be responsible for the following:

1. Organizing and running the trial

2. Asking questions of the accused witches, the afflicted girls, and various witnesses

3. Considering the evidence

4. Deciding on a verdict and sentence*

QUESTIONS YOU SHOULD ASK

Questions to be directed to the afflicted girls

1. Who torments you?

2. How are you tormented?

3. Have you ever been visited by the "shape" or "spirit" of the accused witch? Explain.

Questions to be directed to the witnesses

1. Who are you accusing of witchcraft?

2. How do you know the accused witch?

3. What specific evidence do you have against the accused?

Questions to be directed to the accused witches

1. Have you tormented these afflicted girls or any of these witnesses?

2. Did you ever send your spirit or shape to torment these afflicted girls or witnesses?

3. Do you worship the Devil?

4. Are you in league with other witches?

5. Have you ever performed any evil acts? Explain.

6. Do you confess to witchcraft?

---

*If the accused witch is found guilty and refuses to confess, you must sentence her to death by hanging.

BARTHOLOMEW GEDNEY
MAGISTRATE

You were one of the original magistrates to hear accusations against the accused witches. Like your colleagues, Corwin and Hathorne, you believe in a strict interpretation of Puritan dogma. You believe that there are witches in Salem Village and it is your job to discover them and administer punishment.

At the trial you will serve as one of the magistrates or judges in the Court of Oyer and Terminer. It will be your job to act as both judge and jury during this trial. You will be responsible for the following:

1. Organizing and running the trial

2. Asking questions of the accused witches, the afflicted girls, and various witnesses

3. Considering the evidence

4. Deciding on a verdict and sentence*

QUESTIONS YOU SHOULD ASK

Questions to be directed to the afflicted girls

1. Who torments you?

2. How are you tormented?

3. Have you ever been visited by the "shape" or "spirit" of the accused witch? Explain.

Questions to be directed to the witnesses

1. Who are you accusing of witchcraft?

2. How do you know the accused witch?

3. What specific evidence do you have against the accused?

Questions to be directed to the accused witches

1. Have you tormented these afflicted girls or any of these witnesses?

2. Did you ever send your spirit or shape to torment these afflicted girls or witnesses?

3. Do you worship the Devil?

4. Are you in league with other witches?

5. Have you ever performed any evil acts? Explain.

6. Do you confess to witchcraft?

*If the accused witch is found guilty and refuses to confess, you must sentence her to death by hanging.

JOHN PUTNAM, JR.
Court Officer and Clerk

You are responsible for assisting the Magistrates in running the trial. You will be expected to do the following:

1. Swear in all witnesses, asking them to place their left hand on the Bible, raise their right hand, and say "Yes" to the statement "Do you swear to tell the truth, the whole truth, and nothing but the truth, so help you God."

2. Read aloud to the court any documents that the Magistrates instruct you to enter into the record, including statements of law and evidence introduced as exhibits.

3. Keep a record of the names of all witnesses offering testimony.

4. Assist the Magistrates in maintaining courtroom order. You may be asked to escort the afflicted girls from the court if they become too unruly or hysterical.

COTTON MATHER
MINISTER

You are one of the leading Puritan religious figures and believe that all of New England would become possessed by the Devil and his agents: witches. You constantly preached about the sinister threats of witchcraft for years prior to the trials.

At various points during the trial of the accused, you will ask to make a statement to the court. These speeches are adapted from your actual sermon "Wonders of the Invisible World."

SPEECH ONE (to be given at the beginning of the trial)

"The afflicted state of our poor neighbors, that are now suffering by molestations from the invisible world, we apprehend so deplorable, that we think their condition calls for the utmost help of all persons in the community. We cannot but with all thankfulness acknowledge the success which the merciful God has given unto the hard work of our honorable leaders, to detect the abominable witchcrafts which have been committed in the country, humbly praying that the discovery of these mysterious and mischievous wickednesses may be perfected."

SPEECH TWO (to be given before the witches testify)

"We judge that in the prosecution of these, and all such witchcrafts, there is need of a very critical and exquisite caution, lest too much credulity for things received only upon the Devil's authority, there be a door opened for a long train of miserable consequences, and Satan get an advantage over us, for we should not be ignorant of his evil devices and methods. Nevertheless, we cannot but humbly recommend unto the government the speedy and vigorous prosecution of such as have rendered themselves obnoxious, according to the direction given in the laws of God and the wholesome statutes of the English nation, for the detection of witchcraft."

SPEECH THREE (to be given at the end of the trial if you decide to cast doubt on the use of "spectral" evidence)

"I believe that presumptions whereupon persons may be committed, and much more convictions, whereupon persons may be condemned as guilty or witchcrafts, ought certainly to be more considerable than barely the accused persons being represented by a specter unto the afflicted, inasmuch as 'tis an undoubted and notorious thing that a demon may, by God's permission, appear even to ill purposes in the shape of an innocent, yea, and a virtuous man or woman; nor can we esteem alterations made in the sufferers by look or touch of the accused to be an infallible evidence of guilt, but frequently liable to be abused by the Devil's trickery."

THE WITCHES

"Arresting a witch." Courtesy, Peabody & Essex Museum, Salem, MA.

"I can say before my eternal father that I am innocent, and God will clear my innocence."

—Rebecca Nurse

"You can't prove me a witch."

—Martha Corey

TITUBA
Confessed Witch

You have been accused of witchcraft, one of the most serious crimes in Puritan society. You realize that if you are found guilty of being an unconfessed witch, you could suffer death by hanging.

You and your husband John are slaves in the household of Reverend Samuel Parris of Salem Village. You were originally from Barbados where you learned stories about the Devil, black magic, and voodoo. You told these stories to a group of young girls from Salem.

At the beginning of the trial you will be called before the Magistrates for questioning. You will testify to the following:

1. You told stories of witchcraft, voodoo, black magic, and meetings with the Devil to the afflicted girls Ann Putnam, Jr., Abigail Williams, Elizabeth Parris, Elizabeth Hubbard, and Mercy Lewis. Be prepared to relate some of these stories to the court. Do some additional research on this subject and use your imagination.

2. You will deny hurting the afflicted girls, blaming the other accused witches Sarah Good and Sarah Osborne. You think Rebecca Nurse and Martha Corey were there as well, but you are not completely sure.

3. You will confess to riding through the night on a stick or pole with Sarah Good and Sarah Osborne behind you.

4. You will say that Sarah Good and Sarah Osborne told you to kill Ann Putnam with a knife but you refused.

5. You will confess to attending witches' meetings in the night with the accused Sarah Good and Sarah Osborne.

6. If in doubt, confess to anything the Magistrates want to hear. You realize that admitting to witchcraft and asking for repentance will be your only salvation from the gallows.

SARAH GOOD

ACCUSED WITCH

You were born in 1653 in Wenham, Massachusetts, the daughter of Elizabeth and John Solart. Your father died under suspicious circumstances, probably suicide, in 1672. Your mother remarried and her new husband refused to care for you.

Your first marriage was to a penniless indentured servant named Daniel Poole who died leaving you with a pile of debts. Your second husband, William Good, was not much of an improvement. He was often unemployed. You are the mother of a four-year-old girl, Dorcas, and an infant boy. Your family is so poor that much of your time in Salem was spent begging for food and shelter. You never attended Church services "for want of proper clothes." You often muttered under your breath when refused food. Residents usually interpreted these sounds as curses.

On February 29, 1692 a complaint was filed accusing you, Sarah Osborne, and Tituba of witchcraft. You were arrested on March 1, 1692.

You have been accused of witchcraft, one of the most serious crimes in Puritan society. You realize that if you are found guilty of being a witch, you must either confess or suffer the death penalty by hanging. You know that you are <u>not guilty</u> of this crime and to confess would be against your religious beliefs. You must try to convince the Magistrates at your trial that you are not a witch. It will be difficult since there will be a lot of evidence against you and the Magistrates will not be fair by the standards of modern times—they probably already consider you guilty. Also, events that happen <u>during the trial</u> can be used to convince the Magistrates of your guilt.

At the trial be prepared to say the following:

1. Deny any association with the Devil or other witches.

2. Deny tormenting or afflicting any of the young girls who accuse you of witchcraft by their actions or words.

3. Deny any evil acts like placing curses, attending witches' meetings, worshipping the Devil, or sending your spirit to torment anyone.

4. Try to memorize some passages from the Christian Bible. It will make a favorable impression on the Magistrates.

5. Try to find out any stories the witnesses or afflicted girls might be telling about you so you can be prepared to deny them at the trial.

SARAH OSBORNE
ACCUSED WITCH

You were born in 1643, the daughter of Margaret and John Warren of Watertown. In 1662 you married Robert Prince of Salem Village. He owned a large farm and was considered a wealthy man. He died in 1675, leaving you with two small children and the farm. Two years later you married Alexander Osborne, a young Irish immigrant. Your current husband does not like your children from the previous marriage so there is much tension in the family. To make matters worse, you are gravely ill and have been accused by some Salem teenagers of afflicting them.

On February 29, 1692 a complaint was filed against you, Sarah Good, and Tituba, accusing you of witchcraft. You were arrested on March 1.

You know that witchcraft is one of the most serious crimes in Puritan society. You realize that if you are found guilty of being a witch, you must either confess or suffer the death penalty by hanging. You know that you are <u>not guilty</u> of witchcraft and to confess would be against your religious beliefs. You must try to convince the Magistrates at your trial that you are not a witch. It will be difficult since there will be a lot of evidence against you and the Magistrates will not be fair by the standards of modern legal systems—they probably already consider you guilty. Additionally, anything that happens during the trial can be used as an indication of your guilt.

At your trial you must be prepared to say the following:

1. Deny any association with the Devil.

2. Deny tormenting or afflicting any of the girls who accuse you of witchcraft either by their actions or words.

3. Deny any evil acts like placing curses, calling on the Devil, or sending your spirit to inflict any of these so called evil acts.

4. Deny any association with any other witches or wizards.

5. Try to memorize parts of the Christian Bible since it will make a favorable impression on the Magistrates.

6. Try to find out what stories the witnesses or girls might be making up about you so that you can either deny or discredit them.

MARTHA COREY
Accused Witch

You are an old woman with a reputation for piety. You are a member of the Salem Village Church and usually attend every service. Shortly after the accusation and arrest of Sarah Good, Sarah Osborne, and Tituba, the afflicted girls began accusing you of witchcraft. When you were asked about the three accused witches in jail, you said that you did "not think they were witches. If they were, we could not blame the Devil for making witches of them, for they were idle slothful persons and minded nothing that was good. But you have no reason to think so of me, for I have made a profession of Christ and have rejoiced to go and hear the word of God."

You have been accused of witchcraft, one of the most serious crimes in Puritan society. You realize that if you are found guilty of being a witch, you must either confess or suffer the death penalty by hanging. You also know that you are <u>not guilty</u> of witchcraft and to confess would be against your religious beliefs. You must try to convince the Magistrates at your trial that you are not a witch. It will be difficult since there will be a lot of evidence against you and the Magistrates at your trial will not be fair by the standards of modern legal systems. They probably already consider you guilty. Additionally, anything that happens during the trial can be used as evidence against you.

At your trial you should say the following:

1. Deny any association with the Devil and witches.

2. Deny tormenting or afflicting any of the young girls who accuse you of witchcraft by their actions or words.

3. Deny any evil acts like placing curses, calling on the Devil, or sending your spirit to inflict any of these so-called evil acts.

4. Try to memorize parts of the Christian Bible since it will make a very favorable impression on the Magistrates.

5. Try to find out what stories the witnesses or afflicted girls might be making up about you so that you can either deny or discredit them.

REBECCA NURSE
Accused Witch

You and your friend Martha Corey are both Salem Church members. You are 70 years old, hard of hearing, and so ill that you are often bedridden. In early March, after the arrest and accusation of Sarah Good, Sarah Osborne and Tituba, the afflicted girls in Salem began making accusations against you saying that you sent your "vengeful specter to torment them." On March 24 you were arrested.

You have been accused of witchcraft, one of the most serious crimes in Puritan society. You realize that if you are found guilty of being a witch, you must either confess or suffer the death penalty by hanging. You also know that you are <u>not guilty</u> of witchcraft and to confess would be against your religious beliefs. You must try to convince the Magistrates at your trial that you are not a witch. It will be difficult since there will be a lot of evidence against you and the Magistrates will not be fair by the standards of modern legal systems. They probably already consider you guilty. Additionally, anything that happens during the trial itself can by used as evidence to prove your guilt.

At your trial you will say the following:

1. Deny any association with the Devil or witches.

2. Deny tormenting or afflicting any of the girls who accuse you of witchcraft either by their actions or words.

3. Deny any evil acts like placing curses, calling on the Devil, or sending your spirit to inflict any of these so called evil acts.

4. Try to memorize parts of the Christian Bible since it will make a very favorable impression on the Magistrates.

5. Try to find out what stories the witnesses or afflicted girls might be making up about you so that you can either deny or discredit them.

"Witchcraft in New England," a 19th century engraving, depicting 17th century New England. Courtesy Peabody & Essex Museum, Salem, MA.

"Tituba...she...oh Tituba!"

—Betty Parris

ANN PUTNAM, JR.
Afflicted Girl

You were born in 1680 and are the eldest daughter of Thomas Putnam and his wife Ann. You are intelligent, precocious, and have a quick wit. You were one of the first young girls to be afflicted by the accused witches.

You heard, along with the other girls, Tituba's stories of voodoo and magic. It obviously affected your imagination and has caused you to have visions of demons and devils.

You will accuse all of the arrested women of witchcraft, with particular emphasis on Sarah Good. You saw her spirit come after you with a knife.

During the trial you must do or say any or all of the following:

1. Show a temporary loss of hearing, sight, speech, or memory.

2. Show a choking sensation in the mouth.

3. Act terrified as if you see hallucinations or spirits tormenting you in a variety of ways, including biting and pinching.

4. Occasional body contortions, including twisting your neck or bending your arms and legs in odd positions.

5. Moments in which you are able to relate in clear detail the actions of accused witches that torment you.

6. You should be most active when Sarah Good is being questioned by the Magistrates.

ABIGAIL WILLIAMS
Afflicted Girl

You are a young girl of eleven. Your nickname is "Nabby." Since the death of your parents you have lived with your uncle, Reverend Samuel Parris. He is a strict disciplinarian and you have often been punished for misbehavior. You were part of a group of young girls who heard Tituba's stories of voodoo and magic. These stories gave you nightmares.

You have been afflicted by all of the accused witches, particularly Martha Corey. You saw her giving you an evil eye in church while she was eating a little yellow bird. You were terrified.

During the trial you will do or say the following:

1. Show a temporary loss of hearing, sight, speech, or memory.

2. Show a choking sensation in the mouth.

3. Act terrified as if you see hallucinations or spirits tormenting you in a variety of ways, including biting and pinching.

4. Show occasional body contortions, including twisting your neck or bending your arms and legs in odd positions.

5. Show moments in which you are able to relate in clear detail the actions of the accused witches that torment you.

6. You should be most active when Martha Corey is being questioned by the Magistrates.

ELIZABETH PARRIS
Afflicted Girl

You are called Betty by your friends. At nine years old you are the youngest of the afflicted girls. Your father is the Reverend Samuel Parris. You were part of the group of young girls who heard Tituba's stories of voodoo and magic. It has caused you to have terrifying dreams of demons, devils, and witches.

You have been afflicted by all of the accused witches, especially <u>Sarah Good</u>. Every time you see her you feel sharp pins sticking into your body.

During the trial you will do or say the following:

1. Show a temporary loss of hearing, sight, speech, or memory.

2. Show a choking sensation in the mouth.

3. Act terrified as if you see hallucinations or spirits tormenting you in a variety of ways, including biting and pinching.

4. Show occasional body contortions, including twisting your neck or bending your arms and legs in odd positions.

5. Show moments in which you are able to relate in clear detail the actions of the accused witches that torment you.

6. You should be most active when Sarah Good is being questioned by the Magistrates.

ELIZABETH HUBBARD
AFFLICTED GIRL

You are the great-niece of the wife of Dr. William Griggs and work as a servant in his home. You are seventeen years old. You were part of the nightly group that met in Reverend Samuel Parris' house to hear Tituba's stories of voodoo and magic. Ever since those meetings you have had terrible visions of ghosts, demons, and witches.

You have been afflicted by all of the accused witches, especially <u>Sarah Osborne</u> who you feel sticks you with large pins like knitting needles.

During the trial you will do or say the following:

1. Show a temporary loss of hearing, sight, speech, or memory.

2. Show a choking sensation in the mouth.

3. Act terrified as if you see hallucinations or spirits tormenting you in a variety of ways, including biting and pinching.

4. Show occasional body contortions, including twisting your neck or bending your arms and legs in odd positions.

5. Show moments in which you are able to relate in clear detail the actions of the accused witches that torment you.

6. You should be most active when Sarah Osborne is being questioned by the Magistrates.

MERCY LEWIS
Afflicted Girl

You are Thomas Putnam's seventeen-year-old servant girl. Your parents were killed three years earlier by the Indians and you still suffer horrible dreams about the massacre.

You also have nightmares as a result of the stories you heard from Tituba. You attended the meetings she held, hearing tales of devils, witches, and voodoo magic.

You have been afflicted by all of the accused witches, especially <u>Rebecca Nurse</u>. You often see her spirit hovering over your bed. Sometimes it grabs your head and twists it around causing pain.

During the trial you will do or say the following:

1. Show a temporary loss of hearing, sight, speech, or memory.

2. Show a choking sensation in the mouth.

3. Act terrified as if you see hallucinations or spirits tormenting you in a variety of ways, including biting and pinching.

4. Show occasional body contortions, including twisting your neck or bending your arms and legs in odd positions.

5. Show moments in which you are able to relate in clear detail the actions of the accused witches that torment you.

6. You should be most active when Rebecca Nurse is being questioned by the Magistrates.

THE WITNESSES

"Hang them, they're all witches!"

—John Willard
Deputy Constable

"Of your spectral puppet play
I have traced the cunning wires;
Come what will, I needs must say
God is true, and ye are Liars."

—John Greenleaf Whittier
Calef in Boston, 1692

DR. WILLIAM GRIGGS
WITNESS

You are the doctor for Salem Village. You occupy a position of respect in the community. You have been called to testify against the accused witches.

You will say the following:

1. You have carefully studied all the medical books you have, examined the afflicted girls, and concluded that their afflictions are not caused by natural illness. You believe they must be caused by witchcraft.

2. You believe that they must be "under the evil hand."

3. You were asked by the Court to examine the witches. Your physical examination revealed that the accused witches Sarah Good and Sarah Osborne had strange dark moles on their arms. These moles have subsequently disappeared.

4. You have never been tormented by any of the accused witches, but you have heard plenty of stories about them muttering curses, casting spells, and generally acting strange about town.

 -

JONATHAN PUTNAM
WITNESS

You are currently one of Salem's constables. You signed the complaints against the accused witches and you have decided to come forward as a witness against the accused witch Martha Corey.

You will say the following:

1. You often saw Martha Corey staring at your livestock. After one such episode several of your best cows died. They didn't appear to be sick or have any marks on them.

2. Several times in church you saw Martha Corey giving the evil eye to various people, including some young girls. You tried not to look at her because you were afraid she would put a curse on you.

EDWARD PUTNAM
WITNESS

You are the 38-year-old brother of Thomas Putnam and a firm believer in witchcraft. You have decided to come forward and present yourself as a witness against the accused witch Sarah Good.

You will testify to the following:

1. Sarah Good came to your house begging for food several times a week. Usually you gave her whatever was left over from the evening meal. One evening there were no leftovers. When she was turned away empty-handed, you heard her cursing you in a strange language. It didn't sound like English. When you woke up the next morning, you had developed a large dark mole on your arm. It went away when Sarah Good was arrested.

2. You have seen the accused witch Sarah Good wandering around town making strange noises and staring into people's homes.

CAPTAIN JONATHAN WALCOTT
WITNESS

You are one of the village's military leaders. You are also a church deacon, so sometimes people call you Deacon Walcott. You are 52 years old and married to the sister of Thomas and Edward Putnam. You firmly believe in witchcraft and have encouraged others to bring accusations. You have decided to present yourself as a witness against the accused witch Sarah Osborne.

You will testify to the following:

1. You woke up one night last month in a cold sweat and saw the shape of Sarah Osborne hovering over your bed. It said: "Come with me and worship the Devil or I will inflict great pain on you." You ran out of the room. When you came back, the image was gone. The next morning you awoke with a terrible pain in your back. It was so bad that you could not work for several days.

2. You have heard the afflicted girls repeatedly calling out that Sarah Osborne is tormenting them.

JOSEPH HUTCHINSON
Witness

You are a respected citizen of Salem Village. You believe in witchcraft and originally signed a complaint against the accused witches Sarah Good, Sarah Osborne, and Tituba. Now you think that the afflicted girls, especially Abigail Williams, are making up stories. You have decided to come forward to testify on behalf of the accused witch Martha Corey.

You will say the following:

1. You believe that the accused witches Good, Osborne, and Tituba may be guilty.

2. You think that Abigail Williams is lying and you do not believe that the religious woman Martha Corey is guilty.

3. You have always seen Martha Corey in church and have never seen her perform any evil acts. You believe she is unjustly accused.

REVEREND SAMUEL PARRIS
WITNESS

You are the Minister of the Salem Village Church. You were ordained on November 19, 1689, the day the church was organized as a covenanted body with a total of 27 members. All of the church members were either from the Putnam family or friends of the family. You have carefully studied the fits of the afflicted girls and, along with Dr. Griggs, concluded that they are caused by witchcraft.

You have decided to come forward and testify against Sarah Good and Sarah Osborne. You will say the following:

1. You never knew that the confessed witch Tituba was telling stories about devils, voodoo, and witchcraft to the young afflicted girls at secret meetings in your house. If you had known, you would have put a stop to it immediately.

2. You have repeatedly heard the afflicted girls complaining about horrible pains caused by the accused witches Sarah Good and Sarah Osborne. You have seen them writhing in agony whenever the names of these witches are mentioned or they have actually seen them.

3. You believe that the Devil has sent these witches as his agents on Earth and that there are probably other witches yet to be discovered.

✂ -

THOMAS PRESTON
WITNESS

You believe in witchcraft and originally signed the complaint against the accused witches Sarah Good, Sarah Osborne and Tituba. However, you are the son-in-law of Rebecca Nurse and you now believe that there must be some kind of evil conspiracy against the good, pious women of Salem Village. Sarah Good, Sarah Osborne, and Tituba may be witches, but certainly not the godly Rebecca Nurse.

You have decided to testify on behalf of Rebecca Nurse, saying the following:

1. Your mother-in-law is an honest, caring, religious woman who would do no harm to anyone.

2. She is an old sick woman who hardly knows the afflicted girls. How could she hurt them?

3. You have never seen her perform any kind of action that would be considered evil. She is constantly reading the Bible.

THOMAS PUTNAM
WITNESS

You are 39 years old. Your wife's name is Ann and your daughter, also named Ann, is one of the afflicted girls. You and your wife both maintain that your daughter has suffered greatly at the hands of these accused witches. They have been tormenting her for months. You believe that one of the worst offenders is Rebecca Nurse. You have decided to come forward as a witness against this accused witch. You will say the following:

1. You believe that all of the accused witches are tormenting these afflicted girls, including your daughter Ann.

2. You heard your daughter, on several occasions, when she was in pain call out that Rebecca Nurse was causing her pain.

3. You saw Rebecca Nurse's shape in your barn. It was tormenting the animals. For several days afterwards your cows refused to give milk and one of your horses died.

4. You cannot even look at the accused witches without feeling the presence of the Devil.

EXHIBITS

"For Satan himself is transformed into an Angel of Light."

—Cotton Mather

CONFESSION OF A WITCH IN 1692

Mrs. Mary Osborn of Dover, Massachusetts was examined for witchcraft, September 8, 1692 by a group of Magistrates who reported:

"She confesses that, about eleven years ago, when she was in a melancholy state and condition, she used to walk abroad in her orchard; and upon a certain time she saw the appearance of a cat, at the end of the house, which yet she thought was a real cat. However, at that time, it diverted her from praying to God, and instead thereof she prayed to the Devil; about which time she made a covenant with the Devil, who, as a dark man, came to her and presented her a book, upon which she laid her finger, and that left a red spot: and that upon her signing, the Devil told her he was her God, and that she should serve and worship him, and she believes she consented to it. She says, further, that about two years ago, she was carried through the air, in the company with Deacon Frye's wife, Elizabeth Baker, and Goody Tyler, to Five Mile Pond, where she was baptized by the Devil, who dipped her face in the water and made her renounce her former baptism, and told her she must be his, soul and body, forever, and that she must serve him, which she promised to do."

RECANT OF A CONFESSED WITCH

On October 19, 1692 Mrs. Mary Osborn was examined for witchcraft by Reverend Increase Mather, who reported:

"Mrs. Osborn freely and relentingly said that the confession she made upon her examination for witchcraft (September 8, 1962) and afterwards acknowledged before the honourable judges, was wholly false, and that she was brought to the said confession by the violent urging and unreasonable pressings that were used toward her; she asserted that she never signed the Devil's book, was never baptized by the Devil, never afflicted any of the accusers, or gage her consent for their being afflicted."

EXHIBIT C

TRANSCRIPT OF THE PRELIMINARY EXAMINATION OF SARAH GOOD BY MAGISTRATES JOHN HATHORNE AND JONATHAN CORWIN

Magistrates: Sarah Good, what evil spirit have you familiarity with?
Sarah Good: None.

Magistrates: Why do you hurt these children?
Sarah Good: I do not hurt them. I scorn it.

Magistrates: Who do you employ, then, to do it?
Sarah Good: I employ nobody.

Magistrates: Why did you go away muttering from Mr. Parris' house?
Sarah Good: I did not mutter, but I thanked him for what he gave my child.

Magistrates: Who was it, then, who tormented the children?
Sarah Good: It was Osborne.

Magistrates: What is it that you say with your mutterings?
Sarah Good: If I must tell, it is the Commandments. I may say my Commandments, I hope.

Magistrates: What Commandment is it?
Sarah Good: It is a psalm.

Magistrates: Who do you serve?
Sarah Good: I serve God.

TRANSCRIPT OF THE PRELIMINARY EXAMINATION OF TITUBA BY MAGISTRATES JOHN HATHORNE AND JONATHAN CORWIN

Magistrates: Tituba, what evil spirit have you familiarity with?
Tituba: None.

Magistrates: Why do you hurt these children?
Tituba: I do not hurt them.

Magistrates: Who is it, then?
Tituba: The Devil, for aught I know.

Magistrates: Did you ever see the Devil?
Tituba: The Devil came to me and bid me serve him.

Magistrates: Who have you seen?
Tituba: Four women sometimes hurt the children.

Magistrates: Who were they?
Tituba: Goody Osborne and Sarah Good, and I do not know who the others were. Sarah Good and Sarah Osborne would have me hurt the children, but I would not.

Magistrates: What attendants hath Sarah Good?
Tituba: A yellow bird, and she would have given me one. It did suck between her fingers.

Magistrates: What hath Sarah Osborne?
Tituba: Yesterday she had a thing with a head like a woman, with two legs and wings.

Magistrates: Do you see who torments these children?
Tituba: Yes, it is Good and Osborne. They sent their shapes to pinch and hurt the children.

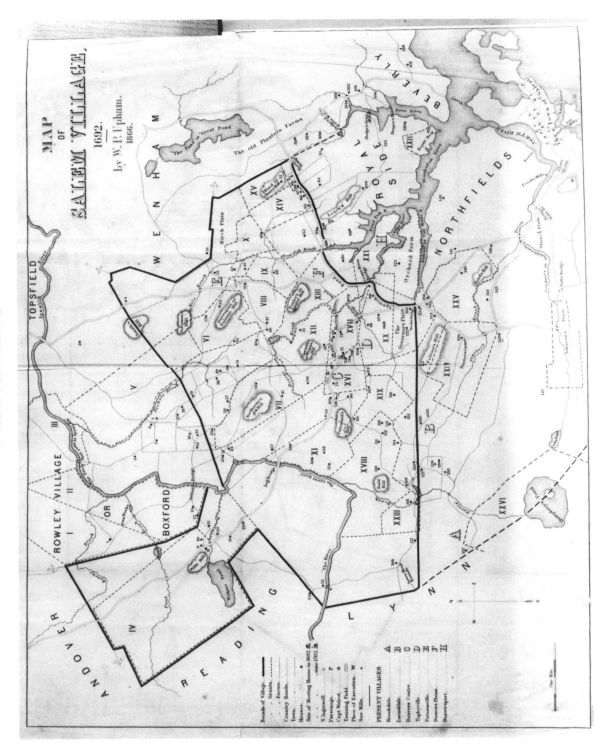

Map of Salem village, 1692, drawn by William P. Upham, 1866, from data obtained from early Essex County, Massachusetts, records. Courtesy, Peabody & Essex Museum, Salem, MA.

ADDITIONAL INFORMATION

"For spell and charm had power no more
The specters ceased to roam
And scattered households knelt again
Around the hearths of home."

—John Greenleaf Whittier
The Witches of Wenham

MASTER ROLE SHEET

HISTORICAL CHARACTER	ROLE	STUDENT NAME
Tituba	Witch	_____
Sarah Good	Witch	_____
Sarah Osborne	Witch	_____
Rebecca Nurse*	Witch	_____
Martha Corey*	Witch	_____
Ann Putnam Jr.	Afflicted Girl	_____
Abigail Williams	Afflicted Girl	_____
Elizabeth Parris	Afflicted Girl	_____
Elizabeth Hubbard	Afflicted Girl	_____
Mercy Lewis	Afflicted Girl	_____
Thomas Putnam*	Witness	_____
Edward Putnam	Witness	_____
Joseph Hutchinson*	Witness	_____
Thomas Preston*	Witness	_____
Jonathan Putnam*	Witness	_____
Cpt. Jonathan Walcott	Witness	_____
Dr. William Griggs	Witness	_____
Rev. Sam Parris	Witness	_____
Cotton Mather	Minister	_____
John Hathorne**	Magistrate	_____
Jonathan Corwin	Magistrate	_____
Bartholomew Gedney	Magistrate	_____
John Putnam, Jr.	Court Officer/Clerk	_____

* These roles may be eliminated for a shorter trial with fewer participants.

**It is recommended that the teacher play the role of this Magistrate.

Note: There are several optional roles should you wish to conduct a more elaborate simulation.

65

TRIAL PROCEDURE*

1. Magistrates enter the Courtroom.

2. The Constable/Clerk says "All Rise."

3. The Magistrates state that "this Court is meeting to Hear and Decide the guilt or innocence of individuals accused of the horrible crime of witchcraft."

4. The Magistrates begin their examination by questioning the confessed witch Tituba.

5. The Magistrates question the afflicted girls.

6. The Magistrates question the witnesses.

7. The accused witches are questioned.

8. The Magistrates deliberate and reach a verdict.

9. The Magistrates either acquit the accused or sentence them to death for witchcraft.

---

* This is a suggested procedure. Unexpected developments may suggest a different approach. Be flexible.

SUGGESTED COURTROOM SET-UP

MAGISTRATES		CLERK

	WITNESS SEAT	

AFFLICTED GIRLS	WITNESSES AND SPECTATORS	ACCUSED WITCHES

LEGAL TERMS*

DISCOVERED	The process by which the names of other witches and wizards were revealed.
HALLUCINATION	A state of mind whereby a person senses something that in reality does not exist. Hallucinations, dreams, and mere fancies could be accepted in court as factual proof of the behavior of the accused witch.
MAGISTRATE	A public officer invested with judicial power.
OYER AND TERMINER	A special tribunal empowered to hear and determine cases within a defined criminal jurisdiction, especially when the delay involved in ordinary prosecution could not be tolerated.
SPECTER	A visible disembodied spirit.
SPECTRAL EVIDENCE	Proof that an accused witch sent his or her spirit or shape to harm innocent victims. It was accepted that the devil could not assume the shape of an innocent person in doing mischief to mankind.
WITCHCRAFT	The Bible does not define witchcraft, it simply names the offense and a proposed punishment; "thou shalt not permit a witch to live." The Puritans viewed witchcraft as being "in league with the devil" and performing his wishes on earth.

* Puritan law, 1692-1693

SUBPOENA*

YOU _____ are hereby commanded to present yourself before the *MAGISTRATES* at the *COURT of OYER and TERMINER* meeting in *SALEM VILLAGE* on or about March 1692 (_____).
                                                                                             (modern date)

Please present yourself at _____ in _____ and be prepared to
                                  (time)   (room number)

PRESENT EVIDENCE to said *COURT* regarding the case of the *ACCUSED WITCH* _____ .
       (name)

Failure to comply with this *SUMMONS* will result in *CONTEMPT CHARGES.*

Requested by the *HONORABLE MAGISTRATES* of *PURITAN NEW ENGLAND.*

I have served this summons _____
                                  (Court Clerk and Constable)

*Please find attached role sheet or other information related to your requested testimony.

69

MAGISTRATE EVALUATION SHEET

Listen carefully to all the evidence presented by the afflicted girls, the witnesses, and the accused witches. Use this form to help you decide the guilt or innocence of the accused witches.

NAME	COMPLETELY BELIEVABLE	MOSTLY BELIEVABLE	UNBELIEVABLE
<u>Accused Witches</u>			
Tituba	❑	❑	❑
Sarah Good	❑	❑	❑
Sarah Osborne	❑	❑	❑
Rebecca Nurse	❑	❑	❑
Martha Corey	❑	❑	❑
<u>Afflicted Girls</u>			
Ann Putnam, Jr.	❑	❑	❑
Abigail Williams	❑	❑	❑
Elizabeth Parris	❑	❑	❑
Elizabeth Hubbard	❑	❑	❑
Mercy Lewis	❑	❑	❑

MAGISTRATE EVALUATION SHEET, CONTINUED

NAME	COMPLETELY BELIEVABLE	MOSTLY BELIEVABLE	UNBELIEVABLE
Witnesses			
Thomas Putnam	❑	❑	❑
Edward Putnam	❑	❑	❑
Joseph Hutchinson	❑	❑	❑
Thomas Preston	❑	❑	❑
Jonathan Putnam	❑	❑	❑
Cpt. Walcott	❑	❑	❑
Dr. Griggs	❑	❑	❑
Rev. Parris	❑	❑	❑

Based on the evidence, I believe that the following individuals are *GUILTY of WITCH-CRAFT*:

_____

_____

_____

Based on the evidence, I believe that the following individuals are *NOT GUILTY of WITCHCRAFT*:

_____

_____

_____

ADDITIONAL WITCHES OR WIZARDS The individuals assigned these roles will be spectators in the courtroom. They should be assigned to research their character, and cautioned that they may be "discovered" as witches or wizards during the course of the trial.

MARTHA CARRIER
BRIDGET BISHOP
ELIZABETH PROCTOR
GILES COREY
GEORGE BURROUGHS

ADDITIONAL MAGISTRATES The individuals assigned these roles should follow the questioning guidelines outlined on any of the other magistrate role sheets.

WILLIAM STOUGHTON (biased against the defendants)

ROBERT CALEF (eventually viewed the defendants as innocent)

THOMAS BRATTLE (eventually viewed the defendants as innocent)

ADDITIONAL WITNESSES The individuals assigned these roles should either research a genuine incident, or make an imaginary account consistent with the other testimony against the accused witches.

BENJAMIN ABBOT
SARAH ABBOT
THOMAS FISK
ANN FOSTER

All of the above characters were real individuals involved in the Salem witch trials.

CHRONOLOGY

1620	—Mayflower Compact
1622	—Rebecca Nurse, accused witch, born
1630	—John Winthrop arrives in Salem, later moves to Boston
1641	—John Hathorne, Magistrate, born
1643	—Sarah Osbourne, accused witch, born. First execution for witchcraft takes place in Massachusetts
1653	—Sarah Good, accused witch, born
1675-77	—King Philip's War
1680	—Ann Putnam Jr., afflicted girl, born
1683	—Elizabeth Parris, afflicted girl, born
February 29, 1692	—Complaint filed accusing Sarah Good, Sarah Osbourne and Tituba of witchcraft
March 1, 1692	—Examinations of first accused witches Tituba, Sarah Good and Sarah Osbourne
May 10, 1692	—Sarah Osbourne dies in prison
June 10, 1692	—Bridget Bishop hanged
July 19, 1692	—Sarah Good and Rebecca Nurse hanged
September 19, 1692	—Giles Cory pressed to death
September 22, 1692	—Martha Corey hanged
September 8, 1692	—Mary Osbourne confesses to witchcraft
October 19, 1692	—Mary Osbourne recants her confession
1693	—Witchcraft trials end and hysteria dies down

AFTERMATH

Sarah Good was hanged for witchcraft on July 19, 1692. Her four-year-old daughter, Dorcas, remained jailed in Boston's prison until a kindly Salem citizen bailed her out in December of that year.

Tituba stayed in jail until the end of the witchcraft hysteria and then was sold to a West Indian slave trader.

Sarah Osborne was never found guilty of witchcraft since she died in prison on May 10, 1692 before her trial was completed.

Martha Corey refused to confess and was hanged on September 22, 1692.

On June 29, 1692 Rebecca Nurse was found not guilty of witchcraft but the court was asked by then Chief Justice Stoughton to reconsider the verdict. It was changed to guilty and she was hanged in Salem on July 19, 1692.

The Puritan general public eventually came to see the folly of what had happened in 1692 and by the following year the witchcraft scare was over. With the exception of one magistrate, Samuel Sewall, the Salem judges never publicly admitted remorse or embarrassment for the many unjust deaths.

THE PLACE OF EXECUTION AND THE CREVICE
FOR THE BODIES

The witches were hanged on Proctor Street, Salem, marked on the map by dotted lines. The cross shows where the dead bodies were thrown. To touch a witch was considered dangerous; yet most of the corpses were taken away for burial near their homes.

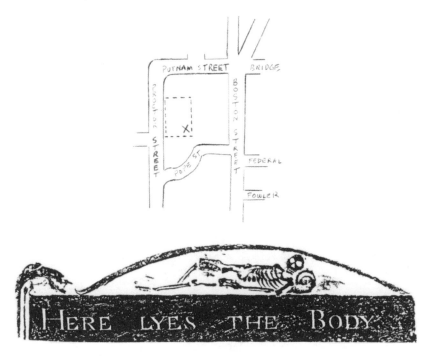

ADDITIONAL INFORMATION ABOUT SALEM IN 1692-1693

1. Nearly all of the accused witches were middle-aged women and most of their accusers were a generation younger.

2. Most of the accused witches were eccentric or had antisocial personalities.

3. Most of the accusers were neighbors of the accused.

4. Most of the accused witches were either married or widowed.

5. Thirty-four persons experienced "fits" or acted "bewitched" during the Salem trials.

6. Eighty-four persons came forward as "witnesses" at one time or another during the trials.

7. Nearly all of the witnesses against the women accused of witchcraft were men.

8. Most of the accused witches came from what we would consider as the lower level of the Puritan social order.

9. Many of the accused witches had a long history of not getting along well with their neighbors and were viewed as nasty people.

10. Most of the accused witches were suspected of conducting witches' meetings or some associations with the Devil.

11. Nearly all of the suspected witches were accused of some sort of aggressive behavior, like sending their spirit to pinch, bite, twist, grab, annoy, or otherwise afflict an unfortunate victim. This hostile behavior could also be directed to livestock or even crops.

12. Over 200 people were arrested for witchcraft in 1692-1693.

13. Of the seven judges originally appointed to the Court of Oyer and Terminer, only one, Bartholomew Gedney, was from Salem Village.

14. The Puritans had a poor regard for attorneys and did not permit the professional practice of law. There were no law schools in Massachusetts and none of the magistrates had any formal legal training.

DISCUSSION QUESTIONS

1. Did the accused witches get a fair trial? Would any of the evidence given be accepted in a court of law today? What aspects would not be admissible? Why?

2. Did any of the testimony against the witches seem believable? Why?

3. Why did the threat of witchcraft create such a problem for the 17th-century Puritans?

4. How were the lives of the accused witches, the afflicted girls, the witnesses, and the magistrates interconnected?

5. Some historians have suggested that there was a deliberate plot or conspiracy to get certain individuals by accusing them of witchcraft. Does this seem likely with the evidence presented in the trial?

6. Did the harsh environment and strict religious standards of the Puritans instigate the afflicted girls' behavior toward the accused adult witches?

7. Some historians think that the events in Salem 1692-1693 were not of much historical consequence. Do you agree or disagree? Why?

BIBLIOGRAPHY

Bailey, Thomas A. *The American Spirit, Vol. 1, United States History as Seen by Contemporaries.* Includes Cotton Mather's "Wonders of the Invisible World" Lexington, MA: D.C. Heath & Co., 1978.

Burr, George Lincoln (ed.). *Narratives of the Witchcraft Cases 1648-1706.* NY: Charles Scribner's, 1914.

Duncan, James. *Salem and the Indians.* Boston: Houghton Mifflin Co., 1947.

Essex Institute Historical Collections. Salem, MA.

Ives, William, and George Pease. *Account of the Life and Character of Reverand Samuel Parris of Salem Village and of His Connection with the Witchcraft Delusion of 1692.* Salem Observor, 1857.

Karlsen, Carol F. *The Devil in the Shape of a Woman.* NY: Vantage Press, a Division of Random House, 1987.

Katz, Stanley N. (ed.). *Colonial American: Essays in Politics and Social Development.* Boston: Little, Brown & Co., 1976.

Levin, David. *What Happened in Salem.* NY: Harcourt, Brace, Inc., 1960.

Nevins, Winfield S. *Witchcraft in Salem Village in 1692.* Salem: Salem Press Co., 1916.

Perley, Sidney. *The History of Salem Massachusetts.* Cambridge, MA: Tudor Press, 1924.

Perley, Sidney. *Where the Salem Witches Were Hanged.* Salem: Essex Institute, 1921.

Perley, M.V.B. (ed.). *Verbatim Report of the Trial of Elizabeth Howe.* Salem: M.V.B Perley, 1911.

Phillips, James Duncan. *Salem in the 17th Century.* Boston: Houghton Mifflin Co., 1933.

Publications of the Colonial Society of Massachusetts. Boston: Records of the Suffolk County Court 1671–1680.

Richardson, Katherine W. *The Salem Witchcraft Trials.* Salem: Essex Institute, 1970.

Robinson, Enders A. *The Devil Discovered: Salem Witchcraft 1692.* NY: Hippocrene Books, 1991.

Smith, Joseph H. *The Pynchon Court Record: Colonial Justice in Western Massachusetts (1639-1702).* Cambridge: Harvard University Press, 1961.

Starkey, Marion L. *The Devil in Massachusetts: A Modern Inquiry into the Salem Witch Trials.* NY: Anchor Books, 1969.

Thomas, Halsey M. (ed.). *The Diary of Samuel Sewall.* NY: Farrar, Straus & Giroux Co., 1973.

Trask, Richard B. *The Devil Hath Been Raised: A Documentary History of the Salem Village Witchcraft Outbreak of March 1692.* Danvers, MA: Danvers Historical Society, 1992.

Weisman, Richard. *Witchcraft, Magic, and Religion in 17th Century Massachusetts.* Amherst: University of Massachusetts Press, 1984.

Winsor, Justin (ed.). *The Memorial History of Boston, Including Suffolk County, Massachusetts 1630-1880.* Boston: Clarence F. Jewett, 1882.

REX VS. CAPTAIN PRESTON, ET. AL.:
THE BOSTON MASSACRE

"English Recruits for America" Courtesy Print Collection Miriam and Ira D. Wallach Division of Art, Prints, and Photographs, The New York Public Library, Astor, Lenox and Tilden Foundations

BACKGROUND

AMERICANS!
BEAR IN REMEMBRANCE
The HORRID MASSACRE!
Perpetrated in King-street, Boston,
New-England,
On the Evening of March the Fifth, 1770.
When FIVE of your fellow countrymen,
GRAY, MAVERICK, CALDWELL, ATTUCKS,
and CARR,
Lay wallowing in their Gore!
Being basely, and most inhumanly
MURDERED!
And SIX others badly WOUNDED!
By a Party of the XXIXth Regiment,
Under the command of Capt. Tho. Preston.
REMEMBER!
That Two of the MURDERERS
Were convicted of MANSLAUGHTER!
By a Jury, of whom I shall say
NOTHING,
Branded in the hand!
And dismissed,
The others were ACQUITTED,
And their Captain PENSIONED!
Also,
BEAR IN REMEMBRANCE
That on the 22d Day of February, 1770
The infamous
EBENEZER RICHARDSON, Informer,
And tool to Ministerial hirelings,
Most barbarously
MURDERED
CHRISTOPHER SEIDER,
An innocent youth!
Of which crime he was found guilty
By his Country
On Friday April 20th, 1770;
But remained Unsentenced
On Saturday the 22d Day of February, 1772.
When the GRAND INQUEST
For Suffolk county,
Were informed, at request,
By the Judges of the Superior Court,
That EBENEZER RICHARDSON'S Case
Then lay before his MAJESTY.
Therefore said Richardson
This day, MARCH FIFTH! 1772,
Remains UNHANGED!!!
Let THESE things be told to Posterity!
And handed down
From Generation to Generation,
'Till Time shall be no more!
Forever may AMERICA be preserved,
From weak and wicked monarchs,
Tyrannical Ministers,
Abandoned Governors,
Their Underlings and Hirelings!
And may the
Machinations of artful, designing wretches,
Who would ENSLAVE THIS People,
Come to an end,
Let their NAMES and MEMORIES
Be buried in eternal oblivion,
And the PRESS,
For a SCOURGE to Tyrannical Rulers,
Remain FREE.

"Unhappy Boston! See they sons deplore
Thy hallowed walks besmear'd with guiltless gore!"

—Paul Revere

VIOLENCE IN BOSTON'S NORTH END

On a cold and windy morning in February 1770, eleven-year-old Christopher Seider was one of several hundred adults and youths surrounding the house of Ebenezer Richardson in Boston's North End. Richardson was a known Tory informer for the British customs commissioners who had been sent to Boston in 1767 to collect duties on colonial imports set by Parliament in the Townshend Acts.

In port cities like Philadelphia, New York, and Boston, mob demonstrations against these Acts occurred frequently. Sometimes they were spontaneous but many were organized by "Sons of Liberty" Patriot leaders like Samuel Adams. The mob that was throwing insults as well as eggs, rotten fruit, sticks, snowballs, ice, and stones at Richardson's house had no leader. Flying debris broke most of the windowpanes and a rock hit Richardson's wife. Terrified, he grabbed an unloaded musket and shoved it through a shattered window. Undaunted, the crowd proceeded to break down his door. Richardson then loaded his weapon with small birdshot pellets and fired into the mob. Christopher Seider fell bleeding onto the street with eleven deadly pellets in his chest and abdomen. He died later that evening.

Richardson was arrested and charged with giving Christopher Seider a "very dangerous wound." This indictment was later changed to murder. Seider's death provided Samuel Adams and other Patriot leaders with a young martyr to British tyranny and served as a grim omen for future mob violence in Boston.

SOLDIERS AND CITIZENRY

By 1770 there were nearly 600 redcoat soldiers of the British Army stationed in Boston. Many were Irish Catholic, some were blacks, and all except the officers were uneducated and poor. Ill-mannered and uncouth, the soldiers spent much of their off-duty time drinking "demon rum" and street-fighting. They were brazenly cursed by the citizens, called "lobsters" because of their bright red uniforms, and were often the butt of practical jokes. Most Bostonians hated the redcoat soldiers who they believed had been sent to take away their freedom. In fact, Samuel Adams wrote that he thought it possible that the British "in calling for a military force under pretence of supporting civil authority, secretly intended to introduce a general massacre." That the British soldiers who occupied Boston in early 1770 intended to "massacre" some of Boston's 16,000 citizens seems improbable today, but in March of that year many residents feared otherwise. Tensions were high and each group—soldiers and citizens—anticipated an attack that it believed its opponents had "plotted" well in advance.

INCIDENT AT JOHN GRAY'S ROPEWALK

On March 2, 1770 only four days after Christopher Seider's funeral, a British soldier named Thomas Walker of the 29th Regiment entered John Gray's ropewalk looking for work. It was his day off. Army pay was low and soldiers often sought extra work while off duty. Ropemaker William Green asked him: "Soldier, do you want work?" "Yes, I do," replied Walker. Green shouted in his face, "Well, then go and clean my outhouse." Walker's face turned as red as his coat with humiliation as Green and the other ropemakers roared with laughter. "Empty it yourself, you scum," yelled the angry Walker. Taunts and curses soon changed to fists as Walker and several ropemakers started to exchange blows. One ropemaker, Nicholas Ferriter, finally knocked the soldier on his rearend. Walker got up and ran for help.

He returned a few minutes later with several fellow soldiers and Gray's ropewalk was quickly jammed with soldiers and ropemakers fighting with fists, wooden clubs, and swords. A tall black soldier was asked, "You black rascal! What have you to do with white people's quarrels?" He replied, "I suppose I may look on." Private Walker, Private Kilroy, Nicholas Ferriter, and Sam Gray all distinguished themselves in the fighting. Both sides suffered bloody injuries until the heavily outnumbered soldiers were driven from the ropewalk.

The next day, March 3, three soldiers returned to the ropewalk and renewed the fight until one received a fractured skull. Private John Carroll later recalled hearing a Bostonian ask where the 29th Regiment "planned to bury its dead." A ropemaker, however, swore that he heard a soldier say that "there were a great many townspeople who would eat their dinners on Monday next who would not eat any on Tuesday."

MARCH 5, 1770 ON KING STREET

Like the incident at the ropewalk, this quarrel began with a British soldier and a young British worker. Private Hugh White of the 29th Regiment was on guard duty at the sentry box on King Street near the Custom House. As Edward Garrick, a teenage wigmaker's apprentice, was passing the sentry box he spotted a British officer named Captain Goldfinch. He shouted in Private White's face: "There goes the fellow that will not pay my master for dressing his hair."

Garrick was soon joined by other passing youths who continued the rude criticisms of Captain Goldfinch. Finally, Private White—having had enough of this name calling—defended the officer by saying he was an "officer and a gentleman who always paid his debts." Garrick said sarcastically: "There are no gentlemen in the 29th Regiment!" Private White then said to Garrick: "Let me see your face!" Garrick thrust his jaw out and White immediately smashed his seven-kilo Brown Bess musket into his face. Garrick crashed to the ground bleeding. Within minutes a crowd of over fifty townsmen had gathered and were shouting curses and daring Private White to fight them.

With bayonet fixed, White slowly retreated back to the steps of the Custom House and loaded his musket. "Lobster son-of-a-bitch! Damned rascally scoundrel!" they shouted at Walker as the town bells began to ring signalling the alarm of "fire." As the crowd grew in size it also became more aggressive. People began throwing large chunks of ice at White and screaming: "Kill him, knock him down! Fire, damn you! You dare not fire!" Terrified, White yelled "Turn out the Guard! Main Guard, turn out!"

Elsewhere similar mobs of townsmen were gathering in the streets near the Custom House. Volleys of snowballs were being hurled at soldiers and several British officers, including Captain Goldfinch, were patrolling the streets ordering their men into the barracks to prevent violence.

As the church bells rang, hundreds of Bostonians began to descend on King Street—many carrying buckets since they believed the town was on fire. Others, however, carried clubs, snowballs, and chunks of ice. "There is no fire!" shouted one youth to a man who replied: "Dammit, I am glad of it! I will knock some of them soldiers on the head!" Another was heard to say he "had a sword to chop off a soldier's head."

SHOTS IN THE NIGHT

Hearing what sounded like a riot, Captain Thomas Preston led a column of seven soldiers onto King Street. Their muskets were empty and shouldered, but their bayonets were fixed. They pushed their way through a crowd that now numbered nearly 400 and finally reached the Custom House steps and the besieged Private White. Preston then tried to march the men back to the Main Guard Station, but the crowd would not let them pass. Hammond Green, a well-known Tory, peered tentatively out his office window on the second floor of the Customs House. Someone in the mob shouted, "Fire, damn you! You can't kill all of us!" Preston formed his men into a semi-circle and the soldiers loaded their muskets with double-shot. He then shouted to the crowd to "disperse," but only received in reply curses, laughter, further threats, and snowballs.

Meanwhile, a Tory justice of the peace, James Murray, arrived on King Street to read the "Riot Act." This was a law that forbid riotous gatherings. He was driven away by the mob with showers of snowballs and chunks of ice.

The crowd, including Edward Langford, Sam Atwood, Crispus Attucks, and James Brewer, became even more daring as some used clubs to beat against the soldiers' muskets while others hurled snowballs and ice. Captain Preston was trying hard to keep the terrified soldiers under his command from firing. At one point he even stepped in front of his men so that if they did fire he would be the first victim. A large man (later identified by some as Crispus Attucks) struck out at the Captain with a large cordwood stick crying, "Kill the dogs, knock them over."

Suddenly a club flew from the mob, hitting Private Hugh Montgomery squarely in the face and knocking him to the ground along with his heavy musket. Montgomery rose to his feet, shouted, "Damn you, fire" and pulled the trigger of his weapon. The explosion momentarily silenced the crowd. No one seemed to have been hit. Instants later the crowd surged forward at Preston and his men, swinging with their wooden clubs. Richard Palmes hit Private Montgomery with his club. He then aimed a blow at Captain Preston which was deflected by Private Warren's musket and landed on his arm. During this time—from fifteen seconds to two minutes (accounts vary)—the other soldiers fired their muskets. Private Kilroy pointed his musket at Sam Gray and Edward Langford. Langford yelled, "God damn you, don't fire!" Kilroy fired and Gray fell to the ground dead—his hands in his pockets and a hole in his head the size of a fist. The huge black man, Crispus Attucks, fell to the ground with "two Balls entering his Breast." All the rest of the soldiers fired, reloaded, and fired a second volley into the crowd. Captain Preston finally shoved the smoking gun barrels down as the blood from the wounded and dead citizens of Boston flowed onto King Street.

THE AFTERMATH

Preston's men began to tell him that they had fired after hearing what they believed to be his command to fire. As the crowd drew back carrying dead and wounded citizens, Preston was able to march the men to the Main Guard Station. Then he assembled the entire Guard, marched them in formation to King Street, and set them up in a "street firing position"—the 18th-century tactic for controlling riots in narrow streets. Rows of soldiers stood in a single-file formation. The soldier at the head of the line would shoot, then move to the back of the line, reload, and wait his turn at the front to shoot.

Word spread quickly through the cold night that five men lay dead or dying including a black sailor named Crispus Attucks (described by contemporaries as a powerfully built runaway "mulatto" and a leader of the mob), an Irish-Catholic immigrant named Patrick Carr, Samuel Gray, the son of the ropewalk owner, 17 year old Samuel Maverick and a young sailor named James Caldwell.

Moderate Patriot leaders pleaded with Lt. Governor Hutchinson to order Captain Preston's soldiers from Kings Street before more blood flowed. Hutchinson spoke to Preston and then addressed the crowd from the balcony of Town Hall, asking them to leave peacefully and assuring them that the men responsible for the shooting would be brought before the law. Then Preston's superior officer, Lt. Colonel Maurice Carr, arrived and ordered Preston and his soldiers to abandon the street firing position and return to their barracks. As the troops marched off, the mob, now silent, drifted away and the night was finally silent.

At 2 A.M. on March 6 the town sheriff served a warrant on Captain Preston. Later, the eight redcoat soldiers under his command were arrested and all nine men were charged with murder.

THE TRIALS

Captain Preston's trial began on October 24, 1770 in the new courthouse on Queen (now Court) Street and lasted for six days. It was the first criminal trial in Massachusetts to last more than one day. One of the prosecutors was a well-known Tory named Samuel Quincy. His defense was handled by two of Boston's leading Patriot lawyers, John Adams and Josiah Quincy. It was evident that the Patriot leaders felt it was necessary to prove to the British government and the public that the defendants were getting a fair trial.

The soldiers realized that they would have a better chance of acquittal if they were tried with their commanding officer. They petitioned the superior court saying, "Let us have our trial at the same time with our Captain, for we did our Captain's orders and if we didn't Obey his commands we should have been confined and shot for not doing it." Their request was denied. The second trial, that of the eight soldiers under Preston's command, began nearly a month later on November 27 and ended on December 5. (However, for the purpose of this simulation, the two trials have been combined as "Rex (the King) vs. Preston, et. al.")

You will now have the chance to participate in this historic event.

'5 Coffings for Massacre' by Paul Revere used in *Boston Gazette*, 1770, and broadsides. American Antiquarian Society.

JUDGE AND CLERK

"God sent thee a good deliverance."

—Court Clerk to the Jury

EDMUND TROWBRIDGE

TRIAL JUDGE

You are the most perceptive of a five-judge panel that presided at the trial. For the purposes of the simulation, you will be the only judge. You should enter the court wearing the dignified red robe of a judge.

It will be your task to organize and run the trial according to the following procedures:

1. First, charge the jury by instructing them to listen carefully to the witnesses and remind them that the defendants are considered innocent until proven guilty. You can say: "You shall well and truly try and true deliverance make between our sovereign lord the King and the prisoners at the bar, who you shall have charge according to the evidence, so help you God."

2. Ask the defendants to "rise" and have them answer to the charge "guilty or not guilty" of "murder."

3. The prosecution and defense attorneys may make opening remarks to the court.

4. Prosecution presents its witnesses and cross-examination.

5. Defense presents its witnesses and cross-examination. (In the real trial the defendants were barred from testifying in their own behalf. They may choose to testify in the simulation.)

6. You may allow rebuttal witnesses as time may permit.

7. The prosecution and defense make their closing remarks to the court.

8. You should then instruct the jury prior to their deliberation. In the real trial you told the jury that if they were satisfied "that the sentinel was insulted and that Captain Preston went to assist him, it was doubtless excusable homicide, if not justifiable." You went on to tell them to reject any thought of conspiracy, stating that there had been "no concerted plan on either side," only the provocative actions of a belligerent mob and the frightened reactions of a small group of soldiers. This position could cause "any little spark to kindle a great fire—and five lives were sacrificed to a squabble between the sentry, Private White, and a barber's boy, Edward Garrick."

9. You may allow the jury to find some of the accused guilty and others, innocent. For example, Captain Preston could be declared "innocent" and Private Kilroy "guilty."

10. You may also allow the jury to find some of the accused guilty of the lesser charge of "manslaughter."

11. If the jury fails to reach a verdict in a specified amount of time (for example, 15 minutes), you may follow the common-law rule that "deprived the jurors of food, drink, light, and fire" until they produce a verdict (use your imagination to simulate this rule).

12. After the verdict you must sentence any of the accused found guilty. If a person is found guilty of murder, he would be sentenced to death. If a person is found guilty of manslaughter, he would be sentenced to a year in jail and a "M" branded with a hot-iron on his thumb.

SAMUEL WINTHROP
CLERK AND BAILIFF

You are responsible for assisting the Judge in running the trial.
You will be expected to do the following:

1. At the beginning of the trial, when the jury is seated, you must say to them: "Good men and true, stand together and harken to your evidence."

2. Swear in all witnesses, asking them to place their left hand on the Bible, raise their right hand, and say "Yes" to the statement "Do you swear to tell the truth, the whole truth, and nothing but the truth, so help you God?"

3. Serve any subpoenas that are issued by the judge.

4. Read aloud to the court any documents that the judge instructs you to enter into the court record, including statements of law and evidence introduced as exhibits.

5. Keep a record of the names of all witnesses offering testimony.

6. Assist the jury in any problems or questions they might have regarding court procedure.

7. Assist the judge in maintaining courtroom order. You may be asked to remove unruly witnesses or spectators.

8. At the end of the trial, when the jury has reached their verdict, the judge will ask you to say the following to the foreman of the jury: "Gentlemen of the Jury, look upon the prisoner. How say you is _____ guilty of all
   (name of defendant)

or either of the felonies or murders whereof he stands indicted, or not guilty." The foreman of the jury will then say the defendant is either "guilty" or "not guilty." You will then say: "Harken to your verdict as the Court hath recorded it. You upon your oaths do say that _____ is (guilty, not guilty), and so say you all."
   (name of defendant)

PROSECUTING ATTORNEYS

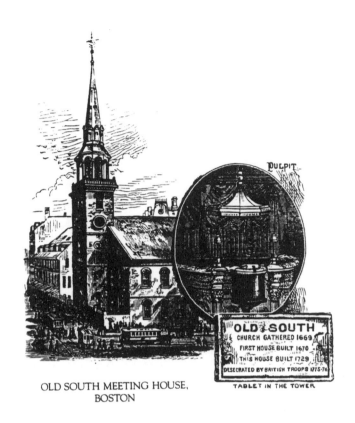

OLD SOUTH MEETING HOUSE,
BOSTON

TABLET IN THE TOWER

"They call me a brainless Tory. But tell me, my young friend, which is better—to be ruled by one tyrant three thousand miles away, or by three thousand tyrants not one mile away."

—Mather Byler
Loyalist Clergyman

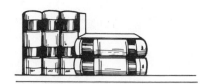

ROBERT TREAT PAINE
Prosecuting Attorney

You are a noted Boston lawyer and a rival of the defense attorney John Adams. Unfortunately, during the trial you become sick and have not been able to present a strong effort.

You will try to marshall enough strength to help your colleague Sam Quincy prove the following:

1. There was a lot of mutual hostility in Boston prior to the shootings on King Street and the soldiers of the 29th Regiment were primarily responsible.

2. It is clear from the evidence that certain Boston citizens like Sam Gray were marked for retaliation because of the fights at the ropewalks.

3. A soldier initiated the whole incident by deliberately striking a young boy with his musket.

4. The crowd was throwing insults and snowballs. The crowd <u>was not</u> throwing ice, stones, or bricks. The crowd was angry for what had been done to the young lad, but they never intended to physically hurt the soldiers.

5. The soldiers loaded their muskets with double-shot and prepared to fire on the command of their officer.

6. One shot was fired and then Captain Preston gave the order to "fire." Surely his men should be able to identify his command.

7. Private Montgomery and Private Kilroy aimed their weapons directly at citizens and killed them. And if one soldier is guilty, they all are guilty.

8. Captain Preston could have stopped his men from firing by giving the order to "recover." He waited until some of the men had reloaded and fired again.

9. There is much evidence to indicate that this was a deliberate conspiracy on the part of the 29th Regiment to murder citizens of Boston.

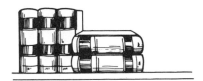

SAMUEL QUINCY
Prosecuting Attorney

You are a well-respected Boston attorney. Your younger brother, Josiah Quincy, is one of the lawyers for the defense. You were once a member of the "Sons of Liberty," but changed your loyalties and became a Tory.

You will help your ailing colleague Robert Treat Paine to prove the following:

1. There was a lot of mutual hostility in Boston prior to the shootings on King Street, and the soldiers of the 29th Regiment were primarily responsible.

2. It is clear from the evidence that certain Boston citizens like Sam Gray were marked for retaliation because of the fights at the ropewalks.

3. A soldier initiated the whole incident by deliberately striking a young boy with his musket.

4. The crowd was throwing insults and snowballs. The crowd <u>was not</u> throwing ice, stones, or bricks. The crowd was angry for what had been done to the young lad, but they never intended to physically hurt the soldiers.

5. The soldiers loaded their muskets with double-shot and prepared to fire on the command of their officer.

6. One shot was fired and then Captain Preston gave the order to "fire." Surely his men should be able to identify his command.

7. Private Montgomery and Private Kilroy aimed their weapons directly at citizens and killed them. And if one soldier is guilty, they all are guilty.

8. Captain Preston could have stopped his men from firing by giving the order to "recover." He waited until some of the men had reloaded and fired again.

9. There is much evidence to indicate that this was a deliberate conspiracy on the part of the 29th Regiment to murder citizens of Boston.

PROSECUTION WITNESSES

"My lads, they will not fire."

—Sam Gray a few moments before his death

EDWARD LANGFORD

WITNESS FOR THE PROSECUTION

You are a Patriot agitator who saw the horrible "Massacre" of five of Boston's citizens. You definitely believe that it was not necessary for the soldiers to fire into the crowd since nobody was going to hurt them.

You will testify to the following:

1. You know that there have been a lot of fights between soldiers and the honest working men of Boston and you blame the uncouth, rum-drinking soldiers.

2. You had nothing to do with the fights at the ropewalk, but you did know Sam Gray, one of the ropemakers killed at the "Massacre." You believe that the soldiers were out to get him.

3. You, Samuel Atwood, James Brewer, and Sam Grey were in the White Horse Tavern near King Street when you heard a tremendous commotion outside.

4. Everyone rushed out and joined a crowd that was heckling a British soldier standing guard in front of the Custom House. A few were throwing snowballs.

5. The fire bells started ringing and the crowd grew.

6. Then a British officer—you learned later it was Captain Preston—arrived with seven men. You saw them load their muskets and form a semi-circle around the front of the Custom House door.

7. You, Sam Atwood, James Brewer, and Sam Gray pushed up close for a better view of what the soldiers were doing.

8. Some people in the crowd were throwing snowballs at them and others were calling them things like "Bloody backs" or "Damn lobsters." A few people had sticks and wooden canes.

9. You saw a British soldier aim his bayonet in the direction of Richard Palmes and then Palmes hit him with his cane. Then you heard the explosion of a musket.

10. The crowd was suddenly silent and surged forward. Then you saw Captain Preston raise his arm and heard "fire."

11. You saw a soldier—you learned later it was Private Kilroy—point his musket at where you and Sam Gray were standing. You yelled, "God damn you, don't fire." You heard a deafening explosion and saw Sam Gray lying on the ground with a huge hole in his head and blood pouring out.

12. You grabbed him under the shoulders and dragged him away from the soldiers.

SAMUEL ATWOOD

WITNESS FOR THE PROSECUTION

You are a Patriot agitator who saw the horrible "Massacre" of five of Boston's citizens. You later related to a newspaper reporter for the <u>Boston Gazette</u> some of your experiences on the evening of March 5. You definitely believe that it was not necessary for the soldiers to fire into the crowd since nobody was going to hurt them.

You will testify to the following:

1. You know that there have been a lot of fights between the soldiers of the 29th Regiment and the citizens of Boston, especially the seamen along the wharves. You believe that both groups are rum-drinking low-lives and share equal blame.

2. You had nothing to do with the fights at the ropewalk. You did know Sam Gray and considered him more of a peacemaker than a troublemaker.

3. You, Sam Gray, Edward Langford, and James Brewer were in the White Horse Tavern near King Street on the night of March 5. Sam Gray told you that certain soldiers of the 29th Regiment had said they planned to "shoot a few ropemakers when they had the chance."

4. You left the tavern and started home. You heard noise in an alley and met a group of soldiers heading in the direction of King Street. You asked them if they intended to murder people and they said, "Yes, by God, root and branch!" Then one of the soldiers hit you on the head.

5. You moved out of their way and then two British officers came by. You said, "Gentlemen, what is the matter?" They answered, "You'll see by and by."

6. You entered King Street and saw a small crowd of thirty or forty men, mostly lads, yelling curses at a lone sentry. A few were throwing snowballs.

7. Shortly, a British officer, Captain Preston, arrived with seven other soldiers and set themselves up in a semi-circular formation in front of the building steps. The soldiers had charged bayonets and pricked some people who got too near them.

8. You joined Edward Langford, Sam Gray, and James Brewer at the front of the crowd to get a better view of the action.

9. More people arrived on King Street. They were shouting insults like "Bloody back, damn lobsters" and throwing snowballs. You didn't see anybody using ice or clubs. Suddenly there was a musket shot, then a momentary silence.

10. You saw Captain Preston raise his arm and within seconds all the soldiers started firing. People seemed to be falling all around you. You turned and ran for the protection of a corner street. You heard later that Sam Gray had been killed along with four others.

JOHN GRAY

WITNESS FOR THE PROSECUTION

You are the owner of a large ropewalk that often hired off-duty British soldiers and unemployed seamen on a daily basis to mend the ropes needed by the hundreds of ships that called at Boston's harbor. Your cousin Sam Gray worked at your ropewalk.

You were involved in the fights on March 2 and 3. You will testify to the following:

1. On March 2 a soldier came to your ropewalk seeking a job. You heard one of your ropemakers, William Green, offer him a job cleaning the "necessary house." This was always the first task for a new employee.

2. He got offended and started yelling insults. Then he started punching people. Finally, Nicholas Ferriter, one of your employees, knocked him down. He got up and ran for help.

3. A short while later he returned with several soldiers armed with clubs and swords. They immediately attacked your employees and were driven off after several minutes of fighting with a lot of cuts and bruises to your men.

4. The next day, March 3, three more soldiers came back to your ropewalk and started another fight. Sam Gray gave one of them a fractured skull and they left muttering threats. William Green, one of your ropemakers, told you he heard one soldier say that "there were a great many townspeople who would eat their dinners on Monday next, who would not eat any on Tuesday."

5. You didn't witness the "Massacre" on March 5, but you believe that Sam Gray was deliberately murdered by the soldiers for his part in the fight. You are sure they would have shot you, too.

NICHOLAS FERRITER

WITNESS FOR THE PROSECUTION

You are a ropemaker who works for John Gray at his ropewalk. You were involved in a fight with soldiers of the 29th Regiment on March 2 and 3.

You will testify to the following:

1. On March 2 you were working at John Gray's ropewalk when you saw William Green talking to a British soldier.

2. You heard him offer the soldier a job cleaning the "necessary house." You and a few other ropemakers started laughing.

3. Then you heard the soldier say, "Empty it yourself, you scum!"

4. You don't think any lowly soldier has the right to insult a respectable man like William Green, so you went over and told him to shut up and leave. He started swinging punches, so you knocked him on his backside.

5. He ran away and returned a little while later with several soldiers. They were armed with clubs and swords. You and the other ropemakers fought them off and they eventually left. You still have a bad cut from a sword slash.

6. The next day three more soldiers returned and started another fight. Again, you and the other ropemakers drove them away after exchanging several blows. One of the soldiers received a fractured skull.

7. You were not at the "Massacre" on March 5, but you heard that one of your friends, Sam Gray, was killed by the soldiers. It didn't surprise you since you knew they were "gunning" for him.

WILLIAM GREEN

WITNESS FOR THE PROSECUTION

You are a ropemaker who works for John Gray at his ropewalk. You were involved in a fight with soldiers of the 29th Regiment on March 2 and 3.

You will testify to the following:

1. On March 2 you were working at John Gray's ropewalk when a British soldier approached you and asked for work. You said, "You want work?" He replied, "Yes, I do." You said, "Then clean the necessary house." This was always the first job that your boss, John Gray, assigned new workers. It was sort of a test of whether they really were a serious worker.

2. The ropemakers who heard the remark started laughing. The British soldier shouted, "Clean it yourself, you scum!"

3. That remark made you angry and you started cursing him and calling him a "Bloody lobster."

4. Then he hit you. You hit him back as Nicholas Ferriter appeared at your side. Ferriter knocked the soldier on his backside.

5. The soldier got up and ran away.

6. He returned a little while later with several soldiers armed with clubs and swords. You and the other ropemakers fought them off and they eventually left. Several ropemakers were hurt.

7. The next day three more soldiers returned and started another fight. Again, you and the other ropemakers drove them away after a brutal fight in which one of the soldiers received a fractured skull. You think that Sam Gray was the ropemaker who inflicted the injury on the soldier.

8. You heard one soldier say as he left that "there were a great many townspeople who would eat their dinners on Monday next, who would not eat any on Tuesday."

EDWARD GARRICK

WITNESS FOR THE PROSECUTION

You are a young wigmaker's apprentice who works in a shop near King Street. You were struck in the face by a British soldier on the evening of March 5 and later witnessed the "Massacre" on King Street.

You will testify to the following:

1. You were on your way home from work near the sentry box at the Custom House when you noticed Captain Goldfinch, an officer in the 29th Regiment, passing on the opposite side of King Street.

2. Your boss had repeatedly told you that Captain Goldfinch was not to be served any more since he never paid his bills.

3. You turned to the sentry and said, "There goes the fellow that will not pay my master for dressing his hair."

4. A few other apprentice lads nearby heard the comment and agreed. Captain Goldfinch had a reputation for not paying his bills on time.

5. The British sentry then said that "Captain Goldfinch was an officer and a gentleman who always paid his debts."

6. You said in jest, "There are no gentlemen in the 29th Regiment."

7. He said, "Let me see your face!" Then he smashed his musket into your head. You fell bleeding to the ground.

8. The other apprentices helped you to your feet and everyone started cursing the British soldier, calling him a "Damn lobster" and "Bloody back." Some started throwing snowballs at him. You heard bells ringing and shouts of "fire," "turn out, fire."

9. The soldier loaded his musket and started shouting, "Turn out the Main Guard!"

10. A large crowd began to form and a friend helped to dress your bleeding head.

11. You heard the crowd shouting curses as a British officer arrived with more men and took up a position in front of the Custom House.

12. You were way in the back of the crowd and couldn't clearly see what was happening.

13. Suddenly a shot rang out. There was a moment of silence and then several shots as people started to run. You saw some men lying in the street bleeding. Then you took cover in an alley and waited until the soldiers had left.

JANE WHITEHOUSE

WITNESS FOR THE PROSECUTION

You are a young chambermaid working for a rich Boston merchant, John Hancock. You are romantically involved with Private Hugh White.

You are a <u>reluctant</u> witness but must testify to the following:

1. On the evening of March 5 you were finishing your chores and heard shouts of "fire" coming from the direction of King Street.

2. You remembered that Private White was on duty near the Custom House and immediately ran out to see what was happening.

3. When you reached King Street you elbowed your way to the front of the crowd. Private White saw you and told you to get home right away because these "rowdy citizens are going to get seriously hurt tonight."

4. You were afraid for his safety, but left immediately. You were scared.

5. You heard the crowd yelling curses and saw them throwing snowballs.

6. As you reached your doorstep you heard shots coming from King Street and feared that your dear Private White had been killed. Later, you learned otherwise.

7. You saw a person dressed like a gentleman walking behind the soldiers urging them to "fire."

JAMES BREWER

WITNESS FOR THE PROSECUTION

You are a Patriot agitator who saw the horrible "Massacre" of five of Boston's citizens. You definitely believe that it was not necessary for the soldiers to fire into the crowd since nobody was going to hurt them.

You will testify to the following:

1. You know that there have been a lot of fights between the soldiers and the honest working men of Boston. You have seen several altercations caused by the uncouth, rum-drinking soldiers of the 29th Regiment.

2. You had nothing to do with the fights at the ropewalk. However, the ropemaker, Sam Gray, killed on March 5 was a good friend. You think that certain soldiers were out to get him.

3. You, Edward Langford, Sam Atwood, and Sam Gray were in the White Horse Tavern near King Street on the night of March 5. You heard shouts of "fire" and, thinking the town was burning, rushed outside.

4. You saw a small crowd teasing a single soldier. They were calling him "Lobster" and "Bloody back." A few snowballs were thrown.

5. The crowd grew and Captain Preston arrived with seven other soldiers. Sam Gray said he recognized one, Matt Kilroy, so you pushed to the front of the crowd to get a better look.

6. You, Sam Atwood, Sam Gray, and Edward Langford were in the front of the crowd which was heckling the soldiers with shouts of "Damn Lobsters, you dare not fire." A few people had wooden canes and snowballs were being thrown.

7. Suddenly, you heard the explosion of a musket. There was a momentary silence and then you heard Captain Preston shout "Damn you, bloods, fire again, let the consequences be what it will!" Then all the soldiers seemed to fire at once.

8. Sam Gray fell to the ground bleeding. You turned and ran for your life. People were running in every direction away from the firing soldiers and several others appeared wounded.

PAUL REVERE

WITNESS FOR THE PROSECUTION

You are a Patriot agitator who saw the horrible "Massacre" of five of Boston's citizens. You are a silversmith and illustrator. You definitely believe that it was not necessary for the soldiers to fire into the crowd since nobody was going to hurt them.

You will testify to the following:

1. You were delivering a finished piece of silver to a customer near King Street when you heard a tremendous commotion and shouts of "fire," "turn out, fire."

2. You immediately ran out and followed a group of other men to King Street.

3. A British officer, Captain Preston, and several soldiers were formed in a semi-circle in front of the Custom House with a large crowd around them. Captain Preston had a sword in his right hand and was shouting at the crowd to "disperse."

4. The crowd was yelling insults like "Bloody backs" and "Lobsters" at the soldiers. Some were throwing snowballs.

5. Suddenly you heard a shot ring out and there was a moment of silence. Then you saw all the soldiers raise their muskets. Captain Preston lifted his sword and shouted "fire" to them. There was a tremendous explosion and a lot of smoke. Several people in the crowd fell to the ground bleeding. A few soldiers reloaded and fired again.

6. Finally, Captain Preston stepped in front of them and pushed their musket barrels down.

7. You tried to memorize everyone's position so that you could later make a drawing of what happened.

8. The next day you made a drawing of the position of the soldiers and the dead citizens. You also made a sketch of what you saw when the soldier opened fire into the crowd.

SAMUEL ADAMS
WITNESS FOR THE PROSECUTION

You are a leading Patriot agitator and one of the founders of the group known as the "Sons of Liberty." You are a well respected lawyer and a former town official. You and Governor Hutchinson are deadly enemies.

You will testify to the following:

1. You know that there have been a lot of fights between the soldiers of the 29th Regiment and the citizens of Boston. You believe that these fights will not end until the British decide to remove these oppressive, uncouth rum-drinking soldiers who are taking away the liberty of the people.

2. You were not present at the March 5 "Massacre," but you did hear a British officer comment prior to the event that "he hoped to God the soldiers would burn the bloody town down."

3. You will deny organizing the crowd to deliberately harass and provoke the soldiers.

DEFENSE ATTORNEYS

"Some call them shavers, some call them geniuses. The plain English is, gentlemen, most probably a motley rabble of saucy boys . . . and outlandish jack tars. And why should we scruple to call such a set of people a mob, I can't conceive, unless the name is too respectable for them. The sun is not about to stand still or go out, nor the rivers to dry up, because there was a mob in Boston on the fifth of March that attacked a party of soldiers."

—John Adams' closing remarks

JOSIAH QUINCY

DEFENSE ATTORNEY

You are a 26-year-old Boston lawyer active in the group known as the "Sons of Liberty." Your older brother, Samuel Quincy, is one of the prosecuting attorneys. Patriot leaders have encouraged you and your colleague John Adams to take the case of these British soldiers to demonstrate to the British the fairness of American justice.

You are a handsome young man who "radiated good will" to nearly everyone except Lt. Governor Hutchinson. You have publicly denounced his administration and, in retaliation, the Governor has denied you the distinctive robes of a legal barrister; you have to plead this case in normal clothes.

At the trial you will work closely with John Adams to prove the following:

1. There was a lot of mutual hostility in Boston prior to the incident with <u>equal</u> blame for soldiers and citizens.

2. Off-duty soldiers and unemployed seamen had to compete for a limited amount of part-time work along Boston's wharves which created mutual hatred.

3. The mob that was harassing the soldiers on the night of March 5 was composed of many individuals trying to settle old scores with the soldiers.

4. Clearly the soldiers were in grave peril from a mob that was armed with sticks, clubs, and swords. Individual soldiers were hit with fists, clubs, sticks, snowballs, and ice.

5. The soldiers never used their bayonets.

6. Various people in the crowd were urging the soldiers to "fire."

7. Captain Preston never ordered his men to fire. In fact, at one point he stepped in front of them to prevent that from happening.

8. The first shot fired was a reflex action as a direct result of being struck by someone in the mob.

9. The rest of the soldiers fired only when they believed Captain Preston had given the order to "fire." Undoubtedly, the alleged "fire" came from someone in the crowd.

10. Captain Preston quickly stopped his men from firing by pushing down their musket barrels.

11. Finally, you admit that Captain Preston may have exceeded his authority by attempting to disperse the mob without orders from Governor Hutchinson, but one of his soldiers was in danger and he believed action was necessary.

JOHN ADAMS

DEFENSE ATTORNEY

You are a 34-year-old Patriot lawyer who was educated at Harvard. You were recommended to Captain Preston because of your reputation in Boston as being a very competent attorney. You are bright, but often intolerant of the views of others. The Patriot organization known as the "Sons of Liberty" encouraged you to take this case to demonstrate to the British the fairness of American justice.

Regardless of your anti-British political feelings, you have a low opinion of the mob that attacked Captain Preston and his men on the night of March 5, referring to them in your closing remarks as a "motley rabble of saucy boys and outlandish jack tars." You should be able to describe in detail the terrifying riot confronting the soldiers.

At the trial you will try to prove the following:

1. There was a lot of mutual hostility in Boston prior to the incident with <u>equal</u> blame for soldiers and citizens.

2. Off-duty soldiers and unemployed seamen had to compete for a limited amount of part-time jobs along Boston's wharves. Thus, the hatred between soldiers and sailors was so great that, in your words, "they fight as naturally when they meet, as the elephant and the rhinoceros."

3. The mob that was harassing the soldiers on the night of March 5 was composed of many individuals trying to settle old scores with the soldiers.

4. Clearly the soldiers' lives were in peril from a mob that was armed with sticks, clubs, and swords. Individual soldiers were hit with fists, clubs, snowballs, and ice.

5. The soldiers never used their bayonets.

6. Various people in the crowd were urging the soldiers to "fire."

7. Captain Preston never ordered his men to fire. In fact, at one point he stepped in front of them to prevent that from happening.

8. The first shot fired was a reflex action as a direct result of being struck by someone in the mob.

9. The rest of the soldiers fired only when they believed Captain Preston had given the order to "fire." Undoubtedly the alleged "fire" came from someone in the mob. Captain Preston said, "Fire, by no means!" In the noise and confusion, prosecution witnesses and his own men might have only heard the word "fire."

10. Captain Preston quickly stopped his men from firing by pushing down their musket barrels.

11. Finally, you admit that Captain Preston may have exceeded his authority by attempting to disperse the mob without orders from Governor Hutchinson, but one of his soldiers was in danger and he believed action was necessary.

12. You might ask the jury, in your closing remarks, what would have happened if Gray, Attucks, and the rest of the crowd had been part of a colonial militia empowered by the governor to keep order against a mob of unruly British soldiers. Would they have had any more restraint?

13. Emphasize that "self-defense" is the major part of the law of nature and if a man who is under assault accidentally kills an innocent bystander, the law should not consider him a murderer.

THE DEFENDANTS

CAPTAIN THOMAS PRESTON

Defendant

You are a 40-year-old British officer. You were born in Ireland and speak with a distinct accent. In addition to your duties as a British soldier, you are also an accomplished musician. You are on trial for murder.

At the trial you will testify to the following:

1. You were the officer on duty when Private White was attacked at the Custom House guard station.

2. You realized at the time that you needed Governor Hutchinson's orders to disperse the mob, but one of your men was in deadly peril. You felt immediate action was necessary to save his life.

3. When you marched the main guard to the Custom House, the crowd was continually hurling insults, snowballs, and ice at the soldiers. You were hit several times by snowballs.

4. At the Custom House you formed the men into a semi-circular formation with fixed bayonets.

5. Alarm bells signaling that the town was on fire were ringing and the mob seemed to grow larger by the minute.

6. The mob's behavior became more outrageous, striking their clubs one against another, and calling out, "Come on, you rascals, damn you bloody backs, you lobsters, fire and be damned, we know you dare not!"

7. You tried to get between the soldiers and the mob to persuade them to leave peacefully. It was to no avail.

8. Some well-behaved persons in the mob asked you if the guns were charged and you said "yes." They asked you if you intended to order the men to fire. You said "no."

9. You saw Private Montgomery struck with a club and then fire his weapon. You asked him why he had fired without orders. Almost immediately you were hit with a club on your arm so hard you couldn't move it.

10. The mob then increased their attack with snowballs and clubs. Some persons at the same time from behind called out, "Damn your bloods, why don't you fire."

11. Instantly three or four of your soldiers fired, one after another, and directly after three more in the same confusion. The mob then ran away, except three unhappy men who were killed instantly.

12. The whole action seemed to last less than half an hour.

13. On asking the soldiers why they fired without orders, they said they heard the word "fire" and supposed it came from you. You think they heard someone in the mob call out "fire."

PRIVATE HUGH WHITE
DEFENDANT

You are a soldier in the 29th Regiment of the British Army stationed in Boston. You are on trial for murder. You will testify to the following:

1. You admit that you had a number of fights with citizens in Boston prior to the incident on the evening of March 5.

2. You will deny participation in any of the ropewalk fights.

3. You were on guard duty at the sentry box on King Street near the Custom House. This is an important station because the Custom House is where the King's money is kept.

4. A young lad insulted one of your officers, so you gave him a tap with your musket. He screamed like a baby and soon there was a huge crowd harassing you with threats and snowballs.

5. You called for the main guard and shortly Captain Preston and seven other soldiers came to your rescue.

6. You and the other soldiers formed a defensive formation around the Custom House steps with Captain Preston in front.

7. King Street was now filled with an unruly mob shouting insults, daring you to fire and hurling missiles. You were terrified.

8. You will say that Captain Preston told you not to fire without a command.

9. You remember seeing Private Montgomery struck by a club and then firing. Then you heard the word "fire." At the time you thought it came from Captain Preston so you fired your musket.

10. You will say that you never meant any harm to the people in the mob. You felt you were just defending yourself.

PRIVATE HUGH MONTGOMERY
Defendant

You are a soldier in the 29th Regiment of the British Army stationed in Boston. You are on trial for murder. You will testify to the following:

1. You admit that you had a number of fights with citizens in Boston prior to the incident on the evening of March 5.

2. You will deny participation in any of the ropewalk fights.

3. You will describe the mob on the night of March 5 as being very hostile and you were afraid for your life.

4. You will describe the events of the evening of March 5, including marching to the rescue of Private White; forming a defensive formation around the Custom House; and being struck with a heavy club.

5. You will admit firing the first shot. You will say that it was a reflex action after being struck with the club. You didn't hear Captain Preston give any order to fire.

6. You will admit that you and the other soldiers fired again when you heard the word "fire." At the time you thought it came from Captain Preston.

7. You will say that you never meant any harm to people in the mob. You felt you were just defending yourself.

✂ --

PRIVATE WILLIAM WARREN
Defendant

You are a soldier in the 29th Regiment of the British Army stationed in Boston. You are on trial for murder. You will testify to the following:

1. You admit that you had a number of fights with citizens in Boston prior to the incident on the evening of March 5.

2. You will deny participation in any of the ropewalk fights.

3. You will describe the mob on the night of March 5 as being very hostile and you were afraid for your life.

4. You will describe the events of the evening of March 5, including marching to the rescue of Private White; forming a defensive formation around the Custom House; and being struck repeatedly with various missiles including snowballs and ice.

5. You will say that Captain Preston told you not to fire without a command.

6. You will admit that you and the other soldiers fired into the mob only when you heard the word "fire." At the time you thought it came from Captain Preston.

7. You will say that you never meant any harm to the people in the mob. You felt you were just defending yourself.

PRIVATE MATTHEW KILROY
DEFENDANT

You are a soldier in the 29th Regiment of the British Army stationed in Boston. You are on trial for murder. You will testify to the following:

1. You admit that you had a number of fights with citizens in Boston prior to the incident on the evening of March 5.

2. You were part of the ropewalk fights, but maintain that you were provoked and had to defend your comrades and the honor of the regiment.

3. You will describe the mob on the night of March 5 as being very hostile and you were afraid for your life.

4. You will describe the events of the evening of March 5, including marching to the rescue of Private White; forming a defensive formation around the Custom House; and being struck with various missiles including snowballs and ice. You were also hit with sticks or clubs.

5. You will say that Captain Preston told you not to fire without a command.

6. You will admit that you and the other soldiers fired into the mob only when you heard the word "fire." At the time you thought it came from Captain Preston.

7. You will deny deliberately aiming at Sam Gray or Edward Langford. You don't recall hearing anybody from the crowd saying "don't fire." In fact, it was the opposite. They were taunting you by saying "why don't you fire."

8. You will say that you never meant any harm to the people in the mob. You felt you were just defending yourself.

PRIVATE JOHN CARROLL
DEFENDANT

You are a soldier in the 29th Regiment of the British Army stationed in Boston. You are on trial for murder. You will testify to the following:

1. You admit that you had a number of fights with citizens in Boston prior to the incident on the evening of March 5.

2. You were involved in a fight at the ropewalk and recall hearing a Bostonian ask a soldier where the 29th Regiment planned to bury its dead.

3. You will describe the mob on the night of March 5 as being very hostile and you were afraid for your life.

4. You will describe the events of the evening of March 5, including marching to the rescue of Private White; forming a defensive formation around the Custom House; and being struck repeatedly with various missiles including snowballs and ice.

5. You will say that Captain Preston told you not to fire without a command.

6. You will admit that you and the other soldiers fired into the mob only when you heard the word "fire." At the time you thought it came from Captain Preston.

7. You will say that you never meant any harm to the people in the mob. You felt you were just defending yourself.

PRIVATE JAMES HARTIGAN

Defendant

You are a soldier in the 29th Regiment of the British Army stationed in Boston. You are on trial for murder. You will testify to the following:

1. You admit that you had a number of fights with citizens in Boston prior to the incident on the evening of March 5.

2. You were part of the fights at the ropewalk and saw a number of injuries. You think these fights were deliberately provoked by the rude behavior and taunts of the ropemakers.

3. You will describe the mob on the night of March 5 as being very hostile and you were afraid for your life.

4. You will describe the events of the evening of March 5, including marching to the rescue of Private White; forming a defensive formation around the Custom House; and being struck repeatedly with various missiles including snowballs and ice. You were also hit with a club.

5. You will say that Captain Preston told you not to fire without a command.

6. You will admit that you and the other soldiers fired into the mob only when you heard the word "fire." At the time you thought it came from Captain Preston.

7. You will say that you never meant any harm to the people in the mob. You felt you were just defending yourself.

PRIVATE WILLIAM McCAULEY
Defendant

You are a soldier in the 29th Regiment of the British Army stationed in Boston. You are on trial for murder. You will testify to the following:

1. You deny having any fights with citizens in Boston prior to the incident on the evening of March 5.

2. You were lucky enough to have a steady part-time job with a barrel-maker on Frog Lane near Beacon Hill. He always treated you fairly.

3. You will describe the mob on the night of March 5 as being very hostile and you were afraid for your life.

4. You will describe the events of the evening of March 5, including marching to the rescue of Private White; forming a defensive formation around the Custom House; and being struck repeatedly with various missiles including snowballs and ice.

5. You will say that Captain Preston told you not to fire without a command.

6. You will admit that you and the other soldiers fired into the mob only when you heard the word "fire." At the time you thought it came from Captain Preston.

7. You deliberately aimed your musket high over the heads of the people.

8. You will say that you never meant any harm to the people in the mob. You felt that you were just defending yourself.

PRIVATE WILLIAM WEEMS
DEFENDANT

You are a tall black soldier in the 29th Regiment of the British Army stationed in Boston. You are on trial for murder. You will testify to the following:

1. You admit that you had a number of fights with citizens in Boston prior to the incident on the evening of March 5.

2. You witnessed the ropewalk fights but only helped to carry away some of your injured comrades.

3. One of the ropemakers called you a "black rascal."

4. You will describe the mob on the night of March 5 as being very hostile and you were afraid for your life.

5. You will describe the events of the evening of March 5, including marching to the rescue of Private White; forming a defensive formation around the Custom House; and being struck repeatedly with various missiles including snowballs and ice.

6. You will say that Captain Preston told you not to fire without a command.

7. You will admit that you and the other soldiers fired into the mob only when you heard the word "fire." At the time you thought it came from Captain Preston.

8. You will say that you never meant any harm to the people in the mob. You felt you were just defending yourself.

DEFENSE WITNESSES

"It is Matter too great Notoriety to need any Proofs, that the arrival of his Majesty's Troops in Boston was extremely obnoxious to its Inhabitants."

—Captain Preston

HAMMOND GREEN
WITNESS FOR THE DEFENSE

You are a customs official and a well-known Tory. On the evening of March 5 you were working late in your office on the second story of the Custom House. You will testify to the following:

1. You heard a lot of commotion out in King Street including the ringing of several bells. You thought that fire had broken out.

2. You looked out the window and saw a British soldier surrounded by a huge mob that was yelling curses and threats. Some were even throwing snowballs and ice. The soldier look terrified and started shouting to "turn out the main guard."

3. As the crowd grew bigger, you saw a British officer and seven soldiers march up to the Custom House and form a defensive formation.

4. The mob now numbered, you think, hundreds of people and they were throwing snowballs and ice; yelling at the soldiers to "fire"; and some even seemed to be striking the soldiers with clubs or sticks.

5. You saw one soldier get knocked down. He rose up and fired. You immediately ducked behind the window.

6. About ten or fifteen seconds later you peered out the window and then a series of shots rang out. The crowd seemed to melt away from the soldiers. You saw Captain Preston trying to push down the barrels of the soldiers' muskets.

7. You never heard Captain Preston give the order to fire and you think the soldiers' lives were in peril from the crowd.

PRIVATE THOMAS WALKER

WITNESS FOR THE DEFENSE

You are a member of the 29th Regiment of the British Army stationed in Boston. You were not involved in the incident on March 5. You will testify about the fights at John Gray's ropewalk. You will say the following:

1. You admit that you had a number of fights with citizens in Boston prior to the incident on the evening of March 5.

2. You went to John Gray's ropewalk on March 2 looking for some honest work. One of the ropemakers, William Green, humiliated you by saying "go clean the outhouse." You told him to empty it himself. Then the ropemakers started punching you. One man, you think his name is Nicholas Ferriter, knocked you to the ground.

3. You ran to the army barracks and several soldiers volunteered to go back and teach these ruffians some respect for the King and the 29th Regiment. There was a big fight with a lot of bruises and bloody noses. Nobody got seriously hurt.

4. You feel that these low-life ropemakers were the cause of not only this fight but the later mob action on March 5.

RICHARD PALMES

WITNESS FOR THE DEFENSE

You are a citizen of Boston and a well-known Patriot agitator. You believe that the British soldiers have no business in Boston other than to oppress the people. You have had fights with British soldiers on several occasions. You will <u>reluctantly</u> testify to the following:

1. On the night of March 5, hearing bells ringing and the sound of a crowd, you grabbed a club and went to King Street.

2. You were yelling curses and taunts at the British soldiers.

3. You admit that some people were throwing snowballs and ice.

4. You were almost face to face with the soldiers when Private Montgomery was hit with a stick. You saw him fall and then fire his musket. Then you hit him with your club. You wanted to prevent him from firing again.

5. You thought Captain Preston was going to give the order to "fire" so you tried to hit him. Your blow was deflected by another soldier.

6. Suddenly all the soldiers started firing. You ran for your life.

7. You admit that even though you were in front of the crowd, you never heard Captain Preston give the order to "fire."

 -

NEWTON PRINCE

WITNESS FOR THE DEFENSE

You are a free black man from the West Indies. You work as a pastry cook in a shop near King Street. You will testify to the following:

1. On the night of March 5, hearing bells ringing and the sound of a crowd, you joined Edward Langford, Sam Atwood, and James Brewer and ran toward King Street. You were carrying a large wooden laddle.

2. You joined the crowd that was yelling curses and taunts at the British soldiers. Some people were throwing snowballs and ice. You just wanted to watch the action.

3. You saw several people begin to hit the soldiers' musket barrels with clubs. At this point you wanted to leave but the crowd was so thick behind you that you couldn't move.

4. You saw a soldier get hit with a stick. He rose and fired. Then all the soldiers seemed to start firing.

5. You admit that many people in the crowd were daring the soldiers to "fire." You confess that although you were nearly in front of Captain Preston, you never heard him give the order to "fire."

JAMES MURRAY
WITNESS FOR THE DEFENSE

You are a Tory justice-of-the-peace. You were alerted that a mob was besieging a group of soldiers on King Street in front of the Custom House. You grabbed a copy of the "Riot Act," which expressly forbids riotous gatherings threatening law and order, and headed in the direction of King Street. You will testify to the following:

1. When you arrived at King Street you saw a scene of utter disorder. A huge mob was screaming insults and throwing snowballs and ice at a small group of soldiers in front of the Custom House.

2. You recognized Captain Preston but not the other soldiers.

3. You raised your voice and tried to read the "Riot Act" to the crowd. They were to "disperse" immediately!

4. Instead, part of the crowd started throwing snowballs and ice at you. Some hurled insults and even threatened you with clubs.

5. You became scared and decided to leave and let the military handle the situation.

6. Later you heard shots from King Street.

7. You fully believe the soldiers were justified in firing to break up this riotous gathering. Their lives were threatened.

LT. GOVERNOR THOMAS HUTCHINSON
WITNESS FOR THE DEFENSE

You are a loyal servant of the King and finally managed to convince the crowd to disperse, promising justice. You will testify to the following:

1. You did not witness the shootings on King Street but you believe firmly in law and order.

2. You ordered Captain Preston to leave King Street after the shootings and told the crowd that there would be a full inquiry as to who was responsible.

3. You believe that rowdy ruffians stirred up trouble and caused the soldiers to fear for their lives.

4. You regret the incident but feel that Captain Preston acted reasonably under the circumstances.

121

CAPTAIN GOLDFINCH
WITNESS FOR THE DEFENSE

You are an officer in the 29th Regiment of the British Army stationed in Boston. You will testify to the following:

1. You didn't hear the rude comments made by the rowdy youth regarding your failure to pay a certain hair bill.

2. Minutes after the incident you began to see groups of citizens forming in the streets.

3. You heard curses and saw snowballs being thrown. You were hit several times.

4. You ordered every soldier you saw to go directly to the barracks and stay there. You didn't want any more fighting like had occurred earlier in the week.

5. When you got to the barracks you learned that the officer of the day, Captain Preston, had taken seven soldiers to King Street to help the lone sentry.

6. You stayed at the barracks to prevent any of the other men from leaving.

7. You believe that you and other British officers did all you could to prevent more violence.

 -

JACK
WITNESS FOR THE DEFENSE

You are the slave of a Boston doctor. You were running an errand for him. You tried to go down King Street but decided it was too dangerous. You will testify to the following:

1. As you approached King Street you heard horrible shouts and cheers of "Kill the soldiers." Some people were yelling: "Fire, you damn bloody backs."

2. You couldn't see the soldiers very well, but you could see hundreds of snowballs and ice filling the cold air.

3. You left before the soldiers fired.

ANDREW

WITNESS FOR THE DEFENSE

You are a slave belonging to Mr. Oliver Wendell, a prominent citizen of Boston. Your master has instructed the court that you have never been known to lie. You will testify to the following:

1. You were part of the crowd on King Street watching the mob harass the soldiers. You heard the mob cheering and crying "Damn them, they dare not fire, we are not afraid of them." Shortly before the firing you were only a few yards and to the left of Captain Preston.

2. You saw a huge black sailor named Crispus Attucks try to hit Captain Preston with a long cordwood stick. You heard him say, "Kill the dogs, knock them over."

3. You saw Attucks fall bleeding to the pavement when the firing started.

4. You heard many people shouting "fire" from the crowd, but you are sure that Captain Preston never said that word.

EXHIBITS

BOSTON MASSACRE

"The Fatal Fifth of March 1770, can never be forgotten—the horrors of that dreadful night are but too deeply impressed on our hearts."

—Dr. Joseph Warren

A PRINT MADE BY PAUL REVERE

A SKETCH BY PAUL REVERE OF KING STREET SHOWING THE POSITION OF THOSE KILLED ON THE EVENING OF MARCH 5, 1770

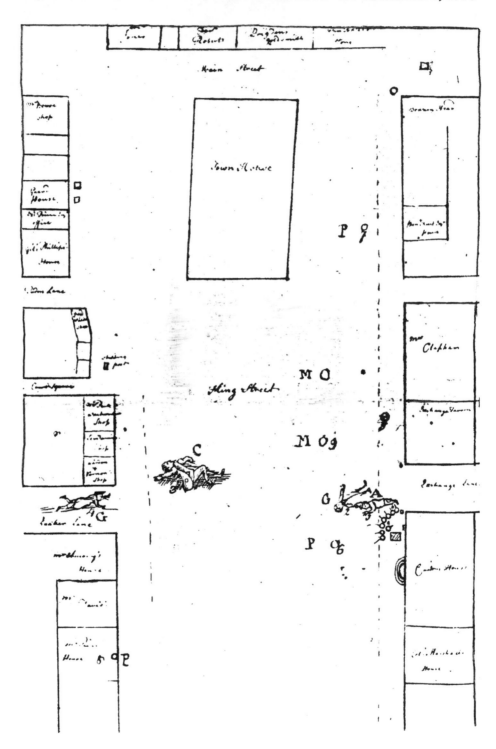

EXHIBIT C

BOSTON IN 1770

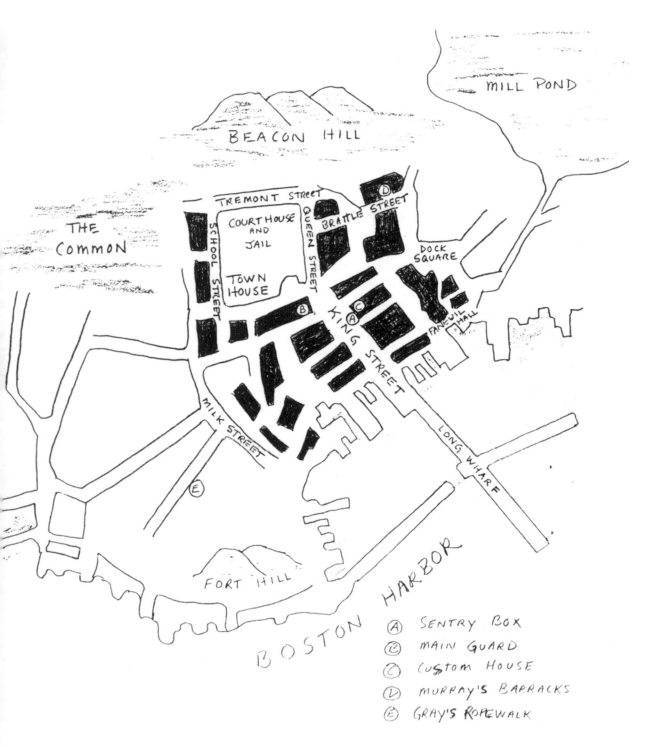

MILL POND

BEACON HILL

THE Common

TREMONT STREET

COURT HOUSE AND JAIL

SCHOOL STREET

QUEEN STREET

BRATTLE STREET

DOCK SQUARE

TOWN HOUSE

Ⓑ

KING STREET

Ⓐ Ⓒ

FANEUIL HALL

MILK STREET

Ⓔ

LONG WHARF

FORT HILL

BOSTON HARBOR

Ⓐ SENTRY BOX
Ⓑ MAIN GUARD
Ⓒ CUSTOM HOUSE
Ⓓ MURRAY'S BARRACKS
Ⓔ GRAY'S ROPEWALK

BOSTON GAZETTE, MARCH 12, 1770[*]

Our readers will doubtless expect a circumstantial Account of the tragical Affair on Monday Night last . . .

On hearing the noise [of the fight in the alley] one Samuel Atwood came up to see what was the matter, and entering the alley . . . heard the latter part of the combat, and when the boys had dispersed he met the ten or twelve soldiers . . . rushing down the alley toward the square, and asked them if they intended to murder people? They answered, "Yes, by G-d, root and branch!" [and struck and wounded Atwood].

Retreating a few steps, Mr. Atwood met two officers and said, "Gentlemen, what is the matter?" They answered, "You'll see by and by."

Immediately after, those heroes [the officers] appeared in the square, asking where were the buggers? Where were the cowards? . . . One of them advanced towards a youth who had a stave in his hand. But the young man, seeing a person near him with a drawn sword and good cane ready to support him, held up his stave [stick] in defiance, and they quietly passed by him up the little alley . . . to King Street, where they attacked single and unarmed persons till they raised such clamor, and then turned down Cornhill Street, insulting all they met . . . and pursuing some to their very doors.

Thirty or forty persons, mostly lads, being by this means gathered in King Street, Capt. Preston, with a party of men with charged bayonets, came from the main guard to the Commissioner's house, the soldiers pushing their bayonets, crying, "Make way!" They took place by the Custom House, and continuing to push to drive the people off, pricked some in several places; on which they were clamorous and, it is said, threw snowballs.

On this, the Captain commanded them to fire, and more snowballs coming, he again said, "Damn you, fire, be the consequences what it will!" One soldier then fired, and a townsman with a cudgel [club] struck him over the hands with such force that he dropped his firelock [musket]: and rushing forward aimed a blow at the Captain's head, which graz'd his hat and fell pretty heavy upon his arm. However, the soldiers continued the fire, successively, till seven or eight or, as some say, eleven guns were discharged.

By this fatal manoeuvre, three men were laid dead on the spot, and two more struggling for life . . . the dead are Mr. Samuel Gray . . . a black man named Crispus Attucks . . . [and] Mr. James Caldwell, mate of Capt. Morton's vessel.

[*]Adapted from the original newspaper article reprinted in Emery, Edwin (ed.), <u>The Story of America as Reported by Its Newspapers 1690-1965</u>.

CAPTAIN PRESTON'S DEPOSITION WRITTEN ON MARCH 12, 1770[*]

On Monday night about 8 o'clock two soldiers were attacked and beat. But the townspeople, in order to carry matters to the utmost length, broke into two meeting houses and rang alarm bells, which I supposed was for fire but was, I believe, to inform the inhabitants to assemble and attack the troops.

This occasioned my repairing immediately to the main guard. In my way there I saw the people in great commotion and heard them use the most cruel and abusive threats against the troops. In a few minutes after I reached the guard, about 100 people passed it and went towards the Custom House where the king's money is kept. They immediately surrounded the sentry posted there, and threatened to execute their vengeance on him.

I immediately sent an officer and twelve men to protect both the sentry and the king's money, and very soon followed myself.

The mob still increased and were more outrageous, striking their clubs one against another, and calling out, "Come on you rascals, G-d damn you bloody backs, you lobsters, fire and be damned, we know you dare not!"

At this time I was between the soldiers and the mob endeavoring to persuade them to retire peaceably, but to no purpose. They advanced to the points of the bayonets, struck some of them and even the muzzles of the pieces, and seemed to be endeavoring to close with the soldiers.

Some well-behaved persons asked me if the guns were charged. I replied, "Yes." They then asked me if I intended to order the men to fire. I answered, "No."

While I was speaking, one of the soldiers, having received a severe blow with a stick, stepped a little to one side and instantly fired, on which asking him why he fired without orders, I was struck with a club on the arm, which for some time deprived me of the use of it.

This general attack was made on the men by a great number of heavy clubs and snowballs being thrown at them. Some persons at the same time from behind called out, "Damn your bloods, why don't you fire."

Instantly three or four of the soldiers fired, one after another, and directly after three more in the same confusion. The mob then ran away, except three unhappy men who instantly expired. One more is since dead, three others are dangerously wounded, and four slightly wounded.

The whole of this melancholy affair was transacted in almost 20 minutes. On my asking the soldiers why they fired without orders, they said they heard the word "fire" and supposed it came from me. This might be the case as many of the mob called out "fire, fire."

[*]Adapted from Captain Preston's original testimony as found in the British Public Record Office, C.O., and reprinted in Jensen, Merrill (ed.), <u>American Colonial Documents to 1776</u>.

THE ALLEGED MURDER WEAPONS–5 LAND SERVICE BROWN BESS BRITISH MUSKETS (.75 CALIBRE) WEIGHING APPROXIMATELY 10 POUNDS EACH.

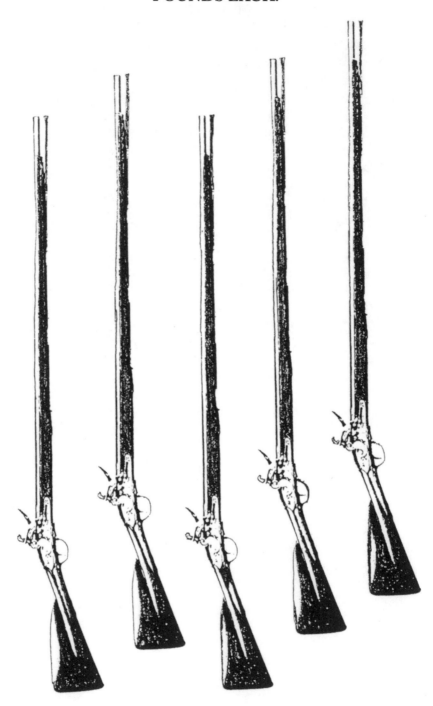

ADDITIONAL INFORMATION

"I take the liberty of wishing you joy of the complete victory obtained over the knaves and foolish villains of Boston."

—General Gage to Captain Preston on learning
of his acquittal

MASTER ROLE SHEET

HISTORICAL CHARACTER	ROLE	STUDENT NAME
Edmund Trowbridge	Judge	_____
Samuel Winthrop	Clerk and Bailiff	_____
Robert Treat Paine	Prosecution Attorney	_____
Samuel Quincy	Prosecution Attorney	_____
Edward Langford	Prosecution Witness	_____
Nicholas Ferriter	Prosecution Witness	_____
James Brewer	Prosecution Witness	_____
Paul Revere	Prosecution Witness	_____
William Green	Prosecution Witness	_____
John Gray	Prosecution Witness	_____
Samuel Adams	Prosecution Witness	_____
Jane Whitehouse	Prosecution Witness	_____
Edward Garrick	Prosecution Witness	_____
Samuel Atwood	Prosecution Witness	_____
Josiah Quincy	Defense Attorney	_____
John Adams	Defense Attorney	_____
Pvt. Thomas Walker	Defense Witness	_____
Richard Palmes	Defense Witness	_____
Hammond Green	Defense Witness	_____
Newton Prince	Defense Witness	_____
James Murray	Defense Witness	_____
Captain Goldfinch	Defense Witness	_____
Lt. Gov. Hutchinson	Defense Witness	_____
Andrew (slave)	Defense Witness	_____
Jack (slave)	Defense Witness	_____

MASTER ROLE SHEET, CONTINUED

HISTORICAL CHARACTER	ROLE	STUDENT NAME
Capt. Thomas Preston	Defendant	_____
Pvt. Hugh Montgomery	Defendant	_____
Pvt. William Warren	Defendant	_____
Pvt. Mathew Kilroy	Defendant	_____
Pvt. Hugh White	Defendant	_____
Pvt. John Carroll	Defendant	_____
Pvt. William McCauley	Defendant	_____
Pvt. James Hartigan	Defendant	_____
Pvt. William Weems	Defendant	_____
John Zenger*#	Newspaper Reporter for "Boston Gazette"	_____
Susan Thatcher*#	Newspaper Reporter for "London Times"	_____
Juror 1	Boston Resident	_____
Juror 2	Boston Resident	_____
Juror 3	Non-Boston Resident	_____
Juror 4	Non-Boston Resident	_____
Juror 5	Non-Boston Resident	_____
Juror 6	Non-Boston Resident	_____
Juror 7	Non-Boston Resident	_____
Juror 8	Tory	_____
Juror 9	Tory	_____
Juror 10	Tory	_____
Juror 11	Tory	_____
Juror 12	Tory	_____

*Fictional Character

#Optional role

Historical and procedural note: In the real trials neither Captain Preston nor the other soldiers gave testimony. Depending on class size and time limitations, only a few of the defendants may give evidence. You may also shorten the length of the trial by allowing the defense and prosecution to present only five witnesses (or some other agreed number). The jury may be reduced in size, too.

TRIAL PROCEDURE

1. Judge enters. All rise.
2. Clerk says to the jury, "Good men and true, stand together and harken to your evidence."
3. Judge charges the jury.
4. Prosecution attorney's opening remarks.
5. Defense attorney's opening remarks.
6. Prosecution presents witnesses and cross-examination.
7. Defense presents witnesses and cross-examination.
8. Rebuttal witnesses (time permitting).
9. Prosecution's closing remarks.
10. Defense's closing remarks.
11. Judge makes final remarks to the jury prior to deliberation.
12. Jury deliberates.
13. Judge imposes sentence on any defendant found guilty.

SUGGESTED COURTROOM SET-UP

CLERK/BAILIFF	JUDGE	WITNESS SEAT

D E F E N D A N T S	DEFENSE ATTORNEY(S)		PROSECUTION ATTORNEY(S)	J U R Y

WITNESSES
AND
SPECTATORS

LEGAL TERMS

1. BENEFIT OF CLERGY   A privilege of exemption from the punishment of death accorded to such persons as were religious "clerks," or who could read. The privilege was claimed after a person's conviction, by a species of motion in arrest of judgment, technically called "praying his clergy." As a means of testing his clerical character, the convicted individual was given a psalm to read (usually Psalm 51) and upon his reading it correctly, he was turned over to the ecclesiastical courts, to be tried by the bishop or a jury of twelve clerks.

2. CONSPIRACY   A combination of two or more persons to commit a criminal or unlawful act, or to commit a lawful act by criminal or unlawful means; or a combination of two or more persons by concerted action to accomplish an unlawful purpose, or some purpose not in itself unlawful by unlawful means.

3. MANSLAUGHTER   Unlawful killing of another human being without "malice aforethought." Heat of passion, such as rage, fright, terror, or wild desperation, is a necessary element of this crime. Voluntary manslaughter is also committed when the killing, although unintentional, resulted from unreasonable and grossly reckless conduct.

4. MURDER   The unlawful killing of another human being with "malice aforethought." This requires a premeditated intent to kill plus an element of hatred.

SUBPOENA

YOU _____ are hereby commanded to appear in the *COURT* of *JUDGE EDMUND TROWBRIDGE* in *BOSTON* on October 24, 1770 (_____)

modern date

Please present yourself at _____ in _____

(time)   (room number)

and be prepared to either   *A. serve as a member of the Jury*

or

                         B. testify as an expert witness
                          (role sheet provided)

Failure to comply with this *SUMMONS* will result in *CONTEMPT CHARGES*.

Requested by _____, Counsel for the _____.

Approved by the Honorable Judge Trowbridge, Presiding Judge,

Criminal Court of Boston, 1770.

I have served this summons _____

(Bailiff's Signature)

JURY

Check one: _____ Boston Citizen _____ Non-Boston Resident _____ Known Tory

At the real trial—after nineteen challenges—a jury was selected that had two Boston citizens, five non-Boston residents of New England, and five known Tories.

One Tory jury member said that "if he had to sit to all eternity he would never convict Preston."

It will be your duty to hear the evidence presented against the accused and decide whether they are "innocent" or "guilty" of the charge of murder. If the judge so instructs, you many find certain individuals guilty of the lesser charge of "manslaughter."

JURY EVALUATION SHEET

WITNESS NAME	TOLD THE TRUTH	MOSTLY TOLD THE TRUTH	LIED
PROSECUTION			
1.	❑	❑	❑
2.	❑	❑	❑
3.	❑	❑	❑
4.	❑	❑	❑
5.	❑	❑	❑
6.	❑	❑	❑
7.	❑	❑	❑
8.	❑	❑	❑
9.	❑	❑	❑
10.	❑	❑	❑

JURY EVALUATION SHEET, CONTINUED

WITNESS NAME	TOLD THE TRUTH	MOSTLY TOLD THE TRUTH	LIED
DEFENSE			
1.	❏	❏	❏
2.	❏	❏	❏
3.	❏	❏	❏
4.	❏	❏	❏
5.	❏	❏	❏
6.	❏	❏	❏
7.	❏	❏	❏
8.	❏	❏	❏
9.	❏	❏	❏
10.	❏	❏	❏
11.	❏	❏	❏
12.	❏	❏	❏
13.	❏	❏	❏
14.	❏	❏	❏
15.	❏	❏	❏
16.	❏	❏	❏
17.	❏	❏	❏
18.	❏	❏	❏

CHRONOLOGY

1761 —Writs of Assistance give customs agents the right to search for smuggled goods in colonial homes without a search warrant.

1763 —End of the French and Indian War. The English are victorious, but issue a proclamation prohibiting Americans from settling in the newly-won Western lands.

1765 —Stamp Act places a tax on legal documents, newspapers, almanacs, dice, and playing cards.

—Quartering Act makes colonists in Boston and elsewhere help support British soldiers by providing rooms, candles, and rum.

March 2, 1770 —Fight at Gray's Ropewalk

March 3, 1770 —Second fight at Gray's Ropewalk

March 5, 1770 —Boston Massacre (five killed on King Street)

March 6, 1770 —Captain Preston and eight soldiers are arrested and charged with murder

October 24, 1770 —Captain Preston's trial begins

October 31, 1770 —Captain Preston is found "not guilty"

November 27, 1770 —Trial of eight soldiers begins

1773 —Boston Tea Party

1774 —The Intolerable Acts

1775 —Battles of Lexington and Concord

1776 —Declaration of Independence

AFTERMATH

On October 31, 1770 Captain Preston was found "not guilty" and released from jail. He returned to England, retired from the Army, and was awarded an annual pension of 200 pounds by the British government. When John Adams was informed of Preston's good fortune, he reputedly muttered, "If Preston is to be reimbursed for his Expenses, I wish his Expenses, at least to his Counsel, had been greater." Years later, after the American Revolution, they crossed paths on a London street without speaking.

All the British soldiers were found "not guilty" of premeditated murder. After the acquittals some relatives of the deceased men considered a measure called "appeal of felony"—an ancient legal custom in which certain close relatives of a dead victim could bring further criminal action against an alleged killer. The idea was quickly dropped when it was pointed out that the accused would then be entitled to claim "trial by combat."

Matthew Kilroy and Hugh Montgomery were found "guilty" of manslaughter. Both soldiers pleaded the "benefit of the clergy," a legacy of the middle ages that permitted a trial by church tribunal. They waived this privilege in favor of a light sentence; both were branded on the right thumb by Sheriff Greenleaf.

Pvt. Kilroy allegedly said later that "he would never miss an opportunity, when he had one, to fire on the inhabitants, and that he had wanted to have an opportunity ever since he landed." Hugh Montgomery later confessed to one of his lawyers that after he was knocked down, he had shouted, "Damn you, fire." Nevertheless, John Adams wrote in 1773 that had any of the soldiers been executed, it "would have been as foul a Stain upon this Country as the Execution of the Quakers or Witches."

"Massacre Day" was observed in Boston as a patriotic holiday until 1776, when it was dropped in favor of the 4th of July.

Crispus Attucks, a black man, is still remembered as the first martyr to American independence. However, few recall the brave testimony offered by three black Americans—the slaves Andrew, Jack and Newton Prince (a West Indian)—that probably prevented the execution of the British soldiers. In 1888 a monument commemorating the Boston Massacre, known as the "Crispus Attucks Monument," was unveiled on the Boston Common.

Today, the actual site of the Boston Massacre is a busy intersection in the downtown commercial district.

HISTORICAL NOTES TO TEACHER

1. At the time of the Boston Massacre trials, English law viewed all homicides as murder. It was the burden of the defense to prove that the murder was either "justified" or "manslaughter." The defendant was <u>guilty</u> until proven <u>innocent</u>. Captain Preston pessimistically noted in his deposition before the trial that "I am perfectly innocent, under most unhappy Circumstances, having nothing in Reason to expect but the Loss of Life in a very ignominious Manner, without the Interposition of his Majesty's Royal Goodness." Clearly, he expected to hang.

2. In the 18th Century, juries made the final decision about whether a killing was justified homicide, manslaughter, or murder. In making their determination, they looked for evidence that the killing was "premeditated." If they viewed the homicide as "justifiable," no blame was attached to the killing. A clear example of "justifiable homicide" was killing in self-defense.

3. Under English law hundreds of offenses including petty theft, shooting a weapon in a house to "cause injury," and kidnapping were punished by hanging. Murder was one of those crimes. Hence, it was the objective of most defendants, if acquittal seemed unlikely, to be convicted of manslaughter. Manslaughter was viewed as unintentional killing in the course of some "idle or dangerous" activity. After 1760 an individual convicted of manslaughter could expect to receive either a short prison sentence or a "burning on the hand" (this punishment was officially abolished in 1779).

DISCUSSION QUESTIONS

1. Was the so-called Boston Massacre merely an accident waiting to happen? Explain.

2. Could the violence on March 5, 1770 have been avoided by better civilian and military leadership? Explain.

3. What examples can you find where the defense and prosecution introduced biased information or blatant propaganda as evidence? Was it effective?

4. Is there sufficient evidence to indicate that the Boston Massacre was nothing more than a overblown fight between two gangs of toughs—one civilian and the other military?

5. Did the defendant(s) get a fair trial? Why or why not?

6. In the real trials the defendant(s) were not allowed to testify in their own behalf. Would that have made a difference in the outcome of your trial? Explain.

7. Is there evidence to suggest that the Boston Massacre was part of a conspiracy initiated by either the "Sons of Liberty" or the "British High Command"? Why would either group want such a tragic event to occur?

8. What was the most damaging evidence against the accused? Explain.

9. Was it "fair" to try soldiers for doing their duty? Explain.

10. If you believe the soldiers heard the word "fire," was it "fair" to try them for obeying orders? Explain.

11. Is it justifiable for citizens to take mob action against lawful measures that they deem harmful or illegal? Explain.

12. This incident took place on a clear moonlit night, before hundreds of people, yet no two witnesses were able to give the same account of what happened. What does this tell you about the struggle for truth in a courtroom? Can we ever be sure about the facts in a highly controversial case?

BIBLIOGRAPHY

Bailey, Thomas A. *The American Pageant*. Boston: Heath & Co., 1983.

Bowen, Catherine Drinker. *John Adams and the American Revolution*. Boston: Little, Brown, Inc., 1950.

Butterfield, L.H. (ed.). *The Book of Abigail and John*. Cambridge: Harvard University Press, 1975.

Chidsey, Donald Barr. *The World of Samuel Adams*. NY: Thomas Nelson Inc., 1974.

Cramer, Kenyon C. *The Causes of War: The American Revolution, the Civil War, and WWI*. NY: Scott, Foresman & Co., 1965.

Cummins, D. Duane and William Gee White. *The American Revolution*. NY: Benziger Brothers, 1968.

Darling, Anthony D. *Red Coat and Brown Bess*. NY: Museum Restoration Service, 1971

Forbes, Ester. *Paul Revere and the World He Lived In*. Boston: Houghton Mifflin Co., 1942.

Frothingham, Richard. *Life and Times of Joseph Warren*. Boston: Little, Brown, Inc., 1865.

Gross, Robert A. *The Minutemen and Their World*. NY: Hill and Wang, 1968.

Hibbert, Christopher. *Redcoats and Rebels: The American Revolution Through British Eyes*. NY: W.W. Norton, 1990.

Jones, Howard Mumford and Bessie Zaban Jones. *The Many Voices of Boston*. Boston: Little, Brown, Inc., 1975.

Kaplan, Sidney. *The Black Presence in the Era of the American Revolution*. Amherst: University of Massachusetts Press, 1989.

Katz, Stanley N. *Colonial American: Essays in Politics and Social Development*. Boston: Little, Brown, Inc., 1976.

Kidder, Frederic. *The History of the Boston Massacre*. Albany, NY: J. Munsell, 1870.

Labaree, Benjamin. *The Road to Independence 1763-1776*. NY: Macmillan Co., 1963.

Ladenberg, Thomas. *The Causes of the American Revolution.* Boston: Brookline-Cambridge Dissemination Center, 1975.

Langguth, A.J. *The Men Who Started the American Revolution.* NY: Simon & Schuster, 1988.

McLynn, Frank. *Crime and Punishment in Eighteenth-Century England.* NY: Oxford University Press, 1991.

Publications of the Colonial Society of Massachusetts, Vol. VII—1900 and Vol. V—1902. Boston.

Schofield, William G. *Freedom By the Bay: The Boston Freedom Trail.* NY: Rand McNally, 1974.

Shenkman, Richard. *I Love Paul Revere, Whether He Rode or Not.* NY: Harper Collins, 1991.

Wahlke, John C. *The Causes of the American Revolution.* Boston, 1973.

Wemms, William. *The Trial of Wemms Et Al.* Boston, 1770. (publisher unknown).

Whitehill, Walter Muir. *Boston: A Topographical History.* Cambridge: Harvard University Press, 1968.

Winsor, Justin (ed.). *The Memorial History of Boston, Including Suffolk County, Massachusetts 1630-1880.* Boston: Clarence F. Jewett, 1882.

Wright, Louis Bocker. *The American Heritage History of the Thirteen Colonies.* NY: American Heritage, 1967.

Zobel, Hiller B. *The Boston Massacre.* NY: W.W. Norton Co., 1970.

THE TRIAL OF SIMEON BUSHNELL FOR VIOLATION OF THE FUGITIVE SLAVE LAW OF 1850

View of the jail at Cleveland, Ohio, where the prisoners were confined.

BACKGROUND

"When I found I had crossed that line. I looked at my hands to see if I was the same person. There was such a glory over everything."

—Harriet Tubman

*"We morn not that man should toil.
'Tis natures need, 'tis God's decree;
But let the hand that tills the soil,
Be like the wind that fans it,
Free."*

—Anonymous

ESCAPE

Sometime between Christmas Day and New Year's 1855–1856 three Kentucky slaves, John and Dinah, owned by John Bacon, and Frank, owned by Richard Loyd, quietly slipped away from their respective farms on stolen horses and raced through the cold Kentucky night north to freedom. It had been a bitter winter and the Ohio River near Maysville was frozen. The shivering slaves reached the riverbank, crossed the dangerous ice into free Ohio, and made their way inland. Luckily, within hours a compassionate Quaker farmer discovered the freezing fugitives, and took them to his farm. They stayed with the kindly man for several weeks, recovering from their dangerous ordeal, and then started north.

Dinah elected to part company with the men. John and Frank headed out together, travelling by night and following the North Star, hopeful of finally reaching Canada and freedom. By February, with the help of the so-called "Underground Railroad," they had reached the shores of Lake Erie. Sadly, it was impassibly clogged with ice. Slavecatchers were rumored to be patrolling the shores. So the two men were led several miles inland to Oberlin, Ohio, an isolated college town with a reputation as a place where black slaves could be secure from capture. By the fall of 1858 John, the slave of John Bacon, was now John Price, living as a free man in Oberlin, Ohio. Nevertheless, John was a fugitive from Federal justice—that of the Fugitive Slave Law.

Eight years earlier, when John was just a young boy, President Millard Filmore and the 31st Congress of the United States were facing the hard reality of a nation bitterly divided over the issue of slavery. Many Southerners openly spoke of secession; flagrant violations of the 1793 Fugitive Slave Act were costing them valuable property. They demanded stronger laws insuring escaped slaves would be returned to their rightful owners. Some Northerners, like Republican Senator John Hale of New Hampshire, agreed. "If this Union, with all its advantages," he said, "has no other cement than the blood of human slavery, let it perish."

Debates raged as the President and Congressional leaders like the Illinois Senator Stephen Douglas tackled this difficult issue. Finally, as part of a legislative compromise designed to assimilate the vast territories taken in the Mexican War, the issue was resolved: California was admitted into the Union as a free state; Utah and New Mexico territories were organized on the basis of popular sovereignty; the slave trade (but not slavery itself) was prohibited from the nation's capitol; and a strict fugitive slave law was enacted. This was the "Compromise of 1850." An appreciative nation that had been on the edge of secession and possible civil war celebrated. But the happiness was short-lived. The "Compromise" proved more a band-aid for the issue of slavery than a cure. The repeated violations of the fugitive slave law would eventually tear that dressing off.

THE LAW

The new Fugitive Slave Law proved to be unenforceable. Ordinary Northern citizens, despite their strong moral, economic and political hostility to slavery were required to aid in the capture of escaped slaves, like John, even in free states like Ohio. Further, the law enabled slavecatchers to travel throughout Northern free states pursuing runaway slaves. Since slavecatchers often operated with no legal warrants or other documents, freemen were just as likely to be captured and taken South as escaped slaves. Yet, according to the statutes of the law, a person could be fined up to $1,000 for merely refusing to assist a slavecatcher. Actually helping a slave escape could result in a fine of $1,000 plus six months in jail. If the runaway slave made it to Canada and freedom, the abettor could be liable an additional $1,000 to the slave's former owner. While this Fugitive Slave Law was tough on paper, it had exactly the opposite effect: Angry Northerners, previously undecided about the issue of slavery, now joined hands with militant abolitionists to help escaped slaves like John. More slave escapes were attempted. Hidden by day in attics and cellars and shuttled by night along an informal escape system known as the "Underground Railroad," slaves either settled in Canada or found refuge in sympathetic communities like Oberlin.

In the late summer of 1858, Oberlin was a quiet college town of nearly 3,000 permanent residents and about 800 students. There were no saloons, no billiard parlors, no gambling halls—even public smoking was prohibited. Most residents were intensely religious. Yet, this could be said of many small towns in America. What really set Oberlin apart was its population. Black men could be seen working side by side with white men on farms and in stores. Blacks and whites attended the same church. Black children played with white children in the public schoolyard. Blacks practiced law, taught school, and were listed on voter registration lists. Blacks and whites lay side by side in the town's cemetery. Oberlin was more than 100 years ahead of the times.

Most people in Oberlin believed that the Fugitive Slave Law, by asking a person to sin against his brother, was contrary to the laws of God. The law should be disobeyed and the town had a history of just that kind of civil disobedience. In 1837 residents helped hide four escaped slaves on their way to Canada. Four years later townspeople foiled an attempt by slavecatchers to hold some escapees by deliberately releasing them from the jail. Oberlin residents were proud that no black person—slave or freeborn—had ever been taken by slavecatchers—and they intended it to stay that way. Strangers were carefully watched and the alarm could be raised at a moment's notice.

CAPTURE

On September 4, 1858, unbeknown to John Price and the residents of Oberlin, John Bacon, and Richard Loyd, the former owners of the slaves John, Dinah, and Frank, were in the town of Maysville, Kentucky drawing up a "power of attorney" that would give authority to Anderson Jennings, a slavecatcher, to act in their behalf in the capture of their slaves under the provisions of the Fugitive Slave Act. They suspected John and Frank were hiding in Oberlin and now they were going to get them back. This "power of attorney" described John as "about 20 years old, about five feet six or eight inches high, heavy set, copper-colored, and will weigh about 140 to 160 pounds." The power of attorney was given to Richard Mitchell, a local farmer and slavecatcher, who would travel to Oberlin and meet Jennings. There they would devise a plan to capture John and Frank.

John Price was living with a black farmer on the outskirts of town, earning a dollar a day as a field-hand helping with the local harvest. It was just barely enough to keep from starving. He had once stated, perhaps in jest, that he might do better as a slave on his old Kentucky farm.

Monday morning, September 13, 1858 John was waiting for an Oberlin teenager, Shakespeare Boynton, to appear with his father's horse and buggy. John and Frank had been promised a day's work digging potatoes at the Boynton farm. However, John knew he would be going alone since Frank had been injured the previous evening and was in bed. What John didn't know was that Shakespeare had been promised $20 by Anderson Jennings, the slavecatcher, to lure John and Frank into an ambush.

Shakespeare and John reached the Oberlin town line, about a mile and a half outside of town, at noon. Glancing over his shoulder down the dirt road, Shakespeare spotted another buggy rapidly coming up behind them. It contained three slavecatchers—Richard Mitchell, Deputy Marshall Jacob Lowe and Samuel Davis—sent by Jennings to make the arrest. Deputy Marshall Lowe was carrying a warrant for John's arrest issued from the U.S. Commissioner for the District of Southern Ohio. Unsuspecting, John was calmly picking his teeth with a pen-knife, when suddenly the carriage with the three men pulled alongside. Davis jumped down from the carriage and grabbed John, ordering him to drop the knife. At the same time Mitchell started to move his coat aside revealing a gun. Obviously frightened, John dropped the knife and said, "I'll go with you." Davis and Mitchell pulled him into their carriage and headed for the nearest train station in Wellington, Ohio, nine miles from Oberlin.

RESCUE

As the slavecatchers were making their way to Wellington, Shakespeare Boynton drove up to Wack's Hotel in Oberlin to tell Anderson Jennings about John's capture. Jennings paid the boy $20, had lunch, settled his hotel bill, and then left on horseback for the nine-mile trip to Wellington. He figured that he would have no trouble making the 5:13 train. John would soon be firmly back in the hands of his master. He didn't know that Ansel Lyman, an Oberlin resident (and an ardent abolitionist), had seen John being taken to Wellington by the slavecatchers and had "immediately aroused the people."

The news spread rapidly that a black man had been seized in Oberlin by Southerners and was being taken to Wellington. Crowds began to form in various locations along Main Street and on College Street near Fitch's Bookstore. Many citizens were armed "with weapons of death." Soon it seemed that every male in Oberlin, white and black, was heading by horse, carriage, or on foot to Wellington. Except for a few "Democrats," like Seth Bartholomew, all were intent on saving John Price at whatever the cost.

In Wellington, the events of the next few hours became so chaotic that no one remembers with clarity what exactly happened. The slavecatchers—

Jennings, Lowe, Mitchell, and Davis—along with their captive, John, had taken refuge in an attic room in Wellington's Wadsworth Hotel. Sympathetic "Democrats" guarded the hotel entrance. They were nervously waiting for the 5:13 train. Meanwhile, the streets around the hotel were rapidly filling with groups of angry men, black and white, shouting "Bring him out!" "Bring out the man!" "Out with him!" Men were milling about everywhere, calling out to friends, waving weapons, and waiting for someone to tell them what to do. However, one thing was clear; most in the crowd did not know that John was an escaped slave and that a power of attorney and a federal warrant were outstanding for his capture. They were simply determined that he would not be carried away. One black man, Charles Langston, was heard to say that the crowd didn't care if he was an ex-slave, "they will have him anyhow."

Finally, William Lincoln and five other men led an assault on the hotel, rushing forward and grappling with the men guarding the hotel entrance. For three minutes they fought hand-to-hand with "heavy breathing, struggles, guns hurled here and there, men on the floor" until Lincoln pointed his revolver at the head of one of the guards and warned, "Quit, or I'll blow your brains out." At the same time, in the back of the building, a group of blacks led by John Scott had launched their own attack. They broke down the rear door and poured into the building. One of Scott's men was heard saying he would shoot "the first Democrat who keeps us from going up the stairs." The two groups converged in the hallway outside the attic room with Lincoln seemingly in charge.

Inside the attic room, the Kentucky slavecatchers, with weapons ready, were by the door. Jennings was holding the door shut with a rope. Several Oberlin men, admitted earlier to examine the slavecatchers' documents, were urging them to let John go. James Patton said, "You had better let the boy go than to lose your life." Suddenly, Lincoln called through the stovepipe hole near the door, "If you don't open this door, I will stave my gun through and shoot you." There was no response so Lincoln shoved the barrel of his pistol through the hole. Jennings head was next to the hole and he was clobbered by the gunbarrel. He stumbled back and released his grip on the rope holding the door. The men burst in. At the same time, the attic window shattered as a ladder hit it. As the captors turned toward the window, someone grabbed John around the waist and pulled him through the door entrance. John was passed from shoulder to shoulder down the stairwell and finally out the hotel door. A tremendous shout went up from the crowd as he emerged. He was immediately placed in a waiting buggy, allegedly driven by Simeon Bushnell, which raced out of town in the direction of Oberlin.

INDICTMENT

President Buchanan was furious. Certainly a citizen was justified in invoking the Fugitive Slave Law to regain his property. It was the law of the land. He had no intention of letting the little town of Oberlin set a precedent for violation of the law. The rescuers of John Price must be punished.

United States District Judge Hiram V. Willson summoned a federal grand jury to hear the case. Curiously, every juror on the panel was a Democrat even though Ohio was overwhelmingly Republican. Thirty-seven persons, "from snowy white to sooty black," were indicted by the grand jury for violating the Fugitive Slave Law of 1850. Simeon Bushnell was the first to be tried.

You are now invited to participate in this historic trial.

THE TRIAL

Simeon Bushnell's trial began at 10:00 A.M. on Tuesday, April 5, 1859.

The presiding Judge was United States District Judge Hiram V. Willson. In charging the grand jury Judge Willson left no one in doubt about his attitude toward this case when he said, "There are some people who oppose the Fugitive Slave Law from a declared sense of conscientious duty. There is, in fact, a sentiment prevalent in the community which arrogates to human conduct a standard of right above, and independent of, human laws; and it makes the conscience of each individual in society the test of his own accountability to the laws of the land. While those who cherish this dogma claim and enjoy the protection of the law for their own lives and property, they are unwilling that the law should be operative for the protection of the constitutional rights of others."

All of the members of the jury were recognized Democrats. They were:

George Knupp
James G. Haley
Salbert Scott
Edward Foster
Daniel P. Rhodes
Andrew Lugenbeel

George W. Slingluff
James Justice
Charles N. Allen
John Cassell
George Harper
Andrew Scott

Note: It was revealed during the trial that Charles Allen, one of the jurors, was an officer of the Court—a Deputy Marshall. The judge overruled the defense objection.

JUDGE AND COURT OFFICER

"This case, like every other which is tried in a court of justice, should be divested of everything that is extraneous. It is to be determined according to the law and the testimony as delivered to you in Court."

—Judge Willson's final remarks to the jury

HIRAM V. WILLSON

United States District Judge

You are a large, obese, gray-haired man who looks much older than your 50 years. You are clearly biased against Oberlin and what it represents. You allowed the selection of an all-Democratic jury despite the fact that the Western Reserve in Ohio was overwhelmingly Republican. Charging the grand jury prior to Bushnell's trial, you said that "there are some people who oppose the Fugitive Slave Law from a declared sense of conscientious duty . . . While those who cherish this dogma claim and enjoy the protection of the law for their own lives and property, they are unwilling that the law should be operative for the protection of the constitutional rights of others."

You must charge the jury at the beginning of the trial, instructing them to listen carefully to the witnesses and reminding them that the defendant is considered innocent until proven guilty by the prosecution.

The defendant is charged with breaking the Fugitive Slave Law of 1850. You should have the Court Clerk read out the section of the Fugitive Slave Law that applies in this case.

After the prosecution and defense have concluded their cases, you should again charge the jury and ask them to render a verdict, saying: "Gentlemen of the jury. You must consider the following and make a decision based on the evidence.

1. Was the Negro John a slave, owing service to John G. Bacon of Kentucky?

2. Did Anderson Jennings hold this fugitive by virtue of the power of attorney given him by Bacon at the time of John's rescue in Wellington on September 13?

3. If you find in the affirmative on the first two facts, then was the defendant, Bushnell, implicated in the rescue?

4. It must be proved, without reasonable doubt, that the defendant acted knowingly and willingly. He knew the Negro was a fugitive from labor and was lawfully detained by the person or person(s) who held him captive. He acted under such circumstances as to show that he might have had such knowledge by exercising ordinary prudence.

5. It is your duty, Gentlemen, to take the case and return a verdict according to the evidence.

Sentence

If the defendant is found innocent, you should immediately declare him free.

If the defendant is found guilty, you should sentence him to 60 days in jail and a fine of $1,000."

FREDERICK G. GREEN
Court Clerk

You are responsible for assisting the Judge in running the trial.
You will be expected to do the following:

1. Swear in all witnesses, asking them to place their left hand on the Bible, raise their right hand, and say "Yes" to the statement "Do you swear to tell the truth, the whole truth, and nothing but the truth, so help you God."

2. Read aloud to the court any documents that the Judge instructs you to enter into the record, including statements of law and evidence introduced as exhibits.

3. Keep a record of the names of all witnesses offering testimony.

4. Assist the jury in any problems or questions they might have regarding court procedure.

5. Assist the Judge (and Bailiff) in maintaining courtroom order.

THE PROSECUTION

AN OBERLIN HOME OF THE FIFTIES
James H. Fairchild's House on Professor Street, now Fairchild Cottage
(Photograph in the Oberlin College Library)

"Here are the Saints of Oberlin, Peck, Plumb, Fitch, to which are to be added Saint Spaulding and Riddle, and subSaint Bushnell—all Saints of the Higher Law."

—George Belden's
closing remarks to the jury

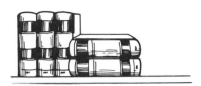

GEORGE BLISS

PROSECUTING ATTORNEY

You are a former Ohio State Judge and a Democratic Congressman to the Ohio Legislature. You believe in a strict interpretation of the Fugitive Slave Law and that the State of Ohio has no right to legislate upon the subjects of fugitives from labor. You have a low opinion of the willingness of Oberlin's citizens to obey the law of the land. You feel that John's escape is "proved by his being found in the common resort of fugitive slaves, to wit, in Oberlin."

You will agree with your partner, Mr. Belden, that the defendant clearly violated the Fugitive Slave Law by aiding in the rescue of the escaped slave John. Your case should take into consideration the following:

1. John was clearly the property of John Bacon of Kentucky, and was living in Oberlin under the name of John Price.

2. There is not sufficient variance in the assorted physical descriptions of John to make a case of mistaken identity.

3. The Oberlin men, including the defendant Bushnell, who came to John's rescue in Wellington knew perfectly well that he was a runaway slave from Kentucky.

4. Jennings was carrying a valid power of attorney from John Bacon.

5. It is not necessary to produce in Court the warrant carried by Marshall Lowe since the defendant's indictment says nothing about John's rescue from a federal warrant. He was rescued from Jennings who was acting under a valid power of attorney.

6. Clearly, Bushnell was a key figure in the crowd that assembled in Oberlin. He induced citizens to go to Wellington armed, and later drove the getaway buggy from the Wellington Hotel. He was instrumental in hiding the slave John and abetting his disappearance from the law.

7. These Oberlin men, including the defendant, went to Wellington proclaiming that there was a "Higher Law" but in reality they were "outraging" the laws of the United States.

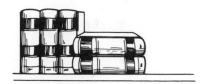

GEORGE W. BELDEN
Prosecuting Attorney

You are a 48-year-old Democratic lawyer from Canton, Ohio. You are an advocate of strict enforcement of the Fugitive Slave Law and are under pressure from the Buchanan administration in Washington to prosecute the case fully. You can be spiteful and easily angered. You want to maintain strict legal procedure and insist that this is a heinous crime. This attitude may cause critics to label you an "imbecile" and "a man of small intellect."

You must prove that Simeon Bushnell violated the Fugitive Slave Law by participating in the rescue of the runaway slave John owned by John Bacon in Kentucky. Your case should take into consideration the following:

1. John was clearly the property of John Bacon. John escaped from Kentucky, even the defense will admit that fact, and many witnesses in Oberlin understood him to be a slave from Kentucky.

2. Jennings had a legal power of attorney to capture John and bring him back to his owner in Kentucky. Clearly, Jennings and Mitchell knew John and were convinced they had captured the correct runaway slave.

3. You should try to ignore the warrant that was acquired by Deputy Marshall Lowe. It was not necessary. John was legally in the custody of Jennings by virtue of the power of attorney.

4. The Court is bound to take notice <u>ex officio</u> of the laws of Kentucky.

5. The "Higher Law" that the defense will allude to is just the law that makes every man's conscience and private opinion his guide, which ultimately leads to chaos.

6. It was perfectly lawful and right for the gentlemen from Kentucky—Jennings and Mitchell—to follow the escaped slave to Oberlin with "Arkansas toothpicks, Bowie knives, and revolvers, if they thought these things best for the purpose of capture."

ARTEMAS HALBERT

WITNESS FOR THE PROSECUTION

You are a 17-year-old Oberlin housepainter who will testify to the following:

1. You have lived in Oberlin for three years.

2. You came into the center of town on September 13 because you heard that Southerners had kidnapped a Negro, contrary to law.

3. You might have seen the Negro called John but you didn't know him well enough to describe his features.

4. You heard Ansel Lyman, standing in front of Watson's General Store, telling the assembling crowd about the captured Negro named John.

5. You will claim you heard the defendant, Bushnell, talking with one Orindatus Wall, a black shoemaker, about getting a horse and going to Wellington.

6. You left for Wellington, out of curiosity, at about 2 or 3 P.M.

7. Later, in Wellington, you saw the defendant in front of the hotel. You heard the defendant say that getting a warrant to arrest the "kidnappers" of John would be the best method of freeing him.

8. You believe the defendant seemed pretty "cool" in comparison with some of the crowd who were noisy and threatening.

9. You witnessed John being carried out of the hotel and being placed in the waiting buggy. You believe the defendant was sitting in the buggy. You will admit that it was dusk and there was a large crowd between you and the buggy.

10. You think the defendant was driving the escape buggy when it left Wellington with John headed for Oberlin.

ROBERT COCHRAN
Witness for the Prosecution

You are the clerk of Mason County Courthouse in Maysville, Kentucky. You have had this post since 1851. You will testify to the following:

1. On September 4, 1858 your Deputy Clerk, Mr. W.H. Richardson, wrote out a "power of attorney" giving Mr. Anderson Jennings the right to act on behalf of Mr. John Bacon and Mr. Richard Loyd in the capture of their escaped slaves John, Frank, and Dinah.

2. Your deputy signed his name on the document because when the gentlemen came to the office, you had stepped out for the moment.

3. You met Mr. Bacon and Mr. Loyd on their way out of the office and you read the "power of attorney" drawn up by your deputy. You found everything in order. However, you did add the words "The said parties are personally known to me, and the said acknowledgment is according to law" to the bottom of the document.

4. You returned the "power of attorney" to them and didn't sign it. You didn't think anything of that at the time since your deputy had the authorization to sign such documents.

5. You have known John Bacon for nine years. You don't remember ever seeing his slave John.

JOHN PARKS GLENN BACON

WITNESS FOR THE PROSECUTION

You have been called as a witness to describe John's physical appearance, to relate the events surrounding his escape from your farm, the power of attorney that was issued for his capture, and your recruitment of Anderson Jennings and John Mitchell to go to Oberlin and retrieve the escaped slaves.

You are a 29-year-old Kentuckian with a moderate-size farm in Mason County near Maysville. The farm is only about a quarter of a mile inland from the Ohio River.

You owned two slaves: a tall slim woman named "Dinah" and her cousin "John." You inherited both slaves from your father who died in 1846.

You will testify at the trial to the following:

1. Your slave John was about 20 years old, about five feet six or eight inches tall, heavy set, copper-colored, and weighing about 140 to 150 pounds. Additionally, he had a huge misshapen foot with an enormous heel.

2. You will testify that you and your wife Jacova decided to visit relatives on a near-by farm on Christmas of 1856. You left John and Dinah in the charge of an Irish hired-hand named Peter. When you returned late on New Year's Day, both slaves had escaped on stolen horses. You later learned that they had met up with another slave, Frank, from your neighbor's farm and fled across the Ohio River.

3. You heard reports from several slavecatchers patrolling in Ohio that your slave John was in Oberlin and calling himself John Price.

4. You and your neighbor, Mr. Loyd, decided to hire men to capture your escaped property.

5. Two neighbors, Anderson Jennings and Richard Mitchell, agreed to go to Ohio and capture the escaped slaves.

6. On September 4, 1858 you went, along with Mr. Loyd and Mr. Mitchell, to the office of the Mason County Clerk in Maysville and made out a "power of attorney" giving Anderson Jennings the right "to capture and return to our service and possession in Kentucky, three Negroes now at large in Ohio." The Clerk was not in the office so the document was drawn up and signed by his deputy. You didn't see any problem with this. Later, leaving the office, you ran into him and he read the document. He added a statement saying he had known you personally for nine years.

7. You gave Mitchell $50 for expenses and indicated that on recapture John would be sold, and he and Jennings would have a share in the sale—perhaps as much as $500.

8. You will insist that you are sure that the "John" who was rescued in Wellington was your slave in Kentucky.

RICHARD P. MITCHELL

Witness for the Prosecution

You are a Kentucky farmer who had previously worked for John Bacon and knew the escaped slave John. You have also worked as a constable and have tracked fugitive slaves into Ohio on a number of occasions. In fact, about a month after John's escape, you traveled nearly fifty miles into Fayette County in pursuit of him.

You are tall, have red hair and whiskers, and speak with a thick Kentucky accent.

You will testify to the following:

1. You recall seeing the escape slave John shortly before Christmas Day 1856.

2. John Bacon told you around New Year's Day that his slaves had escaped, probably to Ohio.

3. You described John as "dark copper color, not jet black," weighing about 150 to 160 pounds, and about five feet eight inches to five feet ten inches tall. He had a "full face" and was "quite good looking."

4. On September 4, 1858 you went with John Bacon to the Mason County Courthouse to make out a "power of attorney" so that you and another Kentucky farmer, Anderson Jennings, could go to Oberlin, Ohio on behalf of Mr. Bacon and Mr. Loyd to retrieve their escaped property. You were given the "power of attorney" (made out in the name of Anderson Jennings) plus $50 to cover expenses.

5. Power of attorney in hand, you took a steamboat from Maysville to Cincinnati and then a train north via Columbus to Wellington. From there you went by carriage to Oberlin where you checked into Wack's Hotel and met with Jennings on September 8.

6. You recognized John immediately when he walked past the hotel shortly after you arrived.

7. You and Jennings decided that more help was needed to capture these slaves since the townspeople were potentially hostile. So while you remained in Oberlin, Jennings went to nearby Columbus to recruit two other slavecatchers: Deputy Marshall Lowe and Assistant Deputy Samuel Davis.

8. A plot was devised in which a young boy would lure John into an ambush.

9. On September 13, about one and a half miles outside of Oberlin you and the two deputies arrested John and took him to nearby Wellington where you met up with Jennings.

10. You always carried a pistol and a knife, but will deny ever showing them to John or threatening anybody.

11. You were present throughout the day in the Wellington Hotel besieged by the Oberlin townspeople intent on rescuing John.

12. You showed the power of attorney and a warrant for John's arrest to several people. You will also claim that John actually wanted to go back to Kentucky to "see his old mistress and master."

13. You saw the men break into the hotel room and take John, but you did not recognize or know any of them.

14. You looked out the hotel window and saw the buggy drive off with John, but you could not identify the driver of the buggy as being the defendant.

164

SETH BARTHOLOMEW

WITNESS FOR THE PROSECUTION

You are a 26-year-old tinware peddler and have lived in Oberlin all your life. You were present in Oberlin prior to the townspeople leaving for Wellington and are prepared to testify about what you heard the crowd and the defendant saying before they left.

Be careful. You have a very bad reputation in town for untruthfulness and you also have a suspicious past that includes indictment for theft. You are not popular in Oberlin.

You will testify to the following:

1. You recall seeing the defendant, Bushnell, outside of Fitch's Bookstore shortly before 1:00 or 2:00 P.M. and overhearing a conversation he was having with Professor Peck, Ralph Plumb, and James Fitch, the defendant's boss.

2. One of the three men, you can't remember which one, said to go out and get ready so they could leave. The defendant left and returned with a buggy and two other men—one of the men had a rifle.

3. You recall that several minutes later the defendant told someone, you think it was a student, to get out of the buggy because "he had no business in there."

4. A short while later, you saw the defendant drive off in the buggy towards Wellington. You saw Oliver Wall, a Negro, sitting next to him armed with a gun.

5. You think the defendant left Oberlin about 3:00 or 4:00 on the afternoon of the rescue in Wellington.

6. You remember the defendant as being a "noisy" member of the crowd in Oberlin, but you can't say exactly what he was saying.

7. You never went to Wellington.

ANDERSON JENNINGS

WITNESS FOR THE PROSECUTION

You are a tall 40-year-old rough-looking Kentucky farmer and slavecatcher. You speak in a coarse drawl that may cause people to laugh. You have a dark complexion and a short bull neck, causing people to refer to you as a "buffalo bull" of a man.

You own a farm near John Bacon and knew the slave John for about two or three years prior to his escape. You identified John as pure black, about 160 pounds, five feet seven inches or five feet eight inches tall and about 20 to 22 years old.

You always carry two pistols, a knife, and several pairs of handcuffs when seeking escaped slaves.

You will testify to the following:

1. You are not normally a slavecatcher. You only did this particular job as a favor to your neighbor John Bacon.

2. John Bacon and Richard Loyd hired you to go to Oberlin and capture the escaped slaves John and Frank. You had a "power of attorney" made out in your name authorizing you to make this arrest.

3. You stayed in Wack's Hotel in Oberlin until a plan was devised to capture the escaped slaves.

4. You sent three men—Marshall Jacob Lowe (holding a federal warrant for John's arrest), his assistant, Samuel Davis, and another slavecatcher, Richard Mitchell—armed with pistols and knives to a prearranged meeting, with Shakespeare Boynton (an Oberlin teenager) driving John in his father's buggy to a day job digging potatoes at their farm. They accomplished the ambush, captured John (Frank was not in the buggy), and brought him to Wellington.

5. Shakespeare returned to Wack's Hotel, told you that John was captured, and was paid $20 for his services.

6. You left shortly after for Wellington.

7. You, Mitchell, Lowe, Davis, and the captured slave, John, were in an attic room in the Wadsworth Hotel in Wellington, waiting for the 5:13 train to Columbus. You will claim that "there was I thought as much as 1,000 armed people around and in the hotel" and "a great many had arms, rifles, and shotguns."

8. You will claim to have shown the power of attorney and warrant for John's arrest to several people in the course of the day.

9. You will testify that John admitted he was a slave and was willing to return to his master in Kentucky. John even went out on the hotel balcony to tell the crowd he would willingly return, but got scared when he saw all the guns.

10. You will claim that the gun barrel shoved through the stovepipe door almost knocked you to the floor and drew blood.

11. You never saw the buggy drive away with John and you never specifically heard the defendant's name mentioned.

EDWARD C. KINNEY

WITNESS FOR THE PROSECUTION

You are an Oberlin student. You were in Oberlin when the crowd was forming and you later went to Wellington to observe the action.

You will testify to the following:

1. You knew that John was a former slave but you had no idea who was his former owner. You don't think anyone in Oberlin knew who had been his master. You don't think that anyone knew anything about a warrant for the arrest of John or about an outstanding "power of attorney." You certainly never saw either of these documents.

2. You were in Oberlin on the afternoon of September 13 and saw the defendant in front of Fitch's Bookstore on College Street near Main Street. You remember that most of the crowd was gathering on Main Street.

3. You saw Bushnell leave with a black man named Wall. They drove off together in a buggy in the direction of Wellington. You didn't notice anything unusual in their manner except that Wall had a rifle. However, you saw many people with guns that day.

4. You remember hearing people in the crowd at Oberlin saying that Southerners had carried off John because "Southerners are men who usually carry off people."

5. You didn't reach Wellington until about sunset because you had to walk. As you reached the edge of town, you saw the defendant in a carriage heading back to Oberlin with two white men and a Negro. You think the black man was John.

THE DEFENSE

SLAVERY IN AMERICA.

"Let Southern oppressors tremble—let their secret abettors tremble—let their Northern apologists tremble—let all the enemies of the persecuted blacks tremble."

—William Lloyd Garrison
Abolitionist leader

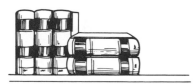

RUFUS PAINE SPAULDING

Defense Attorney

You are the 60-year-old leader of the defense team with a reputation as an outstanding lawyer. You are a former Speaker of the Ohio House of Representatives and a onetime Associate Judge for the Ohio State Supreme Court. You consider yourself a Democrat, but differ with most of your colleagues on the issue of slavery. Like your associate, Albert Riddle, you are a friend and supporter of Ohio's Republican Governor, Salmon P. Chase.

You will work closely with Mr. Riddle to attack the testimony of the prosecution witnesses and the Fugitive Slave Law in general. You will say that "slavery is like a canker eating out the vitals of our liberties, and . . . the Supreme Court of the United States has become the impregnable fortress and bulwark of slavery. No article of the Constitution authorized the passage of such an illegal law."

You will specifically focus on the following in developing your case:

1. Is Bushnell to be convicted merely because he is from the town of Oberlin? Is it a case of guilt by association?

2. Bacon swears that John is his slave, but is that sufficient proof in the Free State of Ohio where the presumption is always in favor of a man's freedom?

3. A person cannot be kidnapped from their home only by virtue of their skin color. The residents of Ohio are always entitled to the benefits of <u>habeas corpus</u> and trial by jury.

4. Whenever and however possible, attack the Fugitive Slave Law.

ALBERT GALLATIN RIDDLE
Defense Attorney

You are a 42-year-old lawyer and have previously served in the Ohio House of Representatives. You are a close friend of Ohio's Republican Governor, Salmon P. Chase, and a bitter opponent of slavery. You believe the best way to deal with this case is to attack the prosecution's arguments by employing technicalities and to make Bushnell's actions into a general indictment against slavery and the odious Fugitive Slave Law.

You should use your witnesses, opening remarks, and closing remarks to make the following points:

1. There is a "Higher Law" that should guide our actions when confronted with obviously immoral laws.

2. You can obey the laws of our country by either obeying them or submitting to the penalty they impose. Both actions reflect obedience.

3. What "right" or "contract" held John as a slave in Kentucky? Was John really Bacon's "property"?

4. The Fugitive Slave Law of September 18, 1850 is illegal, immoral, and unconstitutional. It violated the Fifth Amendment's guarantee that no person could "be deprived of life, liberty, or property, without due process of law."

5. You agree with the prosecution that John the slave ran away from his master. But, you ask, why shouldn't he escape? There is some fault either in the law or in the the whole system that maintains human beings in perpetual bondage.

6. The "power of attorney" held by the slavecatcher Jennings had no official seal and was never executed by a legal officer—merely his assistant. This document was only used to acquire a warrant for John's arrest from the clerk in Columbus—a warrant that was never introduced in evidence and was of dubious authenticity.

7. Jennings, with his "power of attorney," was the only person who could have taken John, yet it was Lowe, Davis and Mitchell who actually kidnapped him. He had no power to confer upon another the authority vested in himself to seize and arrest John.

8. Lowe and Davis did not even testify, yet they were the ones who actually arrested John.

9. Jennings never showed anyone the power of attorney when he was holding John in the Wadsworth Hotel.

10. There are so many differing physical descriptions of John that it is obvious they might have had the wrong man.

11. Oberlin residents went to Wellington entirely convinced that a free black man, John Price, had been illegally kidnapped. No one considered he was an ex-slave.

12. Seth Bartholomew was obviously lying when he related Bushnell's alleged conversations in Oberlin prior to leaving for Wellington. First, Bushnell was not a prominent member of the crowd. Second, he was one of the last men to leave Oberlin on the day of the alleged rescue.

13. John never once said anything about wanting to return to Kentucky and his old master, unless it was out of fear for his life.

14. Finally, you believe the prosecution cannot produce a shred of concrete evidence that Simeon Bushnell ever participated in John's actual escape from the Wadsworth Hotel.

SIMEON BUSHNELL
Defendant

You are a 29-year-old clerk and printer employed in the town of Oberlin by your brother-in-law, James Fitch. You live in a boarding house on the south side of College Street near Fitch's store.

You are a short man with black hair, dark eyes and a beard. You have a wife, an infant daughter, and a reputation around Oberlin as being an unpretentious humble workman. You are very religious and believe that slavery is morally wrong. You are the nephew of Reverend Horace Bushnell of Cincinnati, an anti-slavery missionary. You are suspected of being an active member of the Underground Railroad.

Your attorneys have strongly advised against testifying at the trial. The prosecution must prove you guilty. If you are subjected to cross-examination, it will be nearly impossible to escape conviction since you will have to admit that you were an active participant in John Price's escape.

If you do testify, you must admit to the following:

1. You believe that slavery is morally wrong and the Fugitive Slave Law is evil and must be disobeyed.

2. You were part of the crowd that assembled in Oberlin and later traveled in a buggy to Wellington.

3. You don't recall the specifics of any conversations you had in Oberlin prior to going to Wellington.

4. You were never armed.

5. You were driving the buggy that eventually drove the rescued John out of Oberlin after he was taken by the rescuers from the Wadsworth Hotel.

6. You took him to Oberlin where he was hidden in a "safe place" until he could be spirited away to Canada. You will deny knowing anyone associated with these actions to protect them from prosecution.

7. You will admit that you told people after the rescue that "if rescuing John Price is a crime, I suppose I am guilty."

8. You will, at all times, be true to your beliefs about the immorality of slavery and the necessity to defy the Fugitive Slave Law.

RALPH PLUMB
Witness for the Defense

You are an Oberlin lawyer who was present and witnessed the events on September 13 in Oberlin and Wellington. You are under indictment yourself for having participated in the rescue of John.

You will testify to the following:

1. You were in Oberlin until late in the afternoon of September 13. You only know about John from hearsay. You never actually saw him either in town or later after the alleged rescue.

2. You saw the prosecution witness Bartholomew wandering around the crowd forming on Main Street in Oberlin.

3. You will agree that you had a spirited conversation with your friends Fitch and Peck on the doorstep of Fitch's store prior to leaving for Wellington. But the defendant, Bushnell, was not there. Although he is a clerk in the store, he simply was not there at the time. The doors to the store are glass and you couldn't even see him through the doors.

4. You never saw Bushnell in Wellington and have no knowledge of him driving the alleged slave John away in a buggy after the rescue.

 -

PHILO WEED
Witness for the Defense

You are an Oberlin resident and co-owner of a stove, tin, and hollow-ware store. You will testify to the following:

1. You knew John Price well and will describe him as a very black Negro of about five feet eight inches tall and about 160 pounds. The last time you saw him, however, he seemed to have lost a lot of weight. You think he was sick.

2. You knew Bartholomew well. He had been your apprentice for several months. You consider him nothing short of criminal. He had lied to you several times and had a bad reputation in town. You think he was even indicted a few years back for stealing.

3. You knew the defendant and considered him a man of fine reputation and integrity.

CLARK ELLIOT
Witness for the Defense

You are an Oberlin carpenter. You will testify to the following:

1. You do not know the alleged escaped slave John.

2. You were in Oberlin on September 13 and witnessed the crowd preparing to leave for Wellington to rescue a man taken by Southern kidnappers.

3. You do not recall seeing the defendant in Oberlin on that day.

4. You did see Seth Bartholomew roaming around the crowd. You have known him for about thirteen years and would not believe him under oath, especially if he had an interest in the outcome of the case.

5. You did not go to Wellington and have no knowledge of what happened there except that you heard they rescued a man taken by Southern slavecatchers.

JAMES FITCH
Witness for the Defense

You have lived in Oberlin all your life and own a bookstore in town. You will testify to the following:

1. The defendant is a clerk in your bookstore.

2. You are sure the defendant was not in the store or on the steps of the store when Seth Bartholomew allegedly heard him make statements about going to rescue an escaped slave.

3. You will admit to having a conversation with Plumb and Peck on the bookstore steps about the kidnapping of an Oberlin resident named John Price.

4. You have known Seth Bartholomew for years and believe that he is not capable of telling the truth.

BREWSTER PELTON

WITNESS FOR THE DEFENSE

You are a local merchant and a trustee at Oberlin College. You witnessed the crowd forming in Oberlin prior to leaving for Wellington. You will testify to the following:

1. You do not know John and have never seen him.

2. You know the defendant well and do not recall seeing him in Oberlin on the day in question.

3. You know Seth Bartholomew and have a bad opinion of his general character. You do not think he could be trusted to tell the truth.

LEWIS BOYNTON

WITNESS FOR THE DEFENSE

You have a farm in the town of Russia, about three and a half miles from Oberlin. You are an admitted Democrat. Your son was involved in the capture of John, however, it is unclear whether you knew about the plot. You will admit to the following:

1. You had a meeting with Anderson Jennings on the Sunday prior to John's capture.

2. You can decide to say (a) you just discussed farming or (b) you gave your approval to your son to join the plot to capture John.

3. You can't describe John and you were not present in either Oberlin or Wellington on September 13.

4. You know the defendant but not very well.

SHAKESPEARE BOYNTON

WITNESS FOR THE DEFENSE

You are the 13-year-old son of Lewis Boynton, a farmer from the nearby town of Russia. You were part of the plot to capture John and will testify to the following:

1. You will claim that your father knew nothing of your arrangement with Anderson Jennings to lure the two escape slaves, John and Frank, into an ambush.

2. Jennings had promised you $20 for your part in the plot.

3. You should be able to describe in detail the capture of John on the lonely road outside of Oberlin.

4. Back in Oberlin, Jennings paid you the $20 even though only John was captured, but you will assure the court that it was "good money." In fact, you regretted not being able to help capture Frank, too.

 -

HENRY PECK

WITNESS FOR THE DEFENSE

You are a professor at the college and live in the town of Oberlin. You have also been indicted by the grand jury for involvement in the rescue of John. You will say your recollections are accurate because you are "extraordinarily sensitive about the Fugitive Slave Law." You will testify to the following:

1. You know John Price well and will describe him as five feet five inches tall or less, decidedly black, stoutly built, and weighing about 160 pounds when healthy.

2. You will admit to being in the town of Oberlin on the day of the rescue, but will deny ever seeing the defendant. You never met Bushnell on the steps of Fitch's store either alone or with Plumb and Fitch. You definitely did not have any kind of conversation with him about going to Wellington to rescue the kidnapped John Price.

3. You do remember Seth Bartholomew sneaking around trying to eavesdrop on conversations in the crowd forming in Oberlin on the afternoon of September 13.

4. You have a low opinion of Bartholomew's character and consider him just short of a thief and liar.

JAMES L. PATTON
WITNESS FOR THE DEFENSE

You are an Oberlin student who was present in town on the afternoon of September 13 and later went to Wellington. You will testify to the following:

1. You first heard at about 1:30 that someone had been "carried off by slavecatchers." You didn't know who but decided to go to town and find out.

2. You went to Watson's Store and mingled with the crowd. You never saw the defendant. In fact, you will deny ever seeing the defendant in Oberlin, on the road to Wellington or in the town of Wellington itself.

3. You decided to go in a carriage with a group of men to Wellington. Nobody seemed to know whether the kidnapped black was a slave or a freeman. They were determined, however, to get him back.

4. You were with the crowd in front of the Wellington Hotel. You will admit that many people, including several black men, were armed.

5. Since you are a law student, the slavecatchers allowed you to come up to the attic where they were holding John and examine the warrant for his arrest. You never saw any power of attorney. Jennings merely told you that the boy belonged to him.

6. You heard the crowd respond to the warrant by saying they would have the boy anyway.

7. You saw John go out on the balcony to speak to the crowd, but it was so noisy that nobody could hear anything. He seemed frightened and unable to speak properly.

8. You never saw John's eventual rescue or escape from Wellington.

JOSEPH H. DICKSON
WITNESS FOR THE DEFENSE

You are a Wellington attorney and were present in town on September 13. You were present in front of the Wadsworth Hotel and even entered the hotel itself to examine the documents held by the slavecatchers. You will testify to the following:

1. You saw the crowd assemble in front of the Wadsworth Hotel for the purpose of rescuing John.

2. You did not think the crowd was threatening violence.

3. You were invited into the hotel room where the captive John was being held. Mr. Lowe showed you his warrant for the arrest of the escaped slave John. You read the warrant and found it in order, except that it lacked an official seal. (Lowe claimed that such documents don't normally have an official seal.)

4. You were never shown the power of attorney supposedly held by Mr. Jennings.

5. You were under the impression from the warrant that Jennings, not Bacon, was the alleged owner of John.

6. You will claim to know the defendant, Bushnell, but never saw him in the crowd at Wellington. However, you must admit that you left before the actual rescue.

JOHN J. COX
WITNESS FOR THE DEFENSE

You are a 50-year-old Oberlin construction worker. You have lived in Oberlin for about 20 years and know both John and his alleged rescuer Bushnell very well. You will testify to the following:

1. You know John well because he had worked for you on a number of occasions. He is about five feet four inches or five feet five inches tall and very black.

2. You know Seth Bartholomew and consider him notoriously of bad character. You believe he is a compulsive liar and should never be trusted.

LYSANDER BUTLER

Witness for the Defense

You are an Oberlin law student who was present when the crowd assembled in Oberlin and later went to Wellington to witness the rescue. You will testify to the following:

1. You have seen John around town many times and he was about five feet five inches tall and decidedly black.

2. You have known Seth Bartholomew for about ten years and believe his reputation for truthfulness to be very poor.

3. You never saw the defendant in Oberlin prior to the rescue.

4. You never saw the defendant in Wellington.

5. You were admitted into the hotel to view the federal warrant for John's arrest and were mystified as to why the paper did not have an official seal.

6. You never saw any power of attorney.

 -

ORINDATUS S.B. WALL

Witness for the Defense

You are a black resident of Oberlin. It is questionable whether the judge will allow you to testify since, according to the the Dred Scott Decision, blacks are not considered citizens and have no constitutional rights. Judge Willson may let you testify just to prove that the court is unbiased. You will testify to the following:

1. You know John Price very well. You will describe him as being very black—definitely not a light-skinned Negro. He was about five feet five inches tall and weighed about 150 pounds.

2. You know the defendant well and never saw him on the day of the rescue either in Oberlin or later in Wellington.

EXHIBITS

"Go down Moses,
Way down in Egyptland
Tell old Pharaoh
To let my people go"

—*Go Down Moses*
　slave work song

SECTION 9 of the Fugitive Slave Act of September 18, 1850

"Any person who shall knowingly and willingly obstruct, hinder, or prevent such claimant, his agent or attorney, or any person or persons lawfully assisting him, her, or them from arresting such fugitive from service or labor either with or without process as aforesaid, or shall rescue, or attempt to rescue, such fugitive from service or labor, from the custody of such claimant, his or her agent or attorney, or other person or persons lawfully assisting as aforesaid, when so arrested, pursuant to the authority herein given and declared; or shall aid, abet, or assist such person, so owing service or labor as aforesaid, directly or indirectly, to escape from such claimant, his agent or attorney, or other person or persons legally authorized as aforesaid; or shall harbor or conceal such fugitive so as to prevent the discovery or arrest of such person, after notice or knowledge of the fact that such person was a fugitive from service or labor as aforesaid, shall, for either of said offences, be subject to a fine not exceeding one thousand dollars, and imprisonment not exceeding six months, by indictment and conviction before the District Court."

POWER OF ATTORNEY

KNOW ALL MEN BY THESE PRESENTS, That we, Richard Loyd and John G. Bacon, of the county of Mason, and State of Kentucky, do hereby constitute and appoint Anderson Jennings of the county of Mason and State of Kentucky our attorney: for us and in our name and for our use, to capture and return to our service and possession in Kentucky, three Negroes now at large in the State of Ohio:

Which Negroes answer the following description, viz.:—*Frank*, the property of Richard Loyd, is a large black Negro, full six feet high, large pop eyes, rather thick tongued, about 26 years old. *John,* the property of John G. Bacon, is about 20 years old, about five feet six or eight inches high, heavy set, copper colored, and will weigh about 140 or 150 pounds. *Dinah,* the property of said Bacon, is a tall, slim Negro woman, about 21 or 22 years old, dark copper color, very straight, holds high head, and very quick spoken.

Whatsoever our attorney shall lawfully do in the premises, we do hereby confirm the same, as if we were present and did the same in our own proper names.

IN WITNESS WHEREOF we have hereunto set our hands and seals, the 4th day of September, 1858.

RICHARD LOYD _____

JOHN G. BACON _____

State of Kentucky, Mason County

I, Robert A. Cochran, Clerk of the County Court of the county aforesaid, do hereby certify that this power of attorney, from Richard Loyd and John G. Bacon to Anderson Jennings, was this day produced to me, and acknowledged by the said Richard Loyd and John G. Bacon to be their act and deed. The said parties are personally known to me, and the said acknowledgment is according to law.

Given under my hand and official seal, in the city of Maysville, this 4th day of September, 1858.

ROBERT A. COCHRAN, Clerk, by WILLIAM H. RICHARDSON, D.C.

_____

EXHIBIT C

VIEW OF THE WADSWORTH HOTEL FROM THE FRONT. JOHN PRICE WAS ALLEGEDLY RESCUED FROM AN ATTIC ROOM WHOSE FANTAIL WINDOW CAN BE SEEN DIRECTLY ABOVE THE BALCONY OVER THE FRONT DOOR.

COPY OF A NOTICE ALLEGEDLY CIRCULATED BY ABOLISHIONISTS IN AND AROUND OBERLIN.

CAUTION!!!
COLORED PEOPLE
OF OHIO
ONE AND ALL

KIDNAPPERS
AND
SLAVE CATCHERS,

HAVE ALREADY BEEN EMPLOYED
TO CAPTURE AND RETURN ESCAPED
SLAVES FROM KENTUCKY
THEREFORE,
IF YOU VALUE THE LIBERTY
AND THE WELFARE OF THE
FUGITIVES AMONG YOU

KEEP A SHARP LOOK
OUT FOR SUSPICIOUS
LOOKING MEN

THIS IS THE KIND OF TREATMENT JOHN COULD EXPECT IF HE WERE RETURNED TO HIS MASTER IN KENTUCKY.

ADDITIONAL INFORMATION

"Eliza made her desperate retreat across the river just in the dusk of twilight. The grey mist of evening, rising slowly from the river, enveloped her as she disappeared up the bank, and the swollen current and floundering masses of ice presented a hopeless barrier between her and her pursuers."

—Harriet B. Stowe
Uncle Tom's Cabin

MASTER ROLE SHEET

HISTORICAL CHARACTER	ROLE	STUDENT NAME
Simeon Bushnell	Defendant	_____
Hiram V. Willson*	Judge	_____
George Belden	Pros. Att.	_____
George Bliss	Pros. Att.	_____
Albert Riddle	Def. Att.	_____
Rufus Spaulding	Def. Att.	_____
Frederick Green	Clerk	_____
John Bacon	Pros. Witness	_____
Robert Cochran**	Pros. Witness	_____
Anderson Jennings	Pros. Witness	_____
Seth Bartholomew	Pros. Witness	_____
Artemas Halbert	Pros. Witness	_____
Richard Mitchell	Pros. Witness	_____
Edward Kinney	Pros. Witness	_____
Lewis Boynton**	Def. Witness	_____
Shakespeare Boynton	Def. Witness	_____
Henry Peck	Def. Witness	_____
Ralph Plumb	Def. Witness	_____
James Fitch	Def. Witness	_____
James Patton	Def. Witness	_____
Lysander Butler	Def. Witness	_____
John Cox**	Def. Witness	_____
Philo Weed**	Def. Witness	_____
Brewster Pelton**	Def. Witness	_____

* NORMALLY PLAYED BY THE TEACHER
** OPTIONAL ROLE

Note: The jury can be anywhere from three to twelve members. Additional students can be newspaper reporters covering the trial.

MASTER ROLE SHEET, CONTINUED

HISTORICAL CHARACTER	ROLE	STUDENT NAME
Clark Elliot**	Def. Witness	_____
Orindatus Wall**	Def. Witness	_____
Marshall Johnson**	Bailiff	_____
George Knupp	Juror	_____
James G. Haley	Juror	_____
Salbert Scott	Juror	_____
Edward Foster	Juror	_____
Daniel P. Rhodes	Juror	_____
Andrew Lugenbeel	Juror	_____
George W. Slingluff	Juror	_____
James Justice	Juror	_____
Charles N. Allen	Juror	_____
John Cassell	Juror	_____
George Harper	Juror	_____
Andrew Scott	Juror	_____

* NORMALLY PLAYED BY THE TEACHER
** OPTIONAL ROLE

Note: The jury can be anywhere from three to twelve members. Additional students can be newspaper reporters covering the trial.

TRIAL PROCEDURE

1. The clerk announces "all rise" and the judge enters the courtroom and is seated.

2. The charges are read to the defendant. He is asked to plead "guilty" or "not guilty."

3. The prosecution makes its opening remarks.

4. The defense makes its opening remarks.

5. The prosecution calls witnesses for direct testimony. (After each witness has testified, he can be subject to cross-examination.)

6. The defense calls witnesses for direct testimony. (After each witness has testified, he can be subject to cross-examination.)

7. The prosecution makes its closing remarks to the jury.

8. The defense makes its closing remarks to the jury.

9. The court is declared in "recess" while the jury deliberates a verdict.

10. The jury announces a verdict. If the defendant is found "guilty," then the judge imposes an immediate "sentence."

SUGGESTED COURTROOM SET-UP

CLERK/BAILIFF	JUDGE	WITNESS SEAT

JURY

DEFENDANT

DEFENSE ATTORNEY(S)		PROSECUTION ATTORNEY(S)

WITNESSES AND SPECTATORS

LEGAL TERMS

POWER OF ATTORNEY   An instrument in writing by which one person, as principal, appoints another as his agent and confers upon him the authority to perform certain specified acts or kinds of acts on behalf of the principal. The primary purpose of a power of attorney is not to define the authority of the agent as between himself and his principal, but to evidence the authority of the agent to third parties with whom the agent deals. Powers of attorney may be either *general,* as in the authorization to sell property, or *specific,* as in the authorization to sell to a particular person.

WARRANT   A written order or writ from a competent authority directing the doing of a certain act, especially one directing the arrest of a person or persons, issued by a court, body, or official having authority to issue an arrest warrant.

WRIT   A mandatory precept issued by the authority and in the name of the sovereign or state for the purpose of compelling a person to do something therein mentioned. It is issued by a court or other competent tribunal, and is directed to the sheriff or other officer authorized to execute it. In every case, the writ itself contains directions as to what is required to be done.

WRIT OF HABEAS CORPUS   The writ of habeas corpus, known as the "Great Writ," has varied use in criminal and civil contexts. It is a procedure for obtaining a judicial determination of the legality of an individual's custody. Technically, it is used in the criminal law context to bring the petitioner before the court to inquire into the legality of his confinement. The writ of federal habeas corpus is used to test the constitutionality of a state criminal conviction. It pierces through the formalities of a state conviction to determine whether the conviction is consonant with due process of law. Issues not raised in the state proceeding generally cannot be raised in a federal habeas petition under the doctrine of "exhaustion."

SUBPOENA

YOU; _____, are hereby commanded to appear in the *Court of United States District Judge Willson* in *Cleveland*, on the Date and Time specified below.

Please appear on _____ at _____ and

be prepared to: A. serve as a member of the Jury

                         or

                         B. testify as an expert witness
                            (role sheet provided)

Failure to comply with this *SUMMONS* will result in *CONTEMPT CHARGES*.

Requested by _____, Counsel for the _____.

Approved by the Honorable Judge Willson, Presiding Judge,
United States District Court of Cleveland
September, 1859.

I have served this summons. _____
                                  (Bailiff's Signature)

JURY EVALUATION SHEET

Please mark the appropriate box and write any additional comments on the back of the page.

Prosecution Witnesses

NAME	TOLD THE TRUTH	MOSTLY TOLD THE TRUTH	LIED
Bacon	❏	❏	❏
Cochran	❏	❏	❏
Jennings	❏	❏	❏
Bartholomew	❏	❏	❏
Halbert	❏	❏	❏
Mitchell	❏	❏	❏
Kinney	❏	❏	❏

The *best* prosecution witness was _____. Why?_____

_____

_____

_____

The *worst* prosecution witness was _____. Why? _____

_____

_____

_____

JURY EVALUATION SHEET, CONTINUED

Defense Witnesses

NAME	TOLD THE TRUTH	MOSTLY TOLD THE TRUTH	LIED
L. Boynton	❑	❑	❑
S. Boynton	❑	❑	❑
Peck	❑	❑	❑
Plumb	❑	❑	❑
Fitch	❑	❑	❑
Patton	❑	❑	❑
Butler	❑	❑	❑
Cox	❑	❑	❑
Weed	❑	❑	❑
Pelton	❑	❑	❑
Elliot	❑	❑	❑
Wall	❑	❑	❑

The *best* prosecution witness was _____. Why?_____

_____

_____

The *worst* prosecution witness was _____. Why? _____

_____

_____

I personally feel that the defendant Bushnell is (guilty/not guilty) of breaking the Fugitive Slave Law. Why? _____

_____

_____

CHRONOLOGY

1619	—Slavery is introduced in Virginia
1787	—U.S. Constitution is framed with slavery
1793	—Cotton gin is invented
1808	—Importation of slaves is banned
1820	—Missouri Compromise
1831	—Nat Turner's Rebellion
1850	—Compromise of 1850 includes a strong Fugitive Slave Law
1852	—Harriet Beecher Stowe publishes *Uncle Tom's Cabin*
1854	—Kansas-Nebraska Act
1855	—Slaves John, Dinah, and Frank escape from Kentucky to Ohio
1856	—Kansas erupts in violence over slavery
1857	—Dred Scott decision
1858	—Lincoln-Douglas debates
1859	—Trial of Simeon Bushnell
1860	—Abraham Lincoln is elected President
1861	—Civil War begins
1863	—Emancipation Proclamation
1865	—End of the Civil War
	—13th Amendment to the Constitution

OPTIONAL ROLES

BAILIFF: Assists the Judge and Court Clerk in maintaining courtroom order.

NEWSPAPER REPORTERS: Write a daily account of what happens during the trial. The account should reflect the editorial bias of the specific paper. The following represent possible papers covering this historic trial:

MAYSVILLE TRI-WEEKLY EAGLE (Pro-Prosecution)

THE LIBERATOR (Pro-Defense)

CLEVELAND PLAIN DEALER (Unbiased)

LOUISVILLE DAILY COURIER (Pro-Prosecution)

DAILY CLEVELAND HERALD (Pro-Defense)

THE CLEVELAND MORNING LEADER (Unbiased)

THE DAILY NATIONAL DEMOCRAT (Pro-Prosecution)

THE ANTI-SLAVERY REPORTER (Pro-Defense)

AFTERMATH

Judge Willson charged the jury on the morning of April 15, 1859. The Court reconvened in the afternoon at 2 P.M. The Jury returned shortly after with a verdict. The Judge asked them, "Gentlemen of the Jury, have you agreed upon a verdict?" "We have, your honor." "What is your verdict, Mr. Foreman?" "Guilty."

The defendant, Bushnell, and the rest of the accused rescuers seemed stunned by the decision. Bushnell was sentenced to 60 days in prison and ordered to pay a fine of $600, plus the cost of prosecution.

HISTORICAL NOTES

In order to make the trial manageable for a simulation, some witnesses who testified at Bushnell's trial have not been included.

The attorneys at Bushnell's trial gave closing remarks that covered several days. Their roles in the simulation merely provide guidelines for this rhetoric.

DISCUSSION QUESTIONS

1. What was the most damaging evidence against the defendant?

2. What was the significance of the "power of attorney" and the "federal warrant"?

3. What was the significance of Bushnell's actions in Oberlin prior to the actual rescue?

4. Why do you think it was unwise to have the defendant testify?

5. Do you think the Judge was being biased by allowing a jury of known Democrats?

6. Should a person be allowed to commit a crime, such as kidnapping or breaking any federal law, when the motive is to save someone's life or well-being?

7. Was the Fugitive Slave Law on trial or the defendant? Explain.

8. What was the biggest mistake the defense made? What was the biggest mistake made by the prosecution? Did they affect the outcome of the trial?

9. Was there any evidence that might have been introduced that would have influenced the outcome of the trial?

10. Were you satisfied with the verdict? If so, why? If not, why not?

11. Do you think the trials of the Oberlin rescuers (Bushnell and others) had an impact on the coming of the American Civil War? Why or why not?

12. The Fugitive Slave Law touched dramatically one of the great issues of all times—an issue played out in the ancient world; in India under the Raj; in Hitlerian Germany; and in America of the 1950's, 1960's and 1970's—Is an individual obliged to obey laws that he or she finds morally repugnant?

BIBLIOGRAPHY

Aptheker, Herbert (ed.). *A Documentary History of the Negro People in the United States*. NY: Citadel Press, 1967.

Blockson, L. Charles. *The Underground Railroad*. NY: Berkley Books, 1989.

Bennett, Lerone Jr. *Before the Mayflower: A History of the Negro in America 1619-1964*. Chicage: Johnson Publishing Co., 1962.

Bergman, Peter M. *The Chronological History of the Negro in America*. NY: Harper and Row, 1969.

Brandt, Nat. *The Town that Started the Civil War*. NY: Syracuse University Press, 1990.

Dumond, Dwight Lowell. *Antislavery: The Crusade for Freedom in America*. NY: W.W. Norton & Co., 1961.

Elkins, Stanley M. *Slavery*. Chicago: University of Chicago Press, 1959.

Filler, Louis. *The Crusade Against Slavery 1830-1860*. NY: Harper & Row, 1960.

Foner, Eric. *Free Soil, Free Labor, Free Men: The Ideology of the Republican Party Before the Civil War*. NY: Oxford University Press, 1970.

Franklin, John. *Hope From Slavery to Freedom: A History of Negro Americans*. NY: Alfred Knopf, 1974.

Hamilton, Virginia. *Anthony Burns: The Defeat and Triumph of a Fugitive Slave*. NY: Alfred A. Knopf, 1988.

Hawkins, Hugh (ed.). *The Abolishionists: Means, Ends and Motivations*. Lexington, MA: D.C. Heath & Co., 1972.

Jacobs, Donald (ed.). *Courage and Conscience: Black and White Abolitionists in Boston*. Indianapolis: Indiana University Press, 1993.

Lester, Julius. *To Be a Slave*. NY: Dial Press Inc.,1968.

Rose, Willie Lee (ed.). *A Documentary History of Slavery in North America*. NY: Oxford University Press, 1976.

Shipherd, Jacob R. (ed.). *History of the Oberlin-Wellington Rescue*. Boston: John P. Jewett & Co., 1859.

Stowe, Harriet Beecher. *Uncle Tom's Cabin*. NY: Harper & Row, 1968.

Tyler, Alice Felt. *Freedom's Ferment*. NY: Harper & Row, 1944.

Williams, Harry T. *The Union Sundered*. NY: Time-Life Books, 1963.

THE TRIAL OF CAPTAIN HENRY WIRZ, CSA

BACKGROUND

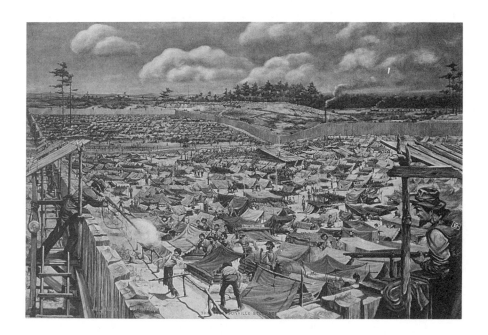

"The Andersonville Stockade Looking Southwest." Courtesy of Anne S.K. Brown Military Collection, Brown University Library, Providence, Rhose Island.

"Gone-ay me!—to the grave
And never one note of song
The Muse would weep for the brave
But how shall she chant the wrong."

—Howard Brownell

"The soldier, be he friend or foe is charged with the protection of the weak and unarmed. It is the very essence and reason of his being . . . a sacred trust."

—Douglas MacArthur

CAMP SUMTER

By the spring of 1864 the South was losing its ability to provide adequate food and medical supplies to its armies and the thousands of prisoners-of-war captured during the preceding years of fighting. One Union army was steadily closing in on the capitol in Richmond and another was marching through the deep South towards Atlanta. Despite shortages of men, food, ammunition, and medical supplies, the defiant Southern armies fought on. This posed a serious dilemma for the Southern leader. What could they do with the continuing flow of captured Union prisoners? They decided to build a new prison camp in a remote location in southwestern Georgia where it could be secure from raiding Union forces. The site lay in the midst of Georgia's cotton growing land that under a war economy had been converted to growing corn. This new prison camp would confine only enlisted men. Officially named "Camp Sumter," it was more often known for the nearby town, Andersonville.

Prisoners were first sent to Andersonville in March of 1864. The camp was designed to hold a maximum of 10,000 men. By August of that year there were over 33,000 sick and malnourished inmates crammed within the stockade walls. By the end of the war in April 1865, a total of 45,000 had passed through the prison's heavy gates. Nearly 13,000 did not leave the prison camp alive. A Union enlisted man had a better chance of surviving the Battle of Antietam than of living through the horror of Camp Sumter.

The new prison camp at Andersonville was located on a tract of twenty-six acres, sloping upon both sides of a small stream, and enclosed with a wooden fence dotted with several tall guard towers. The camp was enclosed by wooden walls of hewn pine logs, from 8 to 10 inches square, 4 feet buried in the ground, 18 feet above, braced on the outside, cross-barred to make one log sustain the other, and a small platform making comfortable standing room for the guards, every 100 feet, with above waist-high space below the top of the stockade, reached by a ladder. Later in 1864 a second stockade was built around the first. There were cannons placed at each corner of the stockade covering all directions. Within the stockade was a line of 4-inch pine boards on posts about 3 feet high, about 17 feet from the walls. It was called the "Dead Line." A prisoner could be shot by a guard for merely stepping into this forbidden zone.

There were about 1,000 Confederate soldiers guarding the prisoners at Andersonville. An Andersonville inmate described them as "the worst looking scalawags . . . from boys just large enough to handle a gun, to old men who ought to have been dead years ago for the good of their country."

Even the camp commander, Captain Wirz, regularly complained of the carelessness and inefficiency of the prison garrison.

DAILY LIFE

For the Union privates, corporals, and sergeants confined in Camp Sumter, daily life was a nightmare of boredom, discomfort, disease, and crime. Within the stockade area the prisoners were compelled to perform all functions of life including cooking, washing, relieving oneself, exercise, and sleeping. One-third of the land was not habitable since it was a virtual swamp of liquid filth. The low grounds bordering the stream were covered with human excrements and filth of all kinds, which in many places seemed alive with maggots. An indescribable sickening stench arose from these fermenting masses of human filth. The small stream that ran through the camp served for most prisoners as the source of drinking water. Some of the earliest prisoners had successfully dug wells that yielded some fresh water, but there were no latrines or bathing facilities. Garbage and human excrement had to be dumped into the stream. New prisoners often had most possessions immediately confiscated by the guards or stolen by gangs of thugs within the stockade. The only shelter from the rain, cold, and blazing sun were mud huts or crude tents, often constructed from the clothing of dead prisoners.

General John Winder, the Commissary General of Confederate prisoners-of-war, officially declared that prisoners' rations were to be "the same in quality and quantity as those furnished to the enlisted men in the Army of the Confederacy." In reality, food and fresh water were grossly inadequate in the camp. The normal daily ration for a prisoner at Andersonville consisted of one-half pint of corn meal (including husk) with a little molasses *or* one pint of stock peas with a little bacon. Less often they received bread or rice. Prisoners were almost entirely without vegetables and fruit. Regardless of the nature of the food received, prisoners learned to eat it immediately lest it be wrenched from their hands by starved-crazy inmates. Vicious brawls were common over mere crusts of bread or rancid meat smuggled in from the outside.

There was a thriving "black market" within the camp and prisoners had to be either clever or criminal to acquire extra food. One Union sergeant whittled objects out of bone that he sold to the guards for extra food. Some prisoners set up washing facilities and hair-cutting operations. Other prisoners were not so skillful or ambitious. They either stole from living comrades, assaulted and robbed the sick, or even committed murder to secure extra food and clothing. In fact, within the camp there was even an execution by hanging of six prisoners who were part of a murdering and thieving gang known as "Mosby's Raiders."

Rather than being "fresh fish," as the newcomers to Andersonville were called by the long-term inmates, most of the Union soldiers who came to the prison camp had been transferred from other prison camps and already suffered from a variety of diseases including incurable diarrhea, dysentery, and scurvy. Conditions at the prison hospital were abysmal. It was located on a 5-acre plot outside the stockade. Sick prisoners were placed in sheds open on all sides, exposed to the weather, with no sheets or blankets. Millions of flies swarmed over everything, and covered the faces of the sleeping patients, crawled down their mouths, and deposited their maggots in the gangrenous wounds of the living. Hospital nurses were normally other prisoners, often more interested in stealing the sick man's possessions than caring for him. Wounds were cleaned merely by pouring water over them and letting everything seep onto the ground on which the men lay. Amputations and other operations were performed without anesthetics or proper sanitation and many died horribly from the effects of gangrene. When a patient died he was carried to the "deadhouse" situated in the southwest corner of the hospital grounds and left on the bare ground, often covered with filth and vermin. Prisoners from the stockade were then detailed to dig and bury them in mass graves.

The prisoners were constantly trying to escape. Tunneling became a daily activity for many prisoners. The tunnels were dug under the stockade and the prisoners then attempted to escape into the thick Georgia pine forest surrounding the camp. Few succeeded. More often than not they ended up in the nearby swampland pursued and captured by guards and savage bloodhound tracking dogs. Dragged bleeding back to camp, they could be subjected to a variety of tortures including the stocks, being tied up and gagged, or having to wear a ball and chain for several weeks. Other prisoners, driven crazy by hunger, thirst and exposure, stumbled into the prohibited "dead line" and were usually shot by one of the guards in the prison towers.

THE TRIAL

Camp Sumter in Andersonville is the most infamous prison camp in American history. Conditions in many Union prison camps were similar in their brutality and deprivation. In fact, Northern prisons retaliated to rumors of starvation in the Southern camps like Andersonville by cutting rations, sometimes in half. Nevertheless, Andersonville stands out because of the many deaths and also that the prison camp commander, Captain Henry Wirz, was placed on trial after the war for war crimes. The shocking conditions that existed at Camp Sumter became public knowledge and a vengeful Northern public demanded justice. Most prisoners, Northern and Southern, regarded their camp commanders as sadistic monsters and Wirz was no exception. He was indicted for murder, conspiracy (with General Winder and other Confederate officers) to commit murder, and willfully allowing the horrible conditions to exist in Andersonville prison camp. On August 23, 1865 he was placed on trial before a military tribunal consisting of senior officers in the Union army.

You will now have the chance to participate in this historic trial.

MEMBERS OF THE COMMISSION
THE COURT CLERK
THE SERGEANT-AT-ARMS

CHARGES AGAINST THE DEFENDANT

CHARGE ONE

Captain Henry Wirz did maliciously, willfully, and traitorously, and in aid of the then-existing armed rebellion against the United States of America, on or before the first day of March, A.D. 1864, and on other days between that day and the tenth day of April, 1865, combining, confederating, and conspiring together with John H. Winder, and others unknown, to injure the health and destroy the lives of soldiers in the military service of the United States, then held and being prisoners-of-war within the lines of the so-called Confederate States and in the military prisons thereof, to the end that the armies of the United States might be weakened and impaired, in violation of the laws and customs of war.

CHARGE TWO

Captain Henry Wirz feloniously, willfully, and of his malice aforethought, did shoot, order to be shot, kick, punch, stomp, and torture several prisoners-of-war resulting in death.

MAJOR-GENERAL LEW WALLACE
HEAD OF MILITARY COMMISSION

You have been selected to serve on a military commission appointed by the United States Army to meet in Washington, D.C. on October 24, 1865 for the trial of Captain Henry Wirz, CSA. You will be the senior officer on the commission and it will be your responsibility to run the trial according to normal courtroom procedure. Since this is a military court, you may allow members of the military commission (including yourself) to ask questions of the witnesses. It will be the commission's task to decide whether the defendant is innocent or guilty of premeditated murder and conspiracy to commit the murder of nearly 13,000 Union prisoners-of-war confined to Camp Sumter in Andersonville, Georgia between the years 1864 and 1865.

This is a military court martial and you represent both judge and jury. Nevertheless, the defendant is considered innocent until proven guilty by the prosecution. If there is any doubt in your mind as to whether the defendant is guilty, you must find him innocent. But remember, this is 1865 and you are the leaders of a victorious army trying an alleged enemy war criminal. After you have heard and evaluated all the evidence presented by the witnesses, you must decide whether the defendant, Captain Henry Wirz, is guilty of any of the forementioned crimes.

The defendant will be considered guilty if a majority of the members of the military commission finds him "guilty". In the event of a tie, you will make the final decision. If Captain Wirz is found guilty of any of the charges, you must sentence him to be hanged.

MAJOR-GENERAL J.W. GEARY
MEMBER OF MILITARY COMMISSION

You have been selected to serve on a military commission appointed by the United States Army to meet in Washington, D.C. on October 24, 1865 for the trial of Captain Henry Wirz, CSA. It will be the commission's task to decide whether the defendant is innocent or guilty of premeditated murder and conspiracy to commit the murder of nearly 13,000 Union prisoners-of-war confined to Camp Sumter in Andersonville, Georgia between the years 1864 and 1865.

This is a military court martial and you represent both the judge and jury. You are permitted to ask questions of the witnesses. As in a civilian trial, the defendant is considered innocent until proven guilty by the prosecution. If there is any doubt in your mind as to whether the defendant is guilty, you must find him innocent. Remember, this is 1865 and you are the leaders of a victorious army trying an alleged enemy war criminal. After you have heard and evaluated all the evidence presented by the witnesses, you must decide whether the defendant, Captain Henry Wirz, is guilty of any of the forementioned crimes.

The defendant will be considered guilty if a majority of the military commission finds him "guilty." In the event of a tie, Major-General Wallace will make the final decision. If the defendant is found guilty of any of the charges, you must sentence him to be hanged.

 -

GENERAL L. THOMAS
MEMBER OF MILITARY COMMISSION

You have been selected to serve on a military commission appointed by the United States Army to meet in Washington, D.C. on October 24, 1865 for the trial of Captain Henry Wirz, CSA. It will be the commission's task to decide whether the defendant is innocent or guilty of premeditated murder and conspiracy to commit the murder of nearly 13,000 Union prisoners-of-war confined to Camp Sumter in Andersonville, Georgia between the years 1864 and 1865.

This is a military court martial and you represent both the judge and jury. You are permitted to ask questions of the witnesses. As in a civilian trial, the defendant is considered innocent until proven guilty by the prosecution. If there is any doubt in your mind as to whether the defendant is guilty, you must find him innocent. Remember, this is 1865 and you are the leaders of a victorious army trying an alleged enemy war criminal. After you have heard and evaluated all the evidence presented by the witnesses, you must decide whether the defendant, Captain Henry Wirz, is guilty of any of the forementioned crimes.

The defendant will be considered guilty if a majority of the military commission finds him "guilty." In the event of a tie, Major-General Wallace will make the final decision. If the defendant is found guilty of any of the charges, you must sentence him to be hanged.

GENERAL G. MOTT
MEMBER OF MILITARY COMMISSION

You have been selected to serve on a military commission appointed by the United States Army to meet in Washington, D.C. on October 24, 1865 for the trial of Captain Henry Wirz, CSA. It will be the commission's task to decide whether the defendant is innocent or guilty of premeditated murder and conspiracy to commit the murder of nearly 13,000 Union prisoners-of-war confined to Camp Sumter in Andersonville, Georgia between the years 1864 and 1865.

This is a military court martial and you represent both the judge and jury. You are permitted to ask questions of the witnesses. As in a civilian trial, the defendant is considered innocent until proven guilty by the prosecution. If there is any doubt in your mind as to whether the defendant is guilty, you must find him innocent. Remember, this is 1865 and you are the leaders of a victorious army trying an alleged enemy war criminal. After you have heard and evaluated all the evidence presented by the witnesses, you must decide whether the defendant, Captain Henry Wirz, is guilty of any of the forementioned crimes.

The defendant will be considered guilty if a majority of the military commission finds him "guilty." In the event of a tie, Major-General Wallace will make the final decision. If the defendant is found guilty of any of the charges, you must sentence him to be hanged.

GENERAL F. FESSENDEN
MEMBER OF MILITARY COMMISSION

You have been selected to serve on a military commission appointed by the United States Army to meet in Washington, D.C. on October 24, 1865 for the trial of Captain Henry Wirz, CSA. It will be the commission's task to decide whether the defendant is innocent or guilty of premeditated murder and conspiracy to commit the murder of nearly 13,000 Union prisoners-of-war confined to Camp Sumter in Andersonville, Georgia between the years 1864 and 1865.

This is a military court martial and you represent both the judge and jury. You are permitted to ask questions of the witnesses. As in a civilian trial, the defendant is considered innocent until proven guilty by the prosecution. If there is any doubt in your mind as to whether the defendant is guilty, you must find him innocent. Remember, this is 1865 and you are the leaders of a victorious army trying an alleged enemy war criminal. After you have heard and evaluated all the evidence presented by the witnesses, you must decide whether the defendant, Captain Henry Wirz, is guilty of any of the forementioned crimes.

The defendant will be considered guilty if a majority of the military commission finds him "guilty." In the event of a tie, Major-General Wallace will make the final decision. If the defendant is found guilty of any of the charges, you must sentence him to be hanged.

BRIGADIER-GENERAL E. BRAGG
MEMBER OF MILITARY COMMISSION

You have been selected to serve on a military commission appointed by the United States Army to meet in Washington, D.C. on October 24, 1865 for the trial of Captain Henry Wirz, CSA. It will be the commission's task to decide whether the defendant is innocent or guilty of premeditated murder and conspiracy to commit the murder of nearly 13,000 Union prisoners-of-war confined to Camp Sumter in Andersonville, Georgia between the years 1864 and 1865.

This is a military court martial and you represent both the judge and jury. You are permitted to ask questions of the witnesses. As in a civilian trial, the defendant is considered innocent until proven guilty by the prosecution. If there is any doubt in your mind as to whether the defendant is guilty, you must find him innocent. Remember, this is 1865 and you are the leaders of a victorious army trying an alleged enemy war criminal. After you have heard and evaluated all the evidence presented by the witnesses, you must decide whether the defendant, Captain Henry Wirz, is guilty of any of the forementioned crimes.

The defendant will be considered guilty if a majority of the military commission finds him "guilty." In the event of a tie, Major-General Wallace will make the final decision. If the defendant is found guilty of any of the charges, you must sentence him to be hanged.

- -

BRIGADIER-GENERAL J. BALLIER
MEMBER OF MILITARY COMMISSION

You have been selected to serve on a military commission appointed by the United States Army to meet in Washington, D.C. on October 24, 1865 for the trial of Captain Henry Wirz, CSA. It will be the commission's task to decide whether the defendant is innocent or guilty of premeditated murder and conspiracy to commit the murder of nearly 13,000 Union prisoners-of-war confined to Camp Sumter in Andersonville, Georgia between the years 1864 and 1865.

This is a military court martial and you represent both the judge and jury. You are permitted to ask questions of the witnesses. As in a civilian trial, the defendant is considered innocent until proven guilty by the prosecution. If there is any doubt in your mind as to whether the defendant is guilty, you must find him innocent. Remember, this is 1865 and you are the leaders of a victorious army trying an alleged enemy war criminal. After you have heard and evaluated all the evidence presented by the witnesses, you must decide whether the defendant, Captain Henry Wirz, is guilty of any of the forementioned crimes.

The defendant will be considered guilty if a majority of the military commission finds him "guilty." In the event of a tie, Major-General Wallace will make the final decision. If the defendant is found guilty of any of the charges, you must sentence him to be hanged.

COLONEL T. ALLCOCK
MEMBER OF MILITARY COMMISSION

You have been selected to serve on a military commission appointed by the United States Army to meet in Washington, D.C. on October 24, 1865 for the trial of Captain Henry Wirz, CSA. It will be the commission's task to decide whether the defendant is innocent or guilty of premeditated murder and conspiracy to commit the murder of nearly 13,000 Union prisoners-of-war confined to Camp Sumter in Andersonville, Georgia between the years 1864 and 1865.

This is a military court martial and you represent both the judge and jury. You are permitted to ask questions of the witnesses. As in a civilian trial, the defendant is considered innocent until proven guilty by the prosecution. If there is any doubt in your mind as to whether the defendant is guilty, you must find him innocent. Remember, this is 1865 and you are the leaders of a victorious army trying an alleged enemy war criminal. After you have heard and evaluated all the evidence presented by the witnesses, you must decide whether the defendant, Captain Henry Wirz, is guilty of any of the forementioned crimes.

The defendant will be considered guilty if a majority of the military commission finds him "guilty." In the event of a tie, Major-General Wallace will make the final decision. If the defendant is found guilty of any of the charges, you must sentence him to be hanged.

LT. COLONEL J. STIBBS
MEMBER OF MILITARY COMMISSION

You have been selected to serve on a military commission appointed by the United States Army to meet in Washington, D.C. on October 24, 1865 for the trial of Captain Henry Wirz, CSA. It will be the commission's task to decide whether the defendant is innocent or guilty of premeditated murder and conspiracy to commit the murder of nearly 13,000 Union prisoners-of-war confined to Camp Sumter in Andersonville, Georgia between the years 1864 and 1865.

This is a military court martial and you represent both the judge and jury. You are permitted to ask questions of the witnesses. As in a civilian trial, the defendant is considered innocent until proven guilty by the prosecution. If there is any doubt in your mind as to whether the defendant is guilty, you must find him innocent. Remember, this is 1865 and you are the leaders of a victorious army trying an alleged enemy war criminal. After you have heard and evaluated all the evidence presented by the witnesses, you must decide whether the defendant, Captain Henry Wirz, is guilty of any of the forementioned crimes.

The defendant will be considered guilty if a majority of the military commission finds him "guilty." In the event of a tie, Major-General Wallace will make the final decision. If the defendant is found guilty of any of the charges, you must sentence him to be hanged.

ELISHA TRAHER
Court Clerk

You are responsible for assisting the officers of the military commission in running the trial. You will be expected to do the following:

1. If Major-General Wallace so directs, read out to the court the charges against the defendant.

2. Swear in all witnesses, asking them to place their left hand on the Bible, raise their right hand, and say "Yes" to the statement "Do you swear to tell the truth, the whole truth, and nothing but the truth, so help you God?"

3. With the help of the sergeant-at-arms, serve any subpoenas that are issued by the military commission.

4. Read aloud to the court any documents that the military commission instructs you to enter into the court record, including statements of law and evidence introduced as exhibits.

5. Keep a record of the names of all witnesses offering testimony.

6. Assist the military commission and sergeant-at-arms in maintaining courtroom order. You may be asked to help remove an unruly witness or spectator.

STEVEN WILLIAMS
Sergeant-at-Arms

You are responsible for assisting the officers of the military commission in running the trial. You will be expected to do the following:

1. Call "Attention, all rise" when the officers of the military commission enter the room.

2. With the help of the court clerk, serve any subpoenas that are issued by the military commission.

3. Assist the military commission and the clerk in maintaining courtroom order. You may be asked to help remove an unruly witness or spectator.

4. Keep a careful eye on Captain Wirz so that he does not escape.

THE PROSECUTION

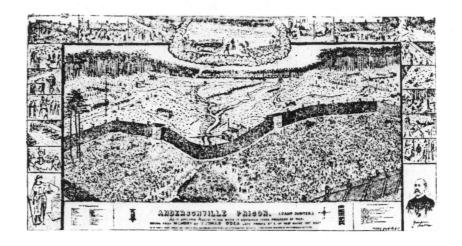

"In many of its aspects and bearings this trial presents features more startling, more extraordinary, and more momentous than are found in the whole annals of jurisprudence . . . this long black catalogue of crimes, these tortures unparalleled, these murders by starvation, implacable as could have been perpetrated had the spirit of darkness controlled them . . . yet . . . there are very many phases of Andersonville prison life that I must leave unnoticed."

—Colonel Chipman's closing remarks

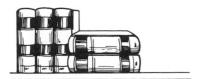

COLONEL N.P. CHIPMAN
Judge-Advocate

You have been assigned to prosecute the case of Captain Henry Wirz, CSA, and to make sure he suffers the full penalty that the law can give for the horrible crimes he committed at Camp Sumter. You should focus on the horrible conditions at Andersonville and how Captain Wirz did little to improve the situation. You have witnesses who will testify to his cruelty; his murder of prisoners; and his conspiracy with other officers to murder prisoners. Be emotional! You should paint Captain Wirz as a real demon!

You will use your opening remarks, witnesses, and closing remarks to make the following points clear to the military tribunal:

Captain Wirz is guilty of conspiracy with other Confederate leaders to murder prisoners-of-war.

1. There is neither doubt that there was a general plan on the part of the Confederate Government to murder the Federal prisoners, nor that Captain Wirz was selected as a fit and willing instrument to further that plot. Camp Sumter was designed to hold a maximum of 10,000 prisoners, yet nearly 35,000 were confined within the stockade in August, 1864.

2. One has merely to consult the medical records to see that the majority of deaths at Andersonville were caused by impure water, improper sanitary conditions, and lack of medical supplies. Clearly, these conditions were deliberate on the part of General Winder and his co-conspirator, Captain Wirz.

3. There is plenty of evidence to suggest that food was abundant in this region of Georgia, yet Captain Wirz failed to supply even the basic allowance needed to survive. Much of the food was of poor quality and prisoners were not given cooking provisions including wood for fires.

4. Many of the deaths were directly attributed to the filthy water supply. Captain Wirz could have saved thousands of lives by merely providing clean fresh water.

5. Sick prisoners were deliberately denied proper health care in a clean hospital area.

6. Prisoners were deliberately used for medical experimentation. They were injected with unknown substances under the most unsanitary conditions, resulting in hundreds of deaths.

7. Prisoners were tormented using a variety of tortures including whippings, buckings, and having to wear a ball and chain.

8. Savage bloodhound dogs were used to track down escape prisoners, often resulting in brutal wounds.

9. Dozens of prisoners were deliberately murdered at the so-called dead-line for merely seeking fresh water.

COLONEL N.P. CHIPMAN

Captain Wirz is guilty of personally committing murder.

1. Several prisoners witnessed Captain Wirz shoot, stomp, bludgeon, kick, and order shot men interned at Camp Sumter.

2. On several occasions he was heard boasting about these murders.

Finally, Captain Wirz cannot be excused from these crimes by simply saying he was just following the orders of his superiors.

1. The horrible conditions at Camp Sumter were vigorously maintained by Captain Wirz. No order was issued to deprive men of clean water; no order was given to load prisoners with balls and chains, and keep them wearing them for weeks; no order was given him to place a sick man on the floor of a vermin infested hospital until he died; no order was given him to shoot defenseless sick men driven crazy with privation and exposure; but he did all these things.

2. The law is clear that if a party remains in a conspiracy—no matter how much he protests—he is still responsible.

3. There is no law, no sympathy, no code of morals, that can warrant anything but full justice and punishment, just because he is the lesser criminal and not the greater.

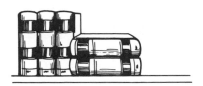

MAJOR A.A. HOSMER
Assistant Judge-Advocate

You have been assigned to help Colonel Chipman prosecute the case of Captain Henry Wirz, CSA, and to make sure he suffers the full penalty that the law can give for the horrible crimes he committed at Camp Sumter. You should focus on the horrible conditions at Andersonville and how Captain Wirz did little to improve the situation. You have witnesses who will testify to his cruelty; his murder of prisoners; and his conspiracy with other officers to murder prisoners. Be emotional! You should paint Captain Wirz as a real demon!

You will use your opening remarks, witnesses, and closing remarks to make the following points clear to the military tribunal:

Captain Wirz is guilty of conspiracy with other Confederate leaders to murder prisoners-of-war.

1. There is neither doubt that there was a general plan on the part of the Confederate Government to murder the Federal prisoners, nor that Captain Wirz was selected as a fit and willing instrument to further that plot. Camp Sumter was designed to hold a maximum of 10,000 prisoners, yet nearly 35,000 were confined within the stockade in August, 1864.

2. One has merely to consult the medical records to see that the majority of deaths at Andersonville were caused by impure water, improper sanitary conditions, and lack of medical supplies. Clearly, these conditions were deliberate on the part of General Winder and his co-conspirator, Captain Wirz.

3. There is plenty of evidence to suggest that food was abundant in this region of Georgia, yet Captain Wirz failed to supply even the basic allowance needed to survive. Much of the food was of poor quality and prisoners were not given cooking provisions including wood for fires.

4. Many of the deaths were directly attributed to the filthy water supply. Captain Wirz could have saved thousands of lives by merely providing clean fresh water.

5. Sick prisoners were deliberately denied proper health care in a clean hospital area.

6. Prisoners were deliberately used for medical experimentation. They were injected with unknown substances under the most unsanitary conditions, resulting in hundreds of deaths.

7. Prisoners were tormented using a variety of tortures including whippings, buckings and having to wear a ball and chain.

8. Savage bloodhound dogs were used to track down escape prisoners, often resulting in brutal wounds.

9. Dozens of prisoners were deliberately murdered at the so-called dead-line for merely seeking fresh water.

MAJOR A.A. HOSMER

Captain Wirz is guilty of personally committing murder.

1. Several prisoners witnessed Captain Wirz shoot, stomp, bludgeon, kick, and order shot men interned at Camp Sumter.

2. On several occasions he was heard boasting about these murders.

Finally, Captain Wirz cannot be excused from these crimes by simply saying he was just following the orders of his superiors.

1. The horrible conditions at Camp Sumter were vigorously maintained by Captain Wirz. No order was issued to deprive men of clean water; no order was given to load prisoners with balls and chains, and keep them wearing them for weeks; no order was given him to place a sick man on the floor of a vermin infested hospital until he died; no order was given him to shoot defenseless sick men driven crazy with privation and exposure; but he did all these things.

2. The law is clear that if a party remains in a conspiracy—no matter how much he protests—he is still responsible.

3. There is no law, no sympathy, no code of morals, that can warrant anything but full justice and punishment, just because he is the lesser criminal and not the greater.

WITNESSES FOR THE PROSECUTION

"Someone has much to answer for."

—John Ransom's Andersonville Diary

SERGEANT JOHN RANSOM
WITNESS FOR THE PROSECUTION

You were captured near Rogersville, East Tennessee, on November 6, 1863 while acting as Quarter-Master Sergeant for the 1st Tennessee Mounted Infantry. You were first imprisoned at the Rebel camp of Belle Isle, near Richmond, Virginia and later taken to Camp Sumter in early March of 1864. You will be able to describe in detail, using the background information provided, the terrible conditions of Camp Sumter and your experiences with Captain Wirz, the camp commander. You are a "star" witness because during the entire time you were a prisoner in Andersonville you kept a written diary and recorded your daily impressions. Portions of your diary may be used as exhibits. You will testify to the following:

1. You were among the first Union prisoners to arrive at Camp Sumter. You noted in your diary: "March 14, arrived at our destination at last and a dismal hole it is, too."

2. You first saw Captain Wirz on March 25 when he replaced Colonel Piersons as the camp commander. You described him as "not a very prepossessing (good-looking) chap, about 35 or 40 years old, rather tall, and a little stoop-shouldered, skin has a pale, white-livered look, with thin lips. He has a sneering sort of cast of countenance, makes a fellow feel as if he would like to go up and boot him."

3. At first Captain Wirz often came into the stockade searching for escape tunnels. The prisoners nicknamed him the "Flying Dutchman" because of his foreign accent.

4. By April nearly everyone was sick with scurvy. New prisoners were made immediately sick by the stench of the camp.

5. You saw men shot by the guards for trying to reach purer water under the dead-line near the creek. A friend of yours, Charlie Hudson, pushed his canteen under the dead-line for some of the fresh water and was shot through the head.

6. By May 10 you noted in your diary that Captain Wirz never came into the stockade anymore since there were thousands of men in there who would willingly die if they could kill him first.

7. You saw some men brought back after an escape attempt. They had been torn by dogs and one of them was bleeding from buckshot wounds.

8. You saw a friend, Sergeant Philo Lewis, die from slow starvation. He was normally a large man weighing over 170 pounds. When he died he weighed less than 90 pounds.

9. By June 8 you noted in your diary that between 100 and 130 men a day were dying. You saw a man with a bullet hole in his head over an inch deep, and you could look down in it and see maggots squirming around at the bottom.

10. On June 17 you noted in your diary that Captain Wirz's commander, General Winder, made an inspection trip to the camp. You described him as an old white-haired man.

SERGEANT JOHN RANSOM

11. Prisoners were constantly writing letters to Captain Wirz, President Jefferson Davis, and other Confederate officials begging for paroles or an ease to their sufferings. The letters were never answered.

12. You do credit Captain Wirz with one good deed. He allowed the capture, arrest, and eventual execution of the "Raiders" who had been terrorizing the other prisoners. But you note that he had to be pressured into it by the threat of a mass prison revolt.

13. You describe August, 1864 in Andersonville as little short of Hell on Earth. Men were dying at a rate of 140 per day with "dead bodies laying around all day in the boiling sun."

14. You believe that Wirz was "but the willing tool of those in higher command. Those who put him there knew his brutal disposition."

PRIVATE GEORGE CONWAY

WITNESS FOR THE PROSECUTION

You were captured in the Battle of Cold Harbor and sent to Andersonville in the middle of June, 1864. You will be able to describe in detail, using the background information provided, the terrible conditions of Camp Sumter and your experiences with Captain Wirz, the camp commander. You will specifically testify to the following:

1. You saw a man deliberately murdered at the "dead-line" by Captain Wirz.

2. No one was allowed, on pain of being shot, to put any part of their body over or under the "dead-line."

3. This man, you think his name was Thompson, was a "new fish" and probably didn't know the rules.

4. You saw him take his drinking cup and reach under the dead-line where it crossed the stream. This was where the stream entered the camp and the water was fairly clear.

5. You heard a shot and saw the cup fall from the man's hand and blood began flowing from his head.

6. You looked at one of the sentry towers and saw Captain Wirz holding a pistol. He seemed to grin and then turned and said something to the guard. They both laughed and then Wirz disappeared from view.

7. The dead man remained partially in the stream until guards ordered some prisoners to take him to the deadhouse, outside the camp.

DR. JOSEPH JONES

WITNESS FOR THE PROSECUTION

You are a surgeon and professor of medical chemistry in the Medical College, in Augusta, Georgia. During the war you heard of the unusually high death rate among prisoners confined at Camp Sumter. You wrote the Confederate Surgeon General, S.P. Moore, and asked if you could visit the camp to investigate the causes of the many prevailing diseases. There were reported cases of smallpox, one of your research interests, and you hoped to be able to study some of the characteristic lesions that mark that disease. Dr. Moore provided a letter of introduction to the surgeons at Andersonville, which asked them to allow you complete freedom to conduct your investigations. You visited the camp in August, 1864 and will testify to the following:

1. You found nearly 5000 seriously ill prisoners in the stockade and the prison hospital. The men were dying from a variety of diseases at a rate that exceeded 100 per day.

2. Nearly all the sick were emaciated from lack of proper food.

3. The most common diseases included incurable diarrhea, dysentery, and scurvy.

4. There was only one medical officer tending the sick whereas, in your medical opinion, there should have been at least twenty.

5. You saw the effects of scurvy on nearly all the prisoners including pale complexion, swollen gums, feeble muscle tone, fetid breath, spongy skin, loose teeth, and large spreading ulcers covered with a dark purplish fungus growth.

6. You observed that from the crowded condition, filthy habits, bad diet, and generally depressed condition of the prisoners, their systems had become so disordered that the smallest abrasion of the sun, or scratch, or mosquito bite often took on a rapid and frightful ulceration and gangrene.

7. Many of the sick and dying were lying on the ground in the hospital literally encrusted with filth and covered with crawling vermin.

8. You saw vaccinations for smallpox performed under extremely unsanitary conditions leading to infection and gangrene.

9. Almost every amputation was followed by death, either from the effects of gangrene, or from the prevailing diarrhea and dysentery.

10. You believe that the abuses you saw were in a large measure caused by the nearly total lack of organized sanitation.

11. You believe that the only means of protecting large bodies of men (like those confined at Camp Sumter) from the ravages of hospital gangrene and other diseases is to furnish a clean water supply, fresh fruit and vegetables, and well-cured meat. Strict rules of hygiene have to be enforced. It is your opinion that none of the above were made available to the soldiers confined at Camp Sumter.

12. You wrote a report to the Surgeon General recommending immediate changes at Camp Sumter. The report was ignored.

PRIVATE MARTIN E. HOGAN
Witness for the Prosecution

You were captured at the Battle of Spotsylvania and sent to Andersonville near the end of May, 1864. You will be able to describe in detail, using the background information provided, the terrible conditions of Camp Sumter and your experiences with Captain Wirz, the camp commander. You will specifically testify to the following:

1. You saw Captain Wirz murder a prisoner of war.

2. You and some other prisoners were being transferred to another prison camp sometime in the middle of September, 1864.

3. One of the prisoners in your group was very sick and walking slowly. He was struggling to keep up with the rest of the prisoners, but was obviously in pain.

4. Wirz came up behind him and kicked him with his heavy boot. The man fell to the ground and Wirz kicked him several times more. He was bleeding from the mouth and nose.

5. The guards forced your group to keep moving. You looked back and saw the man lying in a ditch by the road leading out of the camp.

6. Later, you heard from some other prisoners who passed by the ditch on their way to the train station that the man had died and was taken to the dead-house.

SERGEANT CHARLES FERREN HOPKINS
WITNESS FOR THE PROSECUTION

On June 4, 1861, at the age of 17, you enlisted in Company I, First New Jersey Volunteers. You were badly wounded at the Battle of Gaines' Mill, Virginia, and again at the Battle of the Wilderness in May, 1864. You were captured during this battle and sent to Camp Sumter. You will be able to describe in detail, using the background information provided, the terrible conditions of Andersonville and your experiences with Captain Wirz, the camp commander. You will specifically testify to the following:

1. You arrived at Camp Sumter on May 22, 1864 after a grueling train ride with men "packed in freight cars like sardines."

2. On arrival at the station, you heard Wirz say that these "damn Yanks would not bother Lee again after he was through with them," and "he was doing more for the Confederacy than any regiment at the front."

3. You heard from another prisoner that Wirz's commander, General Winder, had boasted that he had selected the site for Camp Sumter so that death would come quickly to the prisoners by natural causes.

4. You saw many men in the camp go completely insane from hunger, exposure, and disease.

5. Orders were given by Wirz that all prisoners were to be vaccinated. After your vaccination you immediately wiped the vaccination off your arm and sucked out the blood in the area. You believe this vaccination caused many deaths.

6. You were a member of a committee that went to ask Captain Wirz for better drinking water. He met you at the camp gate. He was holding two heavy pistols and said: "The water of the creek is good enough for you God d-mned Yankee sons of b—, go back, or I will blow your damn brains out and send you to Hell!"

7. You managed to escape from the camp by digging a tunnel with several other prisoners.

8. You were quickly captured by Confederate trackers with dogs.

9. You were taken to Captain Wirz who first threatened to shoot you. Then he decided to torture you instead. You were bound, strapped, and suspended in the hot sun until the "pain that racked body and brain" was beyond your power of expression.

10. You were eventually transferred to another prison camp at Florence, South Carolina and finally paroled. You had gone from 226 pounds to 123, and your feet were so swollen you could not wear shoes.

PRIVATE OLIVER B. FAIRBANKS
Witness for the Prosecution

You were captured in the Battle of the Wilderness and sent to Andersonville in late May, 1864. You will be able to describe in detail, using the background information provided, the terrible conditions of Camp Sumter and your experiences with Captain Wirz, the camp commander. You will specifically testify to the following:

1. You believe that you and other inmates were forced to endure medical experimentation.

2. Camp doctors injected prisoners with poisonous substances that caused large open sores on the outside of the arms and armpits.

3. You saw holes eaten big enough for a man to put his fist under the arms of men.

4. A great many of the men who were vaccinated had to have their arms amputated and often died.

5. You heard rebel surgeons laughing and bragging about how the vaccinations were killing the prisoners.

6. You were at the South Gate of the camp one morning when the vaccinations were being performed. While you were watching, one of the surgeons told you to roll up your sleeve so that he could give you a vaccination. You refused. He immediately ordered a guard to escort you to Captain Wirz's office.

7. Wirz came out of his office saying he wanted to know where that "God d-med Yankee son of a b--- was" that refused to be vaccinated. The guard pointed to you. Wirz drew his pistol, put it next to your ear, and said he wanted to know why you refused to obey his orders.

8. You said: "Captain, you are aware that the matter with which I would be vaccinated is poisonous, and therefore I cannot consent to an operation which I know will prove fatal to my life."

9. Wirz pushed the pistol closer and stated that "it would serve me right, the sooner I would die, the sooner he would be rid of me."

10. You were forced to wear a ball and chain for two weeks until you finally consented to the operation.

11. Immediately after the vaccination you went to the cleanest part of the camp stream, scrubbed the spot with soap and water, sucked some blood out, and thereby saved yourself.

SERGEANT CHARLES WHITE

WITNESS FOR THE PROSECUTION

You were a member of Company M, 5th Indiana Cavalry. Your entire company was forced to surrender to the Rebels led by General George Stoneman on July 31, 1864 near Macon, Georgia. You were taken by cattle car to Andersonville. You will be able to describe in detail, using the background information provided, the terrible conditions of Camp Sumter and your experiences with Captain Wirz, the camp commander. You will testify to the following:

1. When you arrived at the station you were met by Captain Wirz and several Rebel guards. They took everything of value. You heard Wirz say: "Yes, strip them! Strip the dogs! Take everything from them. Don't leave them nothing, the raiders."

2. You believe the first day in Andersonville was enough to completely break the spirits of most new prisoners.

3. You saw desperate fights over meager bits of food.

4. Most new prisoners, like yourself, had to drink from the filthy stream. There were some wells with small quantities of fresh water but these were "owned" by gangs of veteran prisoners.

5. You heard a conversation between two guards bragging about shooting a prisoner at the dead-line.

6. You saw prisoners taken out of the stockade every day to the deadhouse. They were usually covered with disgusting sores oozing with maggots. One day you were helping to bury prisoners when Captain Wirz came by the grave site. You heard him comment that the "Yankees are getting the land they came for."

7. You witnessed the hanging of six prisoners known as the "Raiders." They had been stealing and murdering from other prisoners; especially new prisoners and the sick. Captain Wirz had allowed them to be captured, tried, and sentenced.

8. After the hanging a prisoner police force was organized and some order was maintained within the camp.

9. You had been able to secretly hide a small pocket knife from the guards. You used it to carve objects from bone and trade them for extra food and tobacco.

PRIVATE WILLIAM SCOTT
WITNESS FOR THE PROSECUTION

You were captured at the Battle of Cold Harbor in June, 1864 and sent by cattle car to Andersonville in the middle of that month. You will be able to describe in detail, using the background information provided, the terrible conditions of Camp Sumter and your experiences with Captain Wirz, the camp commander. You will specifically testify to the following:

1. You had your crude shelter on the north side of the camp. One day you were down at the south end, near the creek, looking for some fresh water.

2. A sick man was sitting near the creek. You saw Captain Wirz enter the camp with a detail of guards. The sick man asked Captain Wirz if he could get out. He was dying. Captain Wirz said: "Yes, God d-mn it; I will let you out," and with his revolver he struck the man over the head and shoulders several times.

3. A few days later you inquired about the sick man struck by Captain Wirz and were told that he had died.

4. You can't recall for sure which hand Captain Wirz used to strike the man with his pistol and you don't remember the man's name.

5. Sometime in July you and some other prisoners managed to tunnel out of the camp and escape into the thick Georgia pine forest. The guards, using savage bloodhound dogs, tracked you down and caught you and a friend, Private Elmer Jones.

6. Captain Wirz rode up on his horse, and on seeing you and your friend, exclaimed: "I'm glad you captured those sneaking Yankees!" Pvt. Jones shouted back: "To the Devil with you Wirz!"

7. Wirz immediately charged his horse toward the unfortunate man, raised his heavy pistol, and brought it crashing onto his head. Jones collapsed bleeding and died in the camp shortly after.

8. You heard Wirz say as he was riding away: "That's one less Yankee mouth we'll have to feed."

CORPORAL AMOS E. STEARNS

WITNESS FOR THE PROSECUTION

You were captured at the Battle of the Wilderness and sent to Andersonville on May 30, 1864. You were not released from the camp until September 14, 1865. You will be able to describe in detail, using the background information provided, the terrible conditions of Camp Sumter and your experiences with Captain Wirz, the camp commander. You will specifically testify to the following:

1. Your first rations at Camp Sumter consisted of a few slices of moldy bread, four spoonfuls of mush, and a small piece of bacon fat.

2. You and a few other prisoners were able to construct a mud hut that served as your shelter.

3. You hardly ever had any wood to cook your raw rations.

4. You witnessed several men shot while accidentally stepping over the dead-line. You think a lot of them had gone crazy and just wanted to end it all.

5. You were happy when Captain Wirz allowed the capture, trial, and execution of a group of prisoners known as the "Raiders," but you think that there would have been a mass revolt if he hadn't done something.

6. You saw several prisoners punished by Captain Wirz by the torture known as "bucking." This consisted of placing a stick across the back of the knees of a man seated upon the ground, positioning his arms with the elbows under the ends of the stick and binding his wrists in front of his knees with a cord. Men had to endure hours of this torture for attempting escapes or other violations of camp rules.

7. You admit that Captain Wirz at times appeared humane, but he could change at a moment's notice and commit cold wanton cruelties.

THE DEFENDANT

A CONFEDERATE FLAG

"You speak high Colonel—high! Ask them in this room if they can say in their hearts they would have done different if they had been in my place—ask them! (In fury and contempt) You are all the victors here and you make up a morality for the losers!"

—Saul Levitt
The Andersonville Trial

CAPTAIN HENRY WIRZ
Defendant

Your full name is Heinrick Hartmann Wirz and you were born in Switzerland on November 25, 1823. You went to school in Turin, Paris, and Zurich. You are fluent in several languages including Italian, French, German, and English. In 1849 you immigrated to the United States and settled in Cadiz, Kentucky. You later moved to Louisiana where you married a widow and adopted her two young daughters. Later you and your wife had a third child.

You enlisted in the 4th Louisiana Volunteer Infantry on June 16, 1861. You were quickly promoted to sergeant. At the Battle of Seven Pines near Richmond, Virginia on June 12, 1862, you received a severe wound and a battlefield commission. The following year, 1863, you were examined by the chief military surgeon in Richmond and granted a furlough to go to Europe for an operation on your arm and shoulders. You went to Paris and the doctor there removed tissue and bone from your arm and shoulders. After spending several months resting in Switzerland, you took a ship from England to the Confederate States. On shipboard, the wound reopened, and you lost the use of much of your upper body.

When you returned in 1864, despite your poor health, the Confederate High Command ordered you to take command of the new prison camp at Andersonville, Georgia. You arrived at Camp Sumter in March, 1864 and assumed your duties.

By all accounts, Camp Sumter was a nightmare for the Union soldiers confined within its boundaries. Disease, starvation, and death stalked the prisoners daily. Suffering was everywhere. During your tenure as camp commander nearly 13,000 prisoners of war died in less than a year.

You have been indicted for premeditated murder in the deaths of several prisoners. You are also accused of conspiring with several high-level Confederate leaders—including your immediate superior, General Winder—of willfully allowing the terrible conditions at Andersonville which directly contributed to the death of thousands of Union soldiers. You will deny all these charges. You will testify in your defense to the following:

1. You were not part of the decision to locate the camp at Andersonville.

2. General Winder had control over all matters relating to the camp's provisions including food and medical supplies. Your requests for more supplies were repeatedly denied.

3. The poor water supply in the camp was caused by the older prisoners' refusal to share their well water with the new inmates, forcing them into using the sluggish stream running through the camp.

4. Prisoners were issued the same rations as Confederate soldiers. You realize there was a lack of fruits and vegetables in their diet. You and the guards ate the same food and you contracted scurvy. Local farmers were reluctant to bring additional food supplies to the Yankee prisoners when they knew their own soldiers were suffering at the front.

CAPTAIN HENRY WIRZ

5. You had no control over how many prisoners were sent to Camp Sumter. You knew the camp was grossly overcrowded but there was nothing you could do about it.

6. You admit that sometimes you were rough and coarse with your language to the prisoners, but you had to control over 30,000 starving and angry enemy prisoners of war. Sometimes you had to resort to the use of mild physical punishments for prisoners who were constantly escaping or assaulting other inmates. You never used methods that could be called torture. You wished that the Union government had been more willing to accept a prisoner exchange.

7. You never physically assaulted or killed any prisoner. You will claim that the combat wound to your chest, shoulders, and arms prevented you from even raising your arms without grave pain. You certainly could not forcefully strike someone. Using a firearm was equally impossible.

8. You approved the use of the deadline as a means of preventing escape attempts. The deadline was clearly marked and all new prisoners were told what it meant prior to entering the stockade. You never ordered anyone shot at the deadline and you severely punished any guard responsible for indiscriminate shooting of prisoners at this deadline. You instructed the camp guards only to fire on a prisoner if they were sure an escape was being attempted.

9. You repeatedly complained about the poor quality of soldiers who were assigned to your command, but these protests were ignored.

10. You approved the use of vaccination to prevent smallpox from breaking out in the camp. There was no medical experimentation.

11. You helped capture, try, and execute a group of prisoners known as the "Raiders" who were stealing, terrorizing, and murdering their fellow prisoners. Without your intervention in this matter, there would have been even more suffering and death.

12. Finally, you fully believe it was your duty to follow the orders of your commanders to the best of your ability.

DEFENSE ATTORNEYS

"It is simply mockery to get the halter ready for Wirz, while his responsible employers escape the gallows."

—<u>The New York Times</u>
September 11, 1865

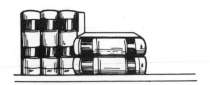

LOUIS SCHADE
Defense Attorney

You have agreed to take this very difficult case. You understand that there is no romance or fame to be gained from defending a man accused of the death of nearly 13,000 Union soldiers. Yet, you are bound by your strong sense of Southern duty to give Captain Wirz the best defense possible, according to the United States justice system. You believe the defendant is not guilty of murder and there is no concrete evidence linking him with any kind of conspiracy. You should ask for an immediate dismissal of the case for lack of evidence (the military commission will undoubtedly deny this motion).

You should focus your case on the obvious bias of the prosecution witnesses (prisoners testifying against their jailor) and the fact that Captain Wirz is an officer in the military where obedience to those above you in the chain-of-command is taken for granted. Captain Wirz could not disobey the orders of his immediate superior, General Winder (now deceased).

You will use your opening remarks, witnesses and closing remarks to make the following points clear to the military tribunal:

Captain Wirz is not guilty of conspiracy with other Confederate leaders to murder prisoners-of-war.

1. There is not a bit of concrete evidence to support the idea of conspiracy; not a scrap of paper found in his office, or a word in the archives of the Confederate government in Richmond, to show that such a conspiracy existed.

2. If the U.S. Government really believed that such a conspiracy existed, why is Captain Wirz the only man indicted? Why aren't other Confederate leaders being placed on trial?

3. Certainly, if there was a conspiracy, the guilt lay more deep and damning on those above the rank of captain.

4. Captain Wirz was merely following the orders of his commanding officer, General Winder.

5. General Winder, unfortunately deceased, is clearly the man responsible for much of the suffering and death at Camp Sumter. He had control over all matters relating to the camp site, food, water, sanitation, and medical supplies.

6. He is on record as saying that "I am killing off more Yankees than twenty regiments in Lee's Army." Captain Wirz complained of the poor quality of his guards and repeatedly asked for more well-trained soldiers. General Winder responded by saying Wirz had more than enough men and the excess soldiers might be "profitably employed at Augusta."

7. On July 21, 1864 General Winder addressed a letter to the Confederate War Department in Richmond in which he stated: "You speak in your endorsement of placing the prisoners properly. I do not exactly comprehend what is intended by it. I know of but one way to place them, and that is to put them into the stockade, where they have four or five square yards to the man."

232

LOUIS SCHADE

8. Captain Wirz had no control over how many prisoners were sent to Camp Sumter. That decision was made by Confederate officers higher in the chain of command and without his approval.

9. Prisoners were issued the same rations as Confederate soldiers. Admittedly they were meager, but under wartime conditions it was the best possible. The local resources were insufficient and farmers in the area were reluctant to bring food to the camp.

10. The poor water was primarily caused by the selfish behavior of the prisoners themselves. Some prisoners had well water and refused to share it with others. Also, had they only used the southern part of the stream for waste disposal the northern part would have been clear.

11. There was no medical experimentation. Some prisoners were vaccinated to prevent smallpox.

12. There were few trained medical doctors assigned to the camp. The sick prisoners suffered worse under the care of other prisoners who robbed them of their food and possessions.

13. A prosecution witness, Mr. Ransom, wrote in his diary that "our own men are worse to each other then the rebels are to us." Captain Wirz, with the full cooperation of the prisoners, tried and hanged six prisoners for terrorizing, stealing, and murdering other men in the stockade.

14. Captain Wirz was simply a junior officer obeying the legal orders of his superiors. He cannot be held responsible for the motives that dictated such orders.

Captain Wirz is not guilty of committing murder.

1. He never personally murdered anyone. He could barely lift his arms without intense pain, much less wield heavy pistols.

2. The dead-line was used to prevent escape attempts. All the prisoners were aware of the dangers of going near this line. Guards were ordered to only shoot at prisoners actually attempting to escape. Wirz never gave orders for indiscriminate shooting at the dead line and he never shot a prisoner at this line.

3. Mild physical punishments, threats, and curses were just a form of discipline to maintain order in the prison camp. What could be expected of a prison camp commander with over 30,000 starving and angry enemy prisoners of war under his command?

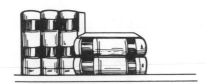

JAMES HUGHES
Assistant Defense Attorney

You have agreed to take this very difficult case. You understand that there is no romance or fame to be gained from defending a man accused of the death of nearly 13,000 Union soldiers. Yet, you are bound by your strong sense of Southern duty to give Captain Wirz the best defense possible, according to the United States justice system. You believe the defendant is not guilty of murder and there is no concrete evidence linking him with any kind of conspiracy. You should ask for an immediate dismissal of the case for lack of evidence (the military commission will undoubtedly deny this motion).

You should focus your case on the obvious bias of the prosecution witnesses (prisoners testifying against their jailor) and the fact that Captain Wirz is an officer in the military where obedience to those above you in the chain-of-command is taken for granted. Captain Wirz could not disobey the orders of his immediate superior, General Winder (now deceased).

You will use your opening remarks, witnesses, and closing remarks to make the following points clear to the military tribunal:

Captain Wirz is not guilty of conspiracy with other Confederate leaders to murder prisoners-of-war.

1. There is not a bit of concrete evidence to support the idea of conspiracy; not a scrap of paper found in his office, or a word in the archives of the Confederate government in Richmond, to show that such a conspiracy existed.

2. If the U.S. Government really believed that such a conspiracy existed, why is Captain Wirz the only man indicted? Why aren't other Confederate leaders being placed on trial?

3. Certainly, if there was a conspiracy, the guilt lay more deep and damning on those above the rank of captain.

4. Captain Wirz was merely following the orders of his commanding officer, General Winder.

5. General Winder, unfortunately deceased, is clearly the man responsible for much of the suffering and death at Camp Sumter. He had control over all matters relating to the camp site, food, water, sanitation, and medical supplies.

6. He is on record as saying that "I am killing off more Yankees than twenty regiments in Lee's Army." Captain Wirz complained of the poor quality of his guards and repeatedly asked for more well-trained soldiers. General Winder responded by saying Wirz had more than enough men and the excess soldiers might be "profitably employed at Augusta."

7. On July 21, 1864 General Winder addressed a letter to the Confederate War Department in Richmond in which he stated: "You speak in your endorsement of placing the prisoners properly. I do not exactly comprehend what is intended by it. I know of but one way to place them, and that is to put them into the stockade, where they have four or five square yards to the man."

JAMES HUGHES

8. Captain Wirz had no control over how many prisoners were sent to Camp Sumter. That decision was made by Confederate officers higher in the chain-of-command and without his approval.

9. Prisoners were issued the same rations as Confederate soldiers. Admittedly they were meager, but under wartime conditions it was the best possible. The local resources were insufficient and farmers in the area were reluctant to bring food to the camp.

10. The poor water was primarily caused by the selfish behavior of the prisoners themselves. Some prisoners had well water and refused to share it with others. Also, had they only used the southern part of the stream for waste disposal the northern part would have been clear.

11. There was no medical experimentation. Some prisoners were vaccinated to prevent smallpox.

12. There were few trained medical doctors assigned to the camp. The sick prisoners suffered worse under the care of other prisoners who robbed them of their food and possessions.

13. A prosecution witness, Mr. Ransom, wrote in his diary that "our own men are worse to each other then the rebels are to us." Captain Wirz, with the full cooperation of the prisoners, tried and hanged six prisoners for terrorizing, stealing, and murdering other men in the stockade.

14. Captain Wirz was simply a junior officer obeying the legal orders of his superiors. He cannot be held responsible for the motives that dictated such orders.

Captain Wirz is not guilty of committing murder.

1. He never personally murdered anyone. He could barely lift his arms without intense pain, much less wield heavy pistols.

2. The dead-line was used to prevent escape attempts. All the prisoners were aware of the dangers of going near this line. Guards were ordered to only shoot at prisoners actually attempting to escape. Wirz never gave orders for indiscriminate shooting at the dead-line and he never shot a prisoner at this line.

3. Mild physical punishments, threats, and curses were just a form of discipline to maintain order in the prison camp. What could be expected of a prison camp commander with over 30,000 starving and angry enemy prisoners of war under his command?

235

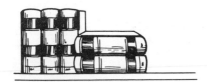

CHARLES PECK

Assistant Defense Attorney

You have agreed to take this very difficult case. You understand that there is no romance or fame to be gained from defending a man accused of the death of nearly 13,000 Union soldiers. Yet, you are bound by your strong sense of Southern duty to give Captain Wirz the best defense possible, according to the United States justice system. You believe the defendant is not guilty of murder and there is no concrete evidence linking him with any kind of conspiracy. You should ask for an immediate dismissal of the case for lack of evidence (the military commission will undoubtedly deny this motion).

You should focus your case on the obvious bias of the prosecution witnesses (prisoners testifying against their jailor) and the fact that Captain Wirz is an officer in the military where obedience to those above you in the chain-of-command is taken for granted. Captain Wirz could not disobey the orders of his immediate superior, General Winder (now deceased).

You will use your opening remarks, witnesses, and closing remarks to make the following points clear to the military tribunal:

Captain Wirz is not guilty of conspiracy with other Confederate leaders to murder prisoners-of-war.

1. There is not a bit of concrete evidence to support the idea of conspiracy; not a scrap of paper found in his office, or a word in the archives of the Confederate government in Richmond, to show that such a conspiracy existed.

2. If the U.S. Government really believed that such a conspiracy existed, why is Captain Wirz the only man indicted? Why aren't other Confederate leaders being placed on trial?

3. Certainly, if there was a conspiracy, the guilt lay more deep and damning on those above the rank of captain.

4. Captain Wirz was merely following the orders of his commanding officer, General Winder.

5. General Winder, unfortunately deceased, is clearly the man responsible for much of the suffering and death at Camp Sumter. He had control over all matters relating to the camp site, food, water, sanitation, and medical supplies.

6. He is on record as saying that "I am killing off more Yankees than twenty regiments in Lee's Army." Captain Wirz complained of the poor quality of his guards and repeatedly asked for more well-trained soldiers. General Winder responded by saying Wirz had more than enough men and the excess soldiers might be "profitably employed at Augusta."

7. On July 21, 1864 General Winder addressed a letter to the Confederate War Department in Richmond in which he stated: "You speak in your endorsement of placing the prisoners properly. I do not exactly comprehend what is intended by it. I know of but one way to place them, and that is to put them into the stockade, where they have four or five square yards to the man."

CHARLES PECK

8. Captain Wirz had no control over how many prisoners were sent to Camp Sumter. That decision was made by Confederate officers higher in the chain-of-command and without his approval.

9. Prisoners were issued the same rations as Confederate soldiers. Admittedly they were meager, but under wartime conditions it was the best possible. The local resources were insufficient and farmers in the area were reluctant to bring food to the camp.

10. The poor water was primarily caused by the selfish behavior of the prisoners themselves. Some prisoners had well water and refused to share it with others. Also, had they only used the southern part of the stream for waste disposal the northern part would have been clear.

11. There was no medical experimentation. Some prisoners were vaccinated to prevent smallpox.

12. There were few trained medical doctors assigned to the camp. The sick prisoners suffered worse under the care of other prisoners who robbed them of their food and possessions.

13. A prosecution witness, Mr. Ransom, wrote in his diary that "our own men are worse to each other then the rebels are to us." Captain Wirz, with the full cooperation of the prisoners, tried and hanged six prisoners for terrorizing, stealing, and murdering other men in the stockade.

14. Captain Wirz was simply a junior officer obeying the legal orders of his superiors. He cannot be held responsible for the motives that dictated such orders.

Captain Wirz is not guilty of committing murder.

1. He never personally murdered anyone. He could barely lift his arms without intense pain, much less wield heavy pistols.

2. The dead-line was used to prevent escape attempts. All the prisoners were aware of the dangers of going near this line. Guards were ordered to only shoot at prisoners actually attempting to escape. Wirz never gave orders for indiscriminate shooting at the dead-line and he never shot a prisoner at this line.

3. Mild physical punishments, threats, and curses were just a form of discipline to maintain order in the prison camp. What could be expected of a prison camp commander with over 30,000 starving and angry enemy prisoners of war under his command?

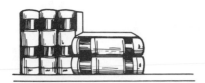

JAMES DENVER
Assistant Defense Attorney

You have agreed to take this very difficult case. You understand that there is no romance or fame to be gained from defending a man accused of the death of nearly 13,000 Union soldiers. Yet, you are bound by your strong sense of Southern duty to give Captain Wirz the best defense possible, according to the United States justice system. You believe the defendant is not guilty of murder and there is no concrete evidence linking him with any kind of conspiracy. You should ask for an immediate dismissal of the case for lack of evidence (the military commission will undoubtedly deny this motion).

You should focus your case on the obvious bias of the prosecution witnesses (prisoners testifying against their jailor) and the fact that Captain Wirz is an officer in the military where obedience to those above you in the chain-of-command is taken for granted. Captain Wirz could not disobey the orders of his immediate superior, General Winder (now deceased).

You will use your opening remarks, witnesses, and closing remarks to make the following points clear to the military tribunal:

*Captain Wirz is not guilty of conspiracy with other Confederate leaders
to murder prisoners-of-war.*

1. There is not a bit of concrete evidence to support the idea of conspiracy; not a scrap of paper found in his office, or a word in the archives of the Confederate government in Richmond, to show that such a conspiracy existed.

2. If the U.S. Government really believed that such a conspiracy existed, why is Captain Wirz the only man indicted? Why aren't other Confederate leaders being placed on trial?

3. Certainly, if there was a conspiracy, the guilt lay more deep and damning on those above the rank of captain.

4. Captain Wirz was merely following the orders of his commanding officer, General Winder.

5. General Winder, unfortunately deceased, is clearly the man responsible for much of the suffering and death at Camp Sumter. He had control over all matters relating to the camp site, food, water, sanitation, and medical supplies.

6. He is on record as saying that "I am killing off more Yankees than twenty regiments in Lee's Army." Captain Wirz complained of the poor quality of his guards and repeatedly asked for more well-trained soldiers. General Winder responded by saying Wirz had more than enough men and the excess soldiers might be "profitably employed at Augusta."

7. On July 21, 1864 General Winder addressed a letter to the Confederate War Department in Richmond in which he stated: "You speak in your endorsement of placing the prisoners properly. I do not exactly comprehend what is intended by it. I know of but one way to place them, and that is to put them into the stockade, where they have four or five square yards to the man."

JAMES DENVER

8. Captain Wirz had no control over how many prisoners were sent to Camp Sumter. That decision was made by Confederate officers higher in the chain-of-command and without his approval.

9. Prisoners were issued the same rations as Confederate soldiers. Admittedly they were meager, but under wartime conditions it was the best possible. The local resources were insufficient and farmers in the area were reluctant to bring food to the camp.

10. The poor water was primarily caused by the selfish behavior of the prisoners themselves. Some prisoners had well water and refused to share it with others. Also, had they only used the southern part of the stream for waste disposal the northern part would have been clear.

11. There was no medical experimentation. Some prisoners were vaccinated to prevent smallpox.

12. There were few trained medical doctors assigned to the camp. The sick prisoners suffered worse under the care of other prisoners who robbed them of their food and possessions.

13. A prosecution witness, Mr. Ransom, wrote in his diary that "our own men are worse to each other then the rebels are to us." Captain Wirz, with the full cooperation of the prisoners, tried and hanged six prisoners for terrorizing, stealing, and murdering other men in the stockade.

14. Captain Wirz was simply a junior officer obeying the legal orders of his superiors. He cannot be held responsible for the motives that dictated such orders.

Captain Wirz is not guilty of committing murder.

1. He never personally murdered anyone. He could barely lift his arms without intense pain, much less wield heavy pistols.

2. The dead-line was used to prevent escape attempts. All the prisoners were aware of the dangers of going near this line. Guards were ordered to only shoot at prisoners actually attempting to escape. Wirz never gave orders for indiscriminate shooting at the dead-line and he never shot a prisoner at this line.

3. Mild physical punishments, threats, and curses were just a form of discipline to maintain order in the prison camp. What could be expected of a prison camp commander with over 30,000 starving and angry enemy prisoners of war under his command?

DEFENSE WITNESSES

A CONFEDERATE FLAG

"Mr. Schade, you know I have always told you that I did not know anything about Jefferson Davis. He had no connection with me as to what was done at Andersonville; and if I knew he had, I would not become a traitor against him, or anybody else, to save my life."

—Captain Wirz's last words to his lawyer, Mr. Schade

COLONEL G.C. GIBBS

WITNESS FOR THE DEFENSE

In October, 1864 you were assigned as commandant of Camp Sumter by General John Winder. Captain Wirz was in command of the prison when you assumed your duties. You were Wirz's superior in rank, but you spent most of your time on official business in Richmond, leaving Captain Wirz to run the prison camp. In fact, General Winder spent more time at the prison camp than you. You will testify to the following:

1. There was enough food available to feed all the prisoners. The rations served to the guards and the prisoners were equal. You don't remember the specific amounts, but they did receive some meat, corn meal, beans, molasses, and flour.

2. You believe that if the quality of the food was unsound, a board of survey would have recommended a change. You will have to admit, however, that to your knowledge Captain Wirz never requested such a survey. Although, he might have made such requests directly to General Winder.

3. You visited the camp in the middle of August and it looked extremely overcrowded—like a human anthill. Captain Wirz told you that nearly 12,000 men had died so far. He blamed the prisoners' complete lack of self-hygiene and outright cruelty to each other. In fact, he said the prisoners finally asked him to try and execute a gang of men who were robbing and murdering the sick and dying in the stockade.

4. A dead-line was established to prevent prisoners from escaping. You don't know if it was under Captain Wirz's orders, General Winder's, or the prior camp commander.

5. You only witnessed one instance of punishment. A man who failed to report the escape of a prisoner was put in the stocks a little while until the doctors interfered.

6. Dogs were kept at the prison, intended for tracking down escaped prisoners. You never heard about them being used to cruelly attack defenseless prisoners.

7. It is your opinion that if Captain Wirz used cruelty against the prisoners, it was probably under the direct orders of General Winder. Captain Wirz *always* obeyed the orders of his superiors.

COLONEL D.T. CHANDLER
Witness for the Defense

You were a medical examiner assigned to report on the prison camp at Andersonville. You visited the camp several times. In your official reports to Richmond you never once attached blame to Captain Wirz for the conditions in the prison hospital or the camp in general. You will testify to the following:

1. Overcrowding, poor sanitation facilities, impure water, inadequate medical supplies, and lack of proper food caused numerous medical problems among the prisoners.

2. They were infected with diarrhea, scurvy, dysentery, and gangrene. Many of the prisoners arrived at Camp Sumter already suffering from these diseases.

3. Clearly, the poor sanitary conditions at the camp contributed to the prisoners' inability to recover from these diseases and caused the high mortality.

4. Most of the prisoners suffered severe malnutrition that also contributed to the high death rate.

5. It is your opinion that Captain Wirz could not have changed the conditions of the camp since he had neither the food nor the medical supplies to deal with the volume of prisoners.

6. Your report to Richmond showed that when the prisoners were asked about their treatment, they never once mentioned Captain Wirz as the cause of their suffering.

7. In your meetings with the defendant, you found him a tired, sick, defeated man. He seemed to be suffering from the symptoms of scurvy. He seemed genuinely concerned about the terrible conditions of the camp, but didn't think there was anything he could do about the situation.

8. You were present at the Andersonville graveyard when an alleged comment was made that "the Yankees are getting the land they came for." You remember the remark was made by another Confederate officer, not Captain Wirz.

9. He never said that he was "doing more for the Confederacy than any regiment at the front." What he said was that his guards were poorly trained, but "he had a larger command than any general at the front."

DR. C.M. FORD

WITNESS FOR THE DEFENSE

You are the acting assistant surgeon in the Army of the United States, in charge of the hospital in Washington, D.C. You have been caring for the defendant, Captain Wirz, since his imprisonment. You have examined his war wounds several times. At the request of defense counsel, you made—in the presence of court-appointed officials—an examination of the physical condition of Captain Wirz on October 24, 1865. You will testify to the following:

1. The defendant's right arm is swollen and inflamed; ulcerated in three places; and has the appearance of being broken. It appears that portions of both bones of the arm are completely dead.

2. You don't know how much strength he has in his right arm, but you believe him incapable of knocking a man down or lifting a heavy object like a pistol, without doing further injury to his arm. It would surely cause him great pain.

3. You have examined his left shoulder and there is a large scar on it. The deltoid muscle is entirely gone and only the front part of the shoulder muscle remains.

4. The loss of the shoulder muscle greatly restricts the strength of the left arm and prevents normal elevation. It has no influence at all on the flexing of the arm at the elbow, or striking out with the forearm from the elbow.

5. The fingers of the defendant's right hand—the little finger and the one next to it—are slightly contracted due to the injury of the nerve leading down to the fingers. This would restrict the defendant's ability to tightly grip any object.

6. You do not believe the injuries to his right arm and hand were any better in 1864 than they are at present. The external appearances would indicate that there had been a very extensive injury to the bones and tissues.

7. There is evidence that the defendant was suffering from scurvy in 1864, which would have made the wounds much worse. Scurvy or similar diseases will often cause the fractures to open again after being reunited.

DR. JOHN C. BATES

WITNESS FOR THE DEFENSE

You were a Confederate medical doctor who saw Captain Wirz several times while making inspection trips of the medical facilities at Andersonville. You have been called by the defense to buttress Dr. Ford's testimony about Captain Wirz's inability to effectively use his upper body and arms. The prosecution may, under cross-examination, ask you questions about the medical care at Andersonville. You will agree that there was inadequate medical supplies, a lack of medical doctors, and generally unsanitary conditions. You reported this to your superiors in Richmond. You will testify to the following:

1. Captain Wirz seemed to have great difficulty using his right arm.

2. When you last saw him in September, 1864, he seemed feeble and in ill health.

3. You never examined him professionally, but it appeared he was suffering from scurvy or some other disease.

4. You agree with Dr. Ford in all that he has said and concur in his opinion in reference to the defendant's left shoulder, the destruction of a portion of the deltoid muscle, and also in his opinion about the right arm. Clearly Captain Wirz could not use it with any considerable degree of force, such as lifting or striking. He could not use the right arm very extensively without injury to the bones, which were already partially destroyed.

5. You do not think it possible for a man in such condition to strike out and hurt anyone else with either of his arms.

COLONEL PIERSONS
Witness for the Defense

You were the Confederate prison camp commander of Camp Sumter prior to Captain Wirz taking command in March. You were in Andersonville while the camp was being constructed and saw the arrival of the first prisoners. You will testify to the following:

1. Captain Wirz had nothing to do with the selection of the site for Camp Sumter. He was not present when the stockade was constructed. The camp was selected and constructed under the direct supervision of other Confederate officers including General Winder.

2. There were only a few thousand prisoners in the camp while you were in command. The camp was designed to hold only 10,000 prisoners at any given time. In order to provide better water supplies, you allowed the prisoners to dig several wells on the north side of the camp.

3. You found great difficulties in gaining prison supplies because the railroad upon which the prison was located was worked to its greatest capacity in feeding General Lee's and General Johnston's armies. You had only infrequent food deliveries.

4. You don't know how it would have been possible for Captain Wirz to provide proper food and medical supplies for so many prisoners.

5. You didn't know Captain Wirz well, but it is your opinion that he must have been an extremely competent man in order to have risen from the rank of private to captain in such a brief time.

PRIVATE HENDERSON R. SHUFFLER
Witness for the Defense

You are a former Confederate prisoner-of-war captured at the Battle of the Wilderness and held at Point Lookout, a Northern prison camp. You were never told the name of the officer in charge of the camp. You only saw various rough and harsh guards strictly enforcing the camp rules. You will testify to the following:

1. You found the camp to be truly horrible. The prisoners were crowded in crude tents and underwent many privations and sufferings.

2. The treatment they received at the hands of those in authority was absolutely barbarous. Reward was given for crime. It was understood that any guard who shot a prisoner attempting to escape would be awarded by promotion or money.

3. Prisoners were allowed only one blanket to several men, and the sufferings from the cold Northern winter was intense.

4. The food was adequate when you first arrived at the camp, but they were soon cut in half. The guards announced that the Rebels were starving their prisoners, so we were going to get the same treatment.

5. Many prisoners suffered from malnutrition and various diseases like scurvy, dysentary, and diarrhea.

6. You saw dead prisoners being carried out of the camp every day.

EXHIBITS

"The vast majority appeared to lose all repulsion to filth, and both sick and well disregarded all the laws of hygiene and personal cleanliness."

—an anonymous Confederate doctor

EXHIBIT A

HOSPITAL REGISTER, ANDERSONVILLE PRISON RECORDS

Whole number of deaths listed by hospital register:	12,462
Total number of deaths in hospital:	8,735
Total number of deaths in stockade:	3,727
Cases returned from hospital to stockade:	3,469

DISEASES AND NUMBER OF DEATHS RESULTING FROM EACH DISEASE

Diarrhea	3,952	Constipation	5
Scurvy	3,574	Ophthahaia	5
Unknown	1,648	Nephritis	4
General Dropsy	377	Vaccine Ulcers	4
Typhoid Fever	229	Laryngitis	4
Pneumonia	221	Ieterus	3
Debility	198	Diphtheria	3
Intermittent and Remittent Fever	177	Scrofula	3
Gun Shot Wounds	149	Asthma	3
Pleurisy	109	Gonorrhea	3
Bronchitis	93	Dyspepsia	2
Rheumatism	83	Homesickness	2
Gangrene	63	Fistula	2
Varioloid	63	Diabetes	1
Catarrh	55	Measles	1
Ulcers	51	Paralysis	1
Phthisis	36	Ague	1
Abdominal Dropsy	24	Consumption	1
Erysipelas	11	Hemorrhoids	1
Syphilis	7	Praeture	1
Asphyxia	7	Stricture	1
Jaundice	6		
Wounds	6		
		TOTAL	12,462

EXHIBIT B

JOURNAL, ANDERSONVILLE PRISON RECORDS

Month and Year	Number of Prisoners received at Camp in Each Month	Total Number of Prisoners on Hand at End of Each Month	Number of Deaths During Each Month	Number of Escapes During Each Month
APRIL, 1864	3,024	9,577	592	8
MAY	3,624	18,451	711	31
JUNE	9,187	26,367	1,203	47
JULY	7,076	31,678	1,742	20
AUGUST	3,085	31,693	2,992	30
SEPTEMBER	282	8,218	2,700	84
OCTOBER	444	4,208	1,560	28
NOVEMBER	49	1,359	485	30
DECEMBER	3,085	4,706	160	26
JANUARY, 1865	743	5,016	200	10
FEBRUARY	1,035	5,016	149	12
MARCH	142	3,819	118	2
APRIL	6,657	51	32	0
TOTAL	**44,882**		**12,644**	**328**

GREATEST NUMBER OF MEN IN PRISON ON A SINGLE DAY WAS:

33,006 ON AUGUST 9, 1864

GREATEST NUMBER OF DEATHS ON A SINGLE DAY WAS;

127 ON AUGUST 23, 1864

EXHIBIT C

Photo of Andersonville Prison, Georgia (N.Y. 1865) by courtesy of the Trustees of the Boston Public Library

250

EXHIBIT D

A FORMER PRISONER OF ANDERSONVILLE AS SEEN BY THE CAMERA OF CAPTAIN A.J. RUSSEL, UNION ARMY. "This living skeleton is a victim of scurvy, gangrene, and malnutrition."

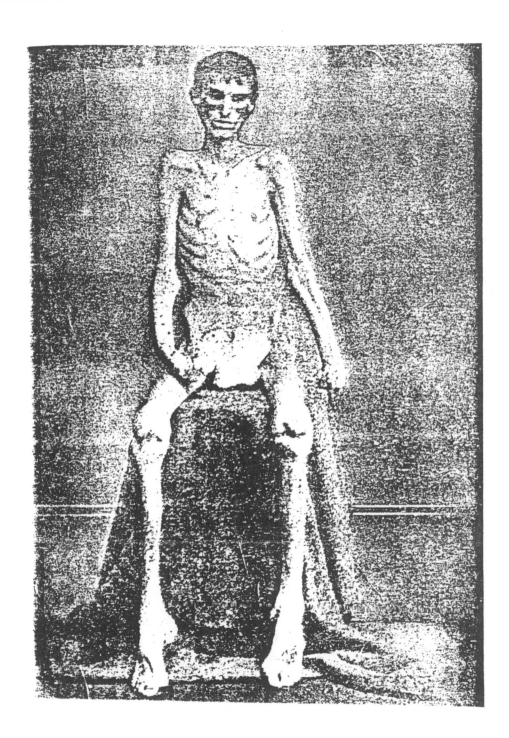

EXHIBIT E

SKETCH OF CAPTAIN HENRY WIRZ

"He was by nature fitted to become distinguished only in the infliction of suffering, and during the entire time he was in charge of Andersonville Stockade, was never known to relent, or manifest the smallest symptom of pity or commiseration for the helpless men consigned to his care."

—Statement of an Andersonville prisoner

EXHIBIT F

SKETCH OF CAPTAIN HENRY WIRZ

"Had he been an angel from heaven, he could not have changed the pitiful tale of privation and hunger unless he had possessed the power to repeat the miracle of the loaves and fishes. Refusing to implicate others, he gave his life of the South, November 10, 1865,"

—Georgia Plaque

CAMP SUMTER AND SURROUNDINGS

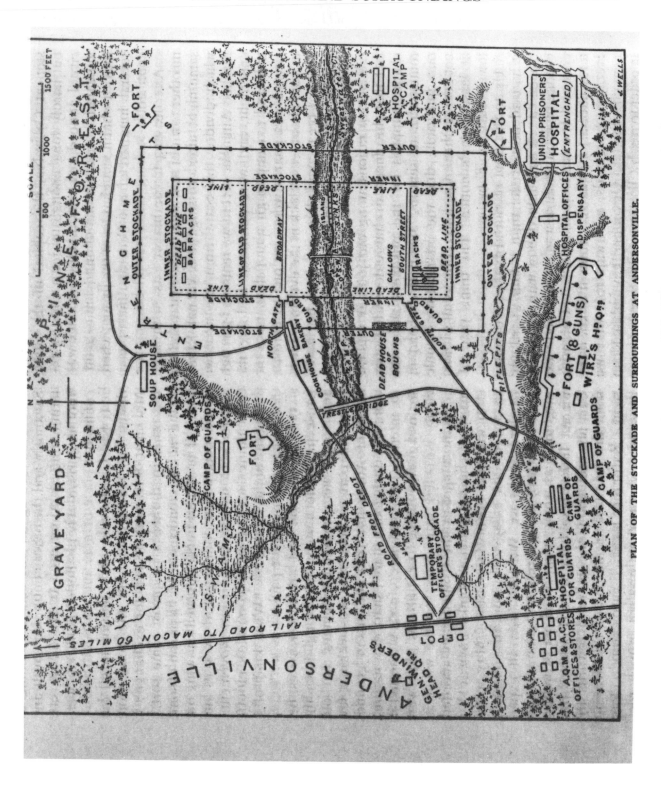

PLAN OF THE STOCKADE AND SURROUNDINGS AT ANDERSONVILLE.

EXHIBIT H

A FRAGMENT OF A DIARY KEPT BY AN ANDERSONVILLE PRISONER DATED, AUGUST 4, 1864

" . . . inside the camp death stalked on every hand. Death at the hands of the cruel guards, though murder in cold blood, was merciful beside the systematic, studied, absolute murder inside, by slow death, inch by inch! . . . *missing section* . . . . As stated before, one-third of the original enclosure was swampy—a mud of liquid filth . . . seething with maggots in full activity. This daily increased by the necessities of the inmates, being the only place accessible for the purpose. Through this mass of pollution passed the only water that found its way through the Bull Pen. It came to us through two sources of pollution, the Confederate camp and the cook house; first, the seepage of the sinks; second, the dirt and filth emptied by the cook house; then was our turn to use it. Today I saw three thousand men wait in line to get water, and the line was added to as fast as reduced, from daylight to dark, yes, even into the night.

The air is loaded with unbearable, fever-laden stench from that poison sink of putrid mud and water, continually in motion by the activity of the germs of death. We cannot get away from the stink—we eat it, drink it and have to sleep in it!

Yesterday I saw a man deliberately jump into the "dead-line" and get immediately shot by the guards. We all know that he preferred a "quick" bullet to the brain than a continuation of this horror.

I heard a rumor that a mere two-hundred feet from the outside stockade is a pure, deep, clear stream of water named "Sweetwater Creek." They say that if we were allowed to get our water from this creek it would save thousands of lives. I know for a fact that Capt. Wirz is afraid to let any prisoner out of the stockade. They may try to escape . . . "

EXHIBIT I

THE LIEBER CODE
Washington, D.C., April 24, 1863

*Instructions for the Government of Armies of the United States
in the Field by Order of the Secretary of War*

Section 3 Article LVI A prisoner of war is subject to no punishment for being a public enemy, nor is any revenge wreaked upon him by the intentional infliction of any suffering, or disgrace, by cruel imprisonment, want of food, by mutilation, death, or any other barbarity.

Section 3 Article LXX The use of poison in any manner, be it to poison wells, or food, or arms, is wholly excluded from modern warfare. He that uses it puts himself out of the pale of the law and usages of war.

Section 3 Article LXXI Whoever intentionally inflicts additional wounds on an enemy already wholly disabled, or kills such an enemy, or who orders or encourages soldiers to do so, shall suffer death, if duly convicted, whether he belongs to the Army of the United States, or is an enemy captured after having committed his misdeed.

Section 3 Article LXXII Prisoners of war are subject to confinement or imprisonment such as may be deemed necessary on account of safety, but they are to be subjected to no other intentional suffering or indignity. The confinement and mode of treating a prisoner may be varied during his captivity according to the demands of safety.

Section 3 Article LXXVI Prisoners of war shall be fed upon plain and wholesome food, whenever practicable, and treated with humanity. They may be required to work for the benefit of the captor's government according to their rank and condition.

Section 3 Article LXXVII A prisoner of war who escapes may be shot or otherwise killed in his flight; but neither death nor any other punishment shall be inflicted upon him simply for his attempt to escape, which the law of war does not consider a crime. Stricter means of security shall be used after an unsuccessful attempt at escape. If, however, a conspiracy is discovered, the purpose of which is a united or general escape, the conspirators may be rigorously punished, even with death, and capital punishment may also be inflicted upon prisoners of war discovered to have plotted rebellion against the authorities of the captors, whether in union with fellow prisoners or other persons.

Section 3 Article LXXIX Every captured wounded enemy shall be medically treated, according to the ability of the medical staff.

EXHIBIT J

ALLEGED MURDER WEAPON: CAPTAIN WIRZ'S REVOLVER

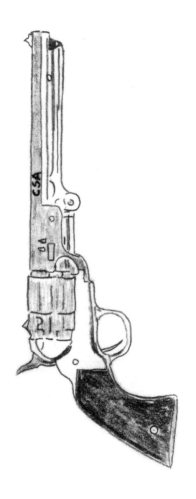

Confederate .44 Cal. Revolver. 2 Lbs. 9 Oz. 7-1/2" Barrel, Overall Length 13-1/4"

EXHIBIT K

SICK AND DYING PRISONERS IN ANDERSONVILLE HOSPITAL

EXHIBIT L

**PRISONER SHOT ATTEMPTING TO CROSS THE DEAD-LINE FOR
A DRINK OF FRESH WATER**

259

EXHIBIT M

ESCAPED PRISONER ATTACKED BY SAVAGE BLOODHOUNDS

View of Andersonville from the stockade. The long sinks, or latrines, run parallel and next to the stream that provided drinking water.

261

EXHIBIT O

BURYING THE DEAD IN LONG TRENCHES AT
ANDERSONVILLE PRISON CAMP

ADDITIONAL INFORMATION

"Count it the greatest sin to prefer life to honor, and for the sake of living to lose what makes life worth having."

—Decimus Junius Juvenalis

"If my life is demanded as an atonement, I will give it and I hope that after a while I will be judged differently from what I am today."

—Captain Henry Wirz shortly before his execution on November 10, 1865

MASTER ROLE SHEET

ROLE   **STUDENT**

Military Commission

Major-General L. Wallace   _____

Major-General J.W. Geary   _____

General L. Thomas   _____

General G. Mott   _____

General F. Fessenden   _____

Brigadier-General E. Bragg   _____

Brigadier-General J. Ballier   _____

Colonel T. Allcock   _____

Lt. Colonel J. Stibbs   _____

Defense Attorneys

Mr. Louis Schade   _____

Mr. James Hughes   _____

Mr. Charles Peck   _____

Mr. James Denver   _____

Defendant

Captain Henry Wirz   _____

Defense Witnesses

Colonel G.C. Gibbs   _____

Colonel D.T. Chandler   _____

Dr. C.M. Ford   _____

Dr. John C. Bates   _____

Colonel Piersons   _____

Private Henderson R. Shuffler   _____

MASTER ROLE SHEET, continued

ROLE   **STUDENT**

Prosecution Attorneys

Colonel N.P. Chipman, Judge-Advocate   _____

Major A.A. Hosmer, Asst. Judge-Advocate   _____

Prosecution Witnesses

Sergeant John Ransom   _____

Dr. Joseph Jones   _____

Sergeant Charles White   _____

Sergeant Charles Ferren Hopkins   _____

Corporal Amos E. Stearns   _____

Private Oliver B. Fairbanks   _____

Private William Scott   _____

Private Martin E. Hogan   _____

Private George Conway   _____

Optional Roles

Court Clerk   _____

Sergeant-at-Arms   _____

Newspaper Reporter (Richmond Times)   _____

Newspaper Reporter (Washington Post)   _____

Photographer/Illustrator (Unbiased)   _____

TRIAL PROCEDURE

1. The officers of the military commission enter the courtroom and are seated.

2. The charges are read to the defendant and he is asked to plead "guilty" or "not guilty."

3. The Judge-Advocate makes his opening remarks.

4. The Defense Attorney makes his opening remarks.

5. The Judge-Advocate calls witnesses for direct testimony. (After each witness has testified, he can be subject to cross-examination and questions from the military commission.)

6. The Defense Attorney calls witnesses for direct testimony. (After each witness has testified, he can be subject to cross-examination and questions from the military commission.)

7. The Judge-Advocate makes his closing remarks.

8. The Defense Attorney makes his closing remarks.

9. The court is called in recess while the military commission deliberates a verdict.

10. The military commission announces a verdict. If the defendant is found "guilty" on either of the two charges, he would be sentenced to be hanged.

SUGGESTED COURTROOM SET-UP

SPECTATORS

SGT.-AT-ARMS	MILITARY COMMISSION	CLERK

DEFENDANT		JUDGE-ADVOCATE

DEFENSE	DEFENSE ATTORNEYS	WITNESS SEAT	PROSECUTION
W I T N E S S E S			W I T N E S S E S

LEGAL TERMS

CONSPIRACY A combination of two or more persons to commit a criminal or unlawful act, or to commit a lawful act by criminal or unlawful means; or a combination of two or more persons by concerted action to accomplish an unlawful act. It is essential that there be two or more conspirators; one cannot conspire with himself. Some jurisdictions, however, permit prosecution of one person for a conspiracy when, for example, the other party(ies) cannot be located or is otherwise unavailable for prosecution.

MILITARY COMMISSION A court appointed by a field commander to try alien enemy combatants for offenses against the laws of war.

MILITARY JURISDICTION Superseding local law and exercised by the military commander under the direction of the President with the express or implied sanction of Congress. It is exercised either outside the boundaries of the United States or in time of rebellion and civil war within states or districts occupied by the rebels. When a military government exists, any offense against the "law of war" is tried before a military court.

MURDER A common-law offense of unlawful homicide; unlawful killing of another human being with malice. This requires a premeditated intent to kill plus an element of hatred.

SUBPOENA

YOU _____ are hereby ordered to appear before the *Military Commission* formed in Washington, D.C. for the trial of *Captain Henry Wirz, CSA,* on August 23, 1865 at 10:30 A.M. (_____)
                                        modern date

Please present yourself at _____ in _____
                                    (time)   *(room number)*

and be prepared to serve as an expert witness for the *PROSECUTION* or *DEFENSE* (circle one).

Failure to comply with this *SUMMONS* will result in *CONTEMPT CHARGES.*

Requested by _____ Counsel for the _____

Approved by *Major-General Lew Wallace,* Senior Officer in Charge of said Military Commission, August 2, 1865.

I have served this summons _____
                                        (Sgt.-at-arms / Court Clerk)

MILITARY COMMISSION EVALUATION SHEET

Prosecution Witnesses

NAME	TOLD THE TRUTH	MOSTLY TOLD THE TRUTH	LIED
John Ransom	❑	❑	❑
Joseph Jones	❑	❑	❑
Charles White	❑	❑	❑
Charles Hopkins	❑	❑	❑
Amos Stearns	❑	❑	❑
Oliver Fairbanks	❑	❑	❑
William Scott	❑	❑	❑
Martin Hogan	❑	❑	❑
George Conway	❑	❑	❑

The *best* prosecution witness was _____

The *worst* prosecution witness was _____

MILITARY COMMISSION EVALUATION SHEET, continued

Defense Witnesses

NAME	TOLD THE TRUTH	MOSTLY TOLD THE TRUTH	LIED
Captain Wirz	❏	❏	❏
Colonel Gibbs	❏	❏	❏
Colonel Piersons	❏	❏	❏
Henderson Shuffler	❏	❏	❏
Dr. Ford	❏	❏	❏
Dr. Bates	❏	❏	❏
Colonel Chandler	❏	❏	❏

The *best* defense witness was _____ Why?

The *worst* defense witness was _____ Why?

VERDICT

I *personally* feel that Captain Wirz is (guilty/not guilty) of the following charge (s)

_____. Why? _____

_____

_____

_____

CHRONOLOGY

April, 1861   —Fort Sumter, South Carolina attacked—Civil War begins

July, 1861   —First Battle of Bull Run

September, 1862   —Battle of Antietam

July, 1863   —Battle of Gettysburg

March, 1864   —First prisoners sent to Camp Sumter, Andersonville

     —Captain Wirz appointed camp commander

May-June, 1864   —Battle of Wilderness

August, 1864   —33,000 prisoners confined to Camp Sumter

October, 1864   —Colonel Gibbs appointed camp commander by General Winder

     —Captain Wirz maintains daily control

April, 1865   —General Lee surrenders to General Grant at Appomattox Court House—Civil War ends

     —Camp Sumter liberated

August, 1865   —Trial of Captain Wirz begins in Washington, D.C.

AFTERMATH

On October 24, 1865 Captain Henry Wirz was found guilty of murdering Union prisoners-of-war and conspiring with other Confederate officers and leaders, including General Winder, to impair, injure, and destroy the health of large numbers of Federal prisoners at Camp Sumter, Andersonville, Georgia. On November 3, 1865 the military commission sentenced him "to be hanged by the neck till he be dead." He was executed at 10:30 in the morning in Washington, D.C. on November 10, 1865.

In 1866, less than a year after Captain Wirz was hanged, in the case of "ex parte Milligan," the Supreme Court ruled against the use of military tribunals where the civilian courts were open and functioning.

In 1927, sixty-five years after the event, Charles Ferren Hopkins was awarded the Congressional Medal of Honor for his gallantry at the Battle of Gaines' Mill. He died in 1936 at the age of 92.

After the war, John Ransom returned to his home in Jackson, Michigan, where he regained his health. He went back to work in the composing room of the "Jackson Citizen," married, and later moved to Clearwater, Michigan, where he continued to follow the printer's trade. Eventually, he moved to Chicago and worked for the Merganthaler Linotype Company. He died in 1919 at the age of 76.

Charles White remained life-loving and healthy well into his mid-80's in spite of the rigors he had suffered as a prisoner-of-war in Andersonville. In his war diary he spoke of his ability as a swimmer allowing him to slip away from the guards and escape the prison camp. His death was due to a rupture he got from plunging into a freezing lake while going to the aid of a boatload of people whose sailboat had capsized. He rescued the only non-swimmer, a 200-pound woman, but sustained the injury that ended his life.

HISTORICAL NOTES TO TEACHER

1. In the real trial there were 135 prosecution witnesses. Obviously, to make the simulation workable, that number had to be reduced.

2. Colonel Gibbs was a prosecution witness in the real trial. His real statements seemed more favorable to Captain Wirz's cause. In order to make the simulation slightly more balanced, I switched him to the defense.

3. Colonel Chipman for the government and Mr. Schade for the defense seemed to bear the bulk of the case, but I have included the other assistant attorneys.

DISCUSSION QUESTIONS

1. What examples can you find where the defense and prosecution introduced biased information or blatant propaganda as evidence? Was it effective? Why or why not?

2. Did Captain Wirz get a fair trial? Why or why not?

3. A defendant does not have to testify in his trial. Would it have made a difference in the outcome of the trial if Captain Wirz had not testified? Why or why not?

4. Do you think there was a "conspiracy" on the part of the Confederate leadership to deliberately murder prisoners-of-war? Was Captain Wirz part of the plot? Why would they want to do such a thing?

5. What was the most damaging evidence against Captain Wirz for the charge of pre-meditated murder? Conspiracy to commit murder?

6. What was the best evidence to support Captain Wirz's claims of innocence?

7. Is it fair for victorious army commanders to try other military officers, like Captain Wirz, for crimes committed during war? Why or why not?

8. After the American officer in charge read the execution order, Captain Wirz allegedly said to him, "I know what orders are, Major, and I am being hanged for obeying them." Is the plea of "following orders" from a superior officer a valid defense? Why or why not?

9. Thousands of Confederate prisoners died in Union prison camps under similar conditions as Andersonville. Would this be a valid defense for Captain Wirz?

10. Can you see any similarities between this trial and twentieth-century war crime trials including Nuremberg, Tokyo, and Lt. Calley?

BIBLIOGRAPHY

Abstracts from "The Report of a Commission of Inquiry Appointed by the United States Sanitary Commission on the Privation and Sufferings of United States Officers and Soldiers While Prisoners of War in the Hands of the Rebel Authorities." Boston, 1864.

American Heritage. "Hell and the Survivor: A Civil War Memoir". Oct./Nov., Vol. 33/Number 6, 1982.

Chipman, General N.P. *The Tragedy of Andersonville.* San Fransisco: Blair-Murdock Co., 1911.

The Civil War Journal of C.M. White. Author's collection.

Davidson, H.M. *Fourteen Months in Southern Prisons.* Milwaukee: Daily Wisconsin Printing House, 1865.

Davis, Burke. *The Long Surrender.* NY: Random House, 1985.

Davis, William C. *The Soldiers of the Civil War.* NY: Maillard Press, 1993.

Friedman, Leon. *The Law of War: A Documentary History, Vol.1.* NY: Random House, 1972.

Futch, Ovid L. *History of Andersonville Prison.* Gainesville: University of Florida Press, 1968.

Hamlin, Augustus C. *Martyria or Andersonville Prison.* Boston: Lee and Shepard, 1866.

Hesseltine, William B. *Civil War Prisons: A Study in War Psychology.* Columbus: Ohio State University Press, 1930.

H.R. Executive Document No. 23, 40th Cong., 2nd Sess (7 December 1867). United States v. Henry Wirz. Washington, 24 October 1865.

Journal of Southern History. Hesseltine, William B., "The Propaganda Literature of Confederate Prisons." Feb–Nov., pp. 56–66, 1935.

Kantor, Mackinlay. *Andersonville.* NY: The World Publishing Co., 1955.

Ketchum, Richard (ed.). *The American Heritage Picture History of the Civil War.* NY: American Heritage, 1960.

Levitt, Saul. *The Andersonville Trial.* NY: Random House, 1960.

McElroy, John. *Andersonville: A Story of Rebel Prisons.* Toledo, Ohio: D.R. Locke, 1879.

McPherson, James M. *Battle Cry of Freedom: The Civil War Era.* NY: Ballantine Books, 1988.

Miers, Earl Schenck. *The American Civil War: Popular Illustrated History of the Years 1861–1865 as Seen by the Artists-Correspondents Who Were There.* NY: Golden Press, 1961.

The New York Times. Aug.–Nov., 1865.

Page, James Madison. *The True Story of Andersonville Prisons: A Defense of Major Wirz.* NY: Neale Publishing Co., 1988.

Ransom, John. *John Ransom's Diary.* NY: Paul S. Erikson, Inc., 1908.

Robertson, James, Jr. *Soldiers: Blue and Grey.* Charlotte: University of South Carolina Press, 1988.

Shuffler, Henderson R. *The Adventures of a Prisoner of War 1863–1864.* Austin: University of Texas Press, 1964.

Spencer, Ambrose. *A Narrative of Andersonville.* NY: Harper and Bros., 1866.

Stevenson, R. Randolph. *The Southern Side; Or, Andersonville Prison.* Baltimore: Turnbull Brothers, 1876.

Wilson, Edmund. *Patriotic Gore.* NY: Oxford University Press, 1966.

THE TRIAL OF JULIUS AND ETHEL ROSENBERG
AND MORTON SOBELL

Julius Rosenberg flanked by FBI agents following his arrest on July 17, 1950.

"To be writing an opinion in a case affecting two lives after the curtain has been rung down upon them has the appearance of pathetic futility. But history also has its claims."

—Justice Felix Frankfurter

BACKGROUND

Post-war America was a time of suspicion, anonymous accusation, and public anxiety. There were intense security checks, forced loyalty oaths, secret FBI investigations, wiretapping of telephones, spy scandals, book-bannings, and government hearings about so-called "un-American" activities. Communists were suspected to be everywhere. The Attorney-General's office in Washington, D.C. provided an "unofficial" list of "subversives" suspected of Communist affiliations. It ruined many lives and careers. Among those on the list identified as suspected "subversives" included the 16th-Century playwright Christopher Marlowe and the actress Shirley Temple.

By 1950 television was becoming common in many American homes. Millions of citizens watched with amazement as Senator Joe McCarthy shook a briefcase at the camera, declaring it contained the names of hundreds of suspected Communists in the American State Department. They viewed news reports showing American Marines fighting against Communist soldiers in Korea. They witnessed what Winston Churchill labelled an "iron curtain" separate Europe into countries dominated by the Soviet Union and those allied to the West.

At the end of World War II in 1945, the United States was the most powerful nation on earth. It alone possessed the secret of atomic weapons. The U.S. wanted this weaponry kept exclusively in the hands of the American military. Yet, on September 23, 1949, four years after an atomic bomb destroyed the Japanese city of Hiroshima, the Soviet Union exploded its own atomic bomb. American officials and scientists wondered how the Soviet Union could have developed this advanced technology so fast. They concluded that the Soviets must have been supplied with information about the atomic bomb from spies in America. An intensive investigation was mounted by the FBI to find the spies.

The first to be arrested was Klaus Fuchs, a British physicist, who was seized in England on February 2, 1950. Fuchs admitted passing atom bomb information during the war to an American agent working for the Soviet Union. On May 23, 1950, Harry Gold, a chemist from Philadelphia, was arrested by the FBI. He confessed that he was the agent who received atom-bomb secrets from Klaus Fuchs, near the end of World War II. Less than a month later, on June 16, 1950, David Greenglass, a former Army sergeant stationed at the atom-bomb facility at Los Alamos, New Mexico was arrested on suspicion of espionage. He was charged with passing classified information about the atomic-bomb project (specifically, the "implosion lens," a vital component installed within the atomic bomb dropped on the Japanese at Nagasaki) to Soviet agents through Harry Gold.

David Greenglass and his wife, Ruth, underwent intensive interrogation sessions. FBI chief, J. Edgar Hoover, was convinced they were merely part of an extensive Communist "conspiracy" to deliver American atomic-bomb secrets to Soviet agents including Anatoli Yakovlev. David Greenglass "cracked" and confessed that he had been recruited to an espionage ring by Ruth's brother-in-law, Julius. On July 17, 1950, Julius Rosenberg was arrested and accused of being the mastermind in a major Communist espionage network operating in the United States. On August 11, 1950, Julius' wife, Ethel, was arrested under suspicion of being part of the conspiracy. Finally, an alleged friend of Julius Rosenberg, Morton Sobell, was implicated. He fled to Mexico; was allegedly "kidnapped" by Mexican secret police; and eventually arrested by the FBI in Laredo, Texas.

David Greenglass, Julius and Ethel Rosenberg, Morton Sobell, Harry Gold, and Anatoli Yakovlev were all indicted by a Federal Grand Jury in 1950 for conspiracy to commit espionage. David Greenglass and Harry Gold both pleaded guilty. Anatoli Yakovlev escaped to the Soviet Union. The Rosenbergs and Morton Sobell denied all the allegations and refused to admit to spying.

The trial of Julius and Ethel Rosenberg and Morton Sobell began on the cold grey morning of March 6, 1951 in the Federal Court House in Foley Square, New York City. The prosecution attorney, Irving Saypol; the presiding judge, Irving Kaufman; the defendants; and their chief accusers, David and Ruth Greenglass were all American Jews. The Rosenbergs and Sobell were charged with "conspiracy to commit espionage during wartime" contrary to the Espionage Act of 1917 and in violation of the Atomic Energy Act of 1946. By charging the defendants with "conspiracy to commit espionage" the government did not have to prove that an actual crime took place, only "intent" to commit the crime. By alleging that the conspiracy took place "during wartime" the defendants could receive the death penalty. Privately, government prosecutors hoped that with the death penalty hanging over their heads, the Rosenbergs and Sobell, as a "plea bargain" for a lighter sentence, would reveal the names of other suspected Soviet agents. The public eagerly awaited the expected courtroom drama of Ethel Rosenberg being confronted by her brother, former U.S. Army Sgt. David Greenglass.

You will now have a chance to participate in what the <u>Columbia Law Review</u> called the "outstanding political trial of this generation."

JUDGE
COURT CLERK
BAILIFF

"What I do not understand and simply cannot fathom is why people seek to undermine the country which gave them every opportunity—opportunity for education, opportunity for livelihood, and an opportunity for a fair trial such as they have received here."

—Judge Kaufman

IRVING R. KAUFMAN

JUDGE

You have a reputation as being one of the most competent of Federal judges. You are known as the "boy judge" since you were only 39 years old when appointed to this prestigious government post.

You will be scrupulously fair throughout the trial. You will repeatedly remind the jury that they must avoid any consideration of the defendants' alleged Communist sympathies as direct evidence of guilt. Additionally, they must not draw any conclusions from your courtroom behavior. They must determine the defendants' guilt or innocence solely on the testimony of the witnesses.

Finally, you will tell the jury that their task is to weigh the evidence and determine whether the defendants are guilty of the charges. You alone will determine the sentence. They should not let consideration of your possible sentence (the death penalty is a possibility) affect their evaluation of whether or not the defendants are innocent or guilty.

During the trial you must specifically do the following:

1. Charge the jury explaining their duty to listen carefully to all evidence.
2. Rule on any objections as the prosecution and defense present their witnesses.
3. After both the prosecution and defense have "rested" their cases, again remind the jury of their duty.
4. If the jury finds the defendants "innocent," then declare them "free to go."
5. If the jury finds the defendants "guilty," you must impose a sentence. Possible penalties include: The death penalty, 30 years in prison without parole, or 15 years in prison.

COURT CLERK

You are responsible for assisting Judge Kaufman in running the trial.
You will be expected to do the following:

1. Swear in all witnesses, asking them to place their left hand on the Bible, raise their right hand, and say "Yes" to the statement: "Do you swear to tell the truth, the whole truth, and nothing but the truth, so help you God."

2. Read aloud to the court any documents that Judge Kaufman instructs you to enter into the record, including statements of law and evidence introduced as exhibits.

3. Keep a record of the names of all witnesses offering testimony.

4. Assist the jury in any problems or questions they might have regarding court procedure.

5. Assist Judge Kaufman and the Bailiff in maintaining courtroom order.

BAILIFF

You are responsible for assisting Judge Kaufman in running the trial.
You will be expected to do the following:

1. Escort the defendants into the courtroom and watch them during the trial. They may try to escape!

2. Assist Judge Kaufman in maintaining courtroom order. (Judge Kaufman may have to ask you to escort out of the courtroom unruly witnesses or spectators.)

THE ATTORNEYS

"The significance of a conspiracy to commit espionage takes on an added meaning here where the defendants are charged with having participated in a conspiracy against our country at the most critical hour in its history, in a time of war."

—Irving Saypol

"The charge here is espionage. It is not that they are members of the Communist Party or that they had any interest in Communism."

—Emmanuel Bloch

IRVING SAYPOL
PROSECUTING ATTORNEY

You are a noted government attorney with a history of successful prosecutions of "Communists" for violations of the 1940 Smith Act, which made it a felony to be a member of any organization that advocated overthrow of the U.S. government by the use of force and violence. You also helped convict Alger Hiss. You realize this case will bring considerable notoriety, so it is important that you do an effective job.

It will be your task to convict the defendants, Julius and Ethel Rosenberg and Morton Sobell, of "espionage" and "conspiracy to commit espionage during wartime" against the United States. You feel that the defendants are, in your own words, "guilty of a terrible disloyalty, proof which transcends any emotional consideration and must eliminate any consideration of sympathy." Unless they are willing to "confess" and name other agents, you will demand the death penalty for these crimes.

You must use your witnesses to demonstrate how the defendants devised and put into operation, with the aid of American collaborators and Soviet agents, an elaborate conspiracy that enabled them to obtain wartime classified information about research on the atomic-bomb project. The defendants delivered to the Soviet Union "the information and the weapons they could use to destroy us." You believe that "the identity of some of the other traitors who sold their country down the river, along with the Rosenbergs and Sobell, remains 'undisclosed'" because the "only living people who can supply the details are the defendants."

Your case should specifically focus on the following:

1. The loyalty and allegiance of Julius and Ethel Rosenberg and Morton Sobell was to Communism and the Soviet Union—not their adopted country, the United States.

2. The statements of your witnesses—especially David and Ruth Greenglass, Harry Gold, and Max Elitcher—are entirely believable. Conspirators are most often brought to justice because of the testimony of former associates who have, willingly or not, come over to the government's side.

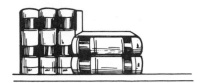

ROY COHN

Assistant Prosecuting Attorney

You are a young aggressive trial lawyer eager to get a successful prosecution under your belt. It will help your career. You will be assisting Irving Saypol in prosecuting the defendants Julius and Ethel Rosenberg and Morton Sobell.

You must use your witnesses to demonstrate how the defendants devised and put into operation, with the aid of American collaborators and Soviet agents, an elaborate conspiracy that enabled them to obtain wartime classified information about research on the atomic-bomb project. The defendants delivered to the Soviet Union "the information and the weapons they could use to destroy us." You believe that "the identity of some of the other traitors who sold their country down the river, along with the Rosenbergs and Sobell, remains 'undiscovered'" because the "only living people who can supply the details are the defendants."

Your case should specifically focus on the following:

1. The loyalty and allegiance of Julius and Ethel Rosenberg and Morton Sobell was to Communism and the Soviet Union—not their adopted country, the United States.

2. The statements of your witnesses—especially David and Ruth Greenglass, Harry Gold, and Max Elitcher—are entirely believable. Conspirators are most often brought to justice because of the testimony of former associates who have, willingly or not, come over to the government's side.

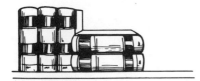

MYLES LANE

Assistant Prosecuting Attorney

You are a young aggressive trial lawyer eager to get a successful prosecution under your belt. It will help your career. You will be assisting Irving Saypol in prosecuting the defendants Julius and Ethel Rosenberg and Morton Sobell.

You must use your witnesses to demonstrate how the defendants devised and put into operation, with the aid of American collaborators and Soviet agents, an elaborate conspiracy that enabled them to obtain wartime classified information about research on the atomic-bomb project. The defendants delivered to the Soviet Union "the information and the weapons they could use to destroy us." You believe that "the identity of some of the other traitors who sold their country down the river, along with the Rosenbergs and Sobell, remains 'undiscovered'" because the "only living people who can supply the details are the defendants."

Your case should specifically focus on the following:

1. The loyalty and allegiance of Julius and Ethel Rosenberg and Morton Sobell was to Communism and the Soviet Union—not their adopted country, the United States.

2. The statements of your witnesses—especially David and Ruth Greenglass, Harry Gold, and Max Elitcher—are entirely believable. Conspirators are most often brought to justice because of the testimony of former associates who have, willingly or not, come over to the government's side.

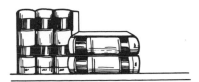

EMMANUEL BLOCH
Defense Attorney

You are the defense attorney for Julius and Ethel Rosenberg. It will be your job to get them acquitted of "espionage" and "conspiracy to commit espionage during wartime." You will need all your best skills as a trial lawyer, since you will have to rely solely on the direct testimony of Julius and Ethel Rosenberg, and the cross-examination of prosecution witnesses. You will be forced into putting Julius and Ethel on the witness stand and leading them through lengthy denials of the stories told by the prosecution witnesses. The Rosenbergs absolutely refuse to allow any of their friends to be called as "character witnesses."

You will try to convince the jury not to be influenced by the hysterical fear of Communism. You will constantly remind them that the defendants are not on trial for their political beliefs.

You will specifically focus on the following:

1. David and Ruth Greenglass are lying. They are implicating the Rosenbergs in David's confessed espionage activities so that David will get a lighter prison sentence. You are personally "revolted" that they would testify against their own relatives to "save their own skins."

2. Harry Gold dealt exclusively with David Greenglass and Anatoli Yakovlev. He really can't directly link Julius Rosenberg into the conspiracy. No direct contact was ever established between Julius Rosenberg and Anatoli Yakovlev.

3. Max Elitcher is obviously an unreliable witness making up fictitious stories. There is no concrete evidence that a conspiracy was established between Julius Rosenberg and Morton Sobell. Julius' association with Sobell and the American Communist Party is not in itself proof of espionage.

4. Elizabeth Bentley cannot really identify the voice of a man calling himself "Julius." There are thousands of people in New York City named "Julius."

5. Harry Gold knew nothing about the Rosenbergs.

6. Whether the Rosenbergs had passport photos taken or not is irrelevant. They never made any attempt to escape the country.

7. The Rosenbergs live a modest life in a small New York apartment. They showed no evidence of receiving money or expensive gifts from the Russians.

8. The Rosenbergs' testimony is more believable than the Greenglasses'. Self-confessed criminals are not reliable witnesses.

9. Ethel Rosenberg never typed any classified documents related to national security or atomic energy.

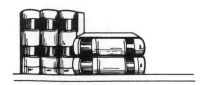

ALEXANDER BLOCH
Assistant Defense Attorney

You are an assistant defense attorney for Julius and Ethel Rosenberg. Your son, Emmanuel, is the defense attorney in charge of the case. It will be your job to get them acquitted of "espionage" and "conspiracy to commit espionage during wartime." You will need all your best skills as a trial lawyer, since you will have to rely solely on the direct testimony of Julius and Ethel Rosenberg, and the cross-examination of prosecution witnesses. You will be forced into putting Julius and Ethel on the witness stand and leading them through lengthy denials of the stories told by the prosecution witnesses. The Rosenbergs absolutely refuse to allow any of their friends to be called as "character witnesses."

You will try to convince the jury not to be influenced by the hysterical fear of Communism. You will constantly remind them that the defendants are not on trial for their political beliefs.

You will specifically focus on the following:

1. David and Ruth Greenglass are lying. They are implicating the Rosenbergs in David's confessed espionage activities so that David will get a lighter prison sentence. You are personally "revolted" that they would testify against their own relatives to "save their own skins."

2. Harry Gold dealt exclusively with David Greenglass and Anatoli Yakovlev. He really can't directly link Julius Rosenberg into the conspiracy. No direct contact was ever established between Julius Rosenberg and Anatoli Yakovlev.

3. Max Elitcher is obviously an unreliable witness making up fictitious stories. There is no concrete evidence that a conspiracy was established between Julius Rosenberg and Morton Sobell. Julius' association with Sobell and the American Communist Party is not in itself proof of espionage.

4. Elizabeth Bentley cannot really identify the voice of a man calling himself "Julius." There are thousands of people in New York City named "Julius."

5. Harry Gold knew nothing about the Rosenbergs.

6. Whether the Rosenbergs had passport photos taken or not is irrelevant. They never made any attempt to escape the country.

7. The Rosenbergs live a modest life in a small New York apartment. They showed no evidence of receiving money or expensive gifts from the Russians.

8. The Rosenbergs' testimony is more believable than the Greenglasses'. Self-confessed criminals are not reliable witnesses.

9. Ethel Rosenberg never typed any classified documents related to national security or atomic energy.

GLORIA AGRIN
Assistant Defense Attorney

You are an assistant defense attorney for Julius and Ethel Rosenberg. It will be your job to get them acquitted of "espionage" and "conspiracy to commit espionage during wartime." You will need all your best skills as a trial lawyer, since you will have to rely solely on the direct testimony of Julius and Ethel Rosenberg, and the cross-examination of prosecution witnesses. You will be forced into putting Julius and Ethel on the witness stand and leading them through lengthy denials of the stories told by the prosecution witnesses. The Rosenbergs absolutely refuse to allow any of their friends to be called as "character witnesses."

You will try to convince the jury not to be influenced by the hysterical fear of Communism. You will constantly remind them that the defendants are not on trial for their political beliefs.

You will specifically focus on the following:

1. David and Ruth Greenglass are lying. They are implicating the Rosenbergs in David's confessed espionage activities so that David will get a lighter prison sentence. You are personally "revolted" that they would testify against their own relatives to "save their own skins."

2. Harry Gold dealt exclusively with David Greenglass and Anatoli Yakovlev. He really can't directly link Julius Rosenberg into the conspiracy. No direct contact was ever established between Julius Rosenberg and Anatoli Yakovlev.

3. Max Elitcher is obviously an unreliable witness making up fictitious stories. There is no concrete evidence that a conspiracy was established between Julius Rosenberg and Morton Sobell. Julius' association with Sobell and the American Communist Party is not in itself proof of espionage.

4. Elizabeth Bentley cannot really identify the voice of a man calling himself "Julius." There are thousands of people in New York City named "Julius."

5. Harry Gold knew nothing about the Rosenbergs.

6. Whether the Rosenbergs had passport photos taken or not is irrelevant. They never made any attempt to escape the country.

7. The Rosenbergs live a modest life in a small New York apartment. They showed no evidence of receiving money or expensive gifts from the Russians.

8. The Rosenbergs' testimony is more believable than the Greenglasses'. Self-confessed criminals are not reliable witnesses.

9. Ethel Rosenberg never typed any classified documents related to national security or atomic energy.

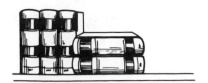

EDWARD KUNTZ
DEFENSE ATTORNEY

You are the defense attorney for Morton Sobell. You are an experienced and aggressive criminal trial lawyer. You will work closely with Emmanuel Bloch and his assistants, but your primary concern will be the acquittal of your client, Morton Sobell.

You should initially appear "puzzled" before the jury. What exactly is the charge against your client? The prosecution has no evidence whatsoever. You don't know why he was even indicted for espionage.

You will repeatedly ask the judge to dismiss the charges against your client because of "lack of evidence."

You may decide not to put Morton Sobell on the witness stand. Remember, it is not necessary for him to testify. A person is "innocent" until proven guilty.

You should focus on the following:

1. Max Elitcher is an unreliable witness. His testimony is unbelievable and flimsy.

2. Morton Sobell's association with the American Communist Party and his friendship with Julius Rosenberg is not evidence of espionage.

3. The fact that your client fled to Mexico was not an admission of guilt, no matter how odd that behavior might seem.

4. There is absolutely no evidence that Morton Sobell had anything to do with David Greenglass and his espionage activities at Los Alamos.

HAROLD PHILLIPS

Assistant Defense Attorney

You are the assistant defense attorney for Morton Sobell. You are an experienced and aggressive criminal trial lawyer. You will work closely with Emmanuel Bloch and his assistants, but your primary concern will be the acquittal of your client, Morton Sobell.

You should initially appear "puzzled" before the jury.

What exactly is the charge against your client? The prosecution has no evidence whatsoever. You don't know why he was even indicted for espionage.

You will repeatedly ask the judge to dismiss the charges against your client because of "lack of evidence."

You may decide not to put Morton Sobell on the witness stand. Remember, it is not necessary for him to testify. A person is "innocent" until proven guilty.

You should focus on the following:

1. Max Elitcher is an unreliable witness. His testimony is unbelievable and flimsy.

2. Morton Sobell's association with the American Communist Party and his friendship with Julius Rosenberg is not evidence of espionage.

3. The fact that your client fled to Mexico was not an admission of guilt, no matter how odd that behavior might seem.

4. There is absolutely no evidence that Morton Sobell had anything to do with David Greenglass and his espionage activities at Los Alamos.

THE DEFENDANTS

"History will record, whether we live or not, that we were victims of the most monstrous frame-up in the history of this country."

—Julius Rosenberg

"I deny guilt."

—Ethel Rosenberg

MORTON SOBELL

DEFENDANT

You are accused of stealing United States secrets about the atomic bomb. You are an alleged member of an espionage conspiracy including Julius and Ethel Rosenberg. The only person with direct evidence against you is your former roommate and friend, Max Elitcher.

You must decide whether to testify in your own behalf. You are "innocent until proven guilty," but if you do not testify, the jury may see this as an admission of guilt.

During the war you were employed by a New York instrument manufacturing company. You were also a member of the American Communist Party.

If you testify, you must be prepared to say the following:

1. You knew Julius Rosenberg in college, but you never discussed the possibilities of committing espionage.

2. You believe that Max Elitcher is making up lies about you merely to "save his own skin."

3. You took your family on a vacation to Mexico in 1950. You were not trying to "escape."

4. While you were in Mexico, you heard that the Rosenbergs had been arrested for spying. You got scared. You feared the FBI would accuse you of spying, too.

5. You will have to admit using various pseudonyms while traveling around Mexico.

6. FBI agents, with the help of the Mexican secret police, illegally captured you in Mexico. They smuggled you over the border into Texas, and you were formally arrested and charged with espionage on August 11, 1950.

7. If in doubt, deny! If you are asked questions about your Communist background you may invoke the "Fifth Amendment" saying, "I refuse to answer on the grounds that it may incriminate me."

297

JULIUS ROSENBERG

Defendant

You are a serious-faced man with a trim black mustache. You are the son of first-generation Russians who emigrated to America after World War I. You grew up in the slums of New York City's lower east side during the Depression. You managed to work your way through college, eventually earning a degree in electrical engineering from the City College of New York. It was at City College that you met and formed a friendship with Morton Sobell.

You married Ethel Greenglass in 1940 and have two young sons. You supported your family through World War II as a civilian junior engineer in the Army Signal Corps. In February of 1945, you lost your job with the Army and went to work for Emerson Radio Corporation in New York City. In the spring of 1946, you became a partner in a small machine shop with Ethel's two brothers—David and Bernard Greenglass.

You will deny every incident related to the alleged espionage scheme. You never knew Anatoli Yakovlev or any other Russian agent. You never received any money or gifts from anyone in exchange for secret government information. You were not even aware of the Los Alamos atomic-bomb project until it was publicly revealed. You never gave any money to either David or Ruth Greenglass.

You will specifically testify to the following:

1. You will admit friendship with Morton Sobell, but deny that you ever plotted espionage with him.

2. You will admit that you were discharged from your job with the Army Signal Corps because of suspicions that you were a member of the American Communist Party.

3. If you are asked about your Communist sympathies, you will say that there are merits to this system of government, but you will completely deny that Communism motivated you to commit espionage against the United States.

4. If you are asked any questions about your alleged American Communist Party membership, you will refuse to answer by taking the "Fifth Amendment." ("I refuse to answer on the grounds that it may incriminate me.")

5. You will deny everything said by David and Ruth Greenglass. You never had any transactions involving secret code words or a divided Jell-O box.

6. You never sent Harry Gold as a messenger to David Greenglass in New Mexico. You don't even know what he looks like. You didn't even know, in 1944, that David was working at Los Alamos, New Mexico.

7. You never had any associations related to espionage with Max Elitcher and Morton Sobell.

8. You will claim that you and your wife have a modest apartment at Knickerbocker Village in New York City. Your rent is 51 dollars a month. You never had an expensive console table with a hollowed out interior allegedly given to you by the Russians. You had a cheap table purchased from Macy's department store.

JULIUS ROSENBERG

9. You will deny receiving any lens mold diagrams and secret documents from David Greenglass in your apartment. Your wife Ethel never typed any secret documents for transmission to Soviet agents.

10. You never gave any money to David or Ruth Greenglass to use in an alleged escape plan involving a flight to Mexico City, Stockholm, and finally the Soviet Union.

11. You never had any passport photos taken prior to your arrest in 1950, and you never contemplated fleeing the country.

12. If in doubt, *deny every charge* or take "the Fifth Amendment."

ETHEL ROSENBERG
Defendant

You are a little woman with soft and pleasant features. Like your husband, Julius, you grew up in the tough slums of the lower east side of New York City. Life was difficult for you during the Depression. After graduation from high school in 1931, you worked as a clerk in a local retail store. You lived at home with your parents until you met Julius Rosenberg.

You married Julius in 1940 and moved into a small apartment in Knickerbocker Village in New York City. Between the years 1940 and 1945 you gave birth to two sons and performed all the chores and duties of a housewife and mother. You are a talented singer. In the "class prophecy" section of your high school yearbook it said that in 1950 you would be "America's leading actress."

You will testify to the following:

1. You will deny any knowledge of Harry Gold, Anatoli Yakovlev, or any other Russian agents, always maintaining that you are just an average housewife.

2. Neither you nor your husband had any contact with Max Elitcher.

3. Your husband spoke about Morton Sobell as a college friend, but you never met him.

4. You will testify that you and your husband always had a good relationship with your brother, David Greenglass, and his wife, Ruth. You do not understand why they are trying to incriminate you and your husband.

5. You will completely deny typing any information for your husband about an atomic weapon. You only used your personal typewriter to type your husband's engineering reports and personal letters.

ETHEL ROSENBERG

6. The fancy console table in your living room (later stored in a closet) was merely a piece of furniture purchased at Macy's department store. It certainly was not a gift from the Russians.

7. You lived a modest lifestyle. You employed a part-time maid for a brief period following the birth of your second child. You were ill during that period and needed help with the housework.

8. You never had any passport photos taken prior to your arrest in 1950, and you never contemplated fleeing the country.

9. You are a loyal citizen of the United States and did not commit espionage.

10. If you are asked any questions about your alleged American Communist Party membership, you will refuse to answer by taking the "Fifth Amendment." ("I refuse to answer on the grounds that it may incriminate me.")

PROSECUTION WITNESSES

"I come from Julius."

—Harry Gold

"The identity of some of the other traitors who sold their country down the river along with Rosenberg and Sobell remains undisclosed."

—Irving Saypol

MAX ELITCHER

WITNESS FOR THE PROSECUTION

You were a boyhood friend of Morton Sobell. You both attended City College of New York City, where you became acquainted with Julius Rosenberg. After graduating from college, you moved to Washington, D.C., where you found work as an electronics engineer with the U.S. Naval Bureau of Ordnance.

You will accuse Julius Rosenberg and Morton Sobell of trying to enlist you in an espionage conspiracy. You will say that you never passed any information to them.

You will be very cooperative all during the trial. You are a former member of the Communist Party. The prosecution knows that you must have lied about your Communist affiliations when you took your loyalty oath prior to accepting work with the Navy. You are fearful they may decide to indict you for this crime.

You will testify to the following:

1. You worked for the U.S. Navy Bureau of Ordnance for ten years beginning in 1938. Morton Sobell also worked for this agency.

2. You shared an apartment in Washington, D.C. with Morton Sobell.

3. You and Sobell both joined the American Communist Party. You will claim that Sobell convinced you that this was the proper thing to do.

4. On several occasions, while you were roommates, Sobell spoke to you about the possibilities your job offered to commit espionage. On one occasion early in the war—you can not recall the exact date—you saw Sobell meeting with Julius Rosenberg.

5. In September 1941, Sobell left Washington to get his master's degree at the University of Michigan. You remained at your job with the Navy.

6. In June 1944, you were contacted by Julius Rosenberg. He asked if he could meet at your apartment to discuss some important matters. You agreed.

7. Rosenberg came to your home a few nights later. He told you that many dedicated Communists were involved in passing classified information to the Soviet Union. He indicated that your friend Morton Sobell was part of this espionage conspiracy. He asked for your help. You refused to give him a definite answer. You said that you would "think about it."

8. You will admit that on one occasion, while you were in New York City in late 1944, you delivered a roll of 35mm film from Sobell to Julius Rosenberg. You did not know what was on the film.

HARRY GOLD

WITNESS FOR THE PROSECUTION

You have already been tried for espionage and sentenced to thirty years in prison. You have agreed to testify for the prosecution in the hope that you will get an early parole.

You are a chemist who worked for a research and development laboratory on Long Island, New York. You were arrested in Philadelphia on May 23, 1950, based on information supplied by a Soviet spy captured in England, Dr. Klaus Fuchs. You later confessed, during your trial, to working for the Soviets as far back as 1935.

You will testify to the following:

1. In the spring of 1945, a Soviet agent named Anatoli Yakovlev contacted you and ordered you to go to Albuquerque, New Mexico.

2. You were told to meet a man named David Greenglass and receive information about a secret weapon that was being developed at Los Alamos.

3. Yakovlev gave you a sheet of paper on which was typed the name "Greenglass," an address in Albuqueque, and the password "I come from Julius."

4. He also gave you a piece of a Jell-O box, cut in an odd shape, and told you that Greenglass would have the other half.

5. You arrived in Albuqueque on Sunday morning, June 3, and registered at the Hilton Hotel. You signed your own name on the hotel registry card, which was then stamped on the front with the date, June 3, 1945.

6. That morning you went to David Greenglass' house and knocked on the door. It was opened by a man about 23 years old. You said: "I come from Julius." Then you showed him your half of the Jell-O box. Greenglass picked up a woman's handbag and took out a piece of a Jell-O box. The two parts fit exactly.

7. Greenglass then told you he would have the information about the bomb ready in a few hours.

8. You left and came back in two hours. Greenglass gave you a folder with several documents.

9. Two days later you turned the information over to Yakovlev in New York City.

DR. WALTER KOSKI

WITNESS FOR THE PROSECUTION

You are a professor at Johns Hopkins and also work for the Brookhaven Laboratory. During World War II, you worked at Los Alamos as a research chemist, specializing in the theories of implosion. You were a member of the scientific team that created the first atom bomb. You have been called to explain the significance of the information that David Greenglass provided to the defendant, Julius Rosenberg.

You will testify to the following:

1. While at Los Alamos, you and other scientists designed possible "lens molds" for testing. The procedure was as follows: You would bring these plans to the Theta machine shop, where David Greenglass was the foreman, and, under his supervision, they would be made into actual molds.

2. The "lens mold" was a metal device that "shaped" explosive charges so that their force was directed along a particular path and in a manner that could be understood mathematically.

3. In your opinion, David Greenglass was just a plain "machinist," but the sketches he made of the lens mold did "illustrate the important principle involved." They certainly revealed that atomic research was being conducted at Los Alamos.

DAVID GREENGLASS

Witness for the Prosecution

You are Ethel Rosenberg's brother. In June 1950 you were arrested by the FBI for suspicion of espionage. After intensive questioning, you confessed. You are technically on the indictment that includes Julius and Ethel Rosenberg and Morton Sobell. Only ten days before the trial, you agreed to testify against the Rosenbergs, hoping that it would get you a lighter sentence.

You will present a picture of a young man recruited into a Communist espionage conspiracy by a respected brother-in-law. You will say that you did not want to commit espionage. You only agreed because of the constant and repeated pressure by Julius and his wife, your sister Ethel. After all, Julius often told you that the Russians were paying the school tuition of a number of young scientists in the United States. Why shouldn't you get something, too?

You will answer questions about your work at Los Alamos; your recruitment into espionage by the Rosenbergs; your meeting with Harry Gold; and Rosenberg's attempts to make you flee the country.

You will specifically testify to the following:

1. You were first enticed to commit espionage by Julius Rosenberg in 1944 when you were working for the Army as a machinist on the Los Alamos atomic energy project. You will say that Ethel Rosenberg told your wife, Ruth, sometime in November 1944, that Julius has finally gotten to the point where he is doing what he wanted to do all along, which was that he was giving information to the Soviet Union.

2. Part of your job in New Mexico involved assembling instruments crucial to the construction of an atomic bomb.

3. While on leave in New York City, you drew a sketch for Julius of a high explosive lens mold. This was part of the triggering mechanism of the atomic bomb. You also agreed to supply Julius with more information when you returned to Los Alamos.

4. Julius took a Jell-O box and cut it in half. He kept one half and gave the other piece to you. He said that the agent he sent to Los Alamos would have his half of the box.

5. On Sunday morning, June 3, 1945, Harry Gold knocked at your apartment door in New Mexico. He asked if you were Mr. Greenglass. He said: "Julius sent me." He showed you his half of the Jell-O box. It matched yours perfectly. You asked him to come back later that afternoon, and you would give him some documents.

DAVID GREENGLASS

6. He returned that afternoon and you gave him two more lens mold sketches and some written material about the atomic bomb project.

7. In September 1945, while you were in New York City, you drew a sketch of the atomic bomb and prepared a twelve-page written report containing your knowledge about its construction. You gave this report to Julius in their apartment. He looked over the papers and said: "This is very interesting. We ought to have this typed immediately."

8. You saw him hand the papers to his wife, Ethel. She went to a console table in the living room and began typing the documents. While Ethel was typing, Julius bragged to you that the attractive console table was "a gift from the Russians." He showed you the hollowed out interior used to store secret documents.

9. After the arrest of Harry Gold by the FBI, Julius urged you and your wife to flee the country. He gave you money (several thousand dollars), and told you to have passport photos taken. He suggested an elaborate escape plan that would involve first fleeing to Mexico City, then Stockholm, and finally, the Soviet Union.

RUTH GREENGLASS

WITNESS FOR THE PROSECUTION

You are the wife of David Greenglass, a confessed agent for the Soviet Union. You have not been indicted by the government, although you are probably just as guilty. You hope that by testifying against the Rosenbergs, your husband will get a lighter sentence for his role in the espionage conspiracy.

You will testify to the following:

1. Everything your husband said about the Rosenbergs' involvement in espionage was true.

2. You overheard many conversations in which Julius Rosenberg spoke to your husband about espionage.

3. You saw Julius Rosenberg accept the lens mold sketches from your husband in New York City. You remember them discussing a method of identification using a divided Jell-O box.

4. You recall your husband answering the door of your New Mexico home on June 3, 1945 and Harry Gold being admitted. You heard him say "Julius sent me." Later you saw your husband turn over several documents to him.

5. You will say that while you and your husband were in New York in September 1945, you visited the Rosenbergs in the living room of their Knickerbocker Village apartment.

6. You saw your husband give Julius Rosenberg several documents. Julius took the information into the bathroom and read it. When he came out he called Ethel and told her to type this information immediately.

7. Ethel then sat down at the typewriter, which he had placed on a console table in the living room, and proceeded to type the documents.

8. Julius always wanted your husband's documents typed because David's handwriting was very poor.

9. After the arrest of Harry Gold, your husband suggested that you both flee to Mexico. He said that Julius urged him to make a quick escape before the FBI tracked him down. He gave him some money and also told him to have passport photos made.

10. You will say that your husband is a good man. He never would have committed espionage if it had not been for the pressure from his sister Ethel and her husband, Julius Rosenberg.

ELIZABETH BENTLEY

WITNESS FOR THE PROSECUTION

You are a confessed ex-Communist and a former agent for the Soviet Union. The newspapers have labelled you the "Red Spy Queen" and some have even alleged that you are a "professional informer." You realize that spying for the Russians was deeply wrong. Your testimony should show how membership in the American Communist Party can lead to espionage. You can be trusted to "remember" the names of American Communist Party members, unsubstantiated details about spies, and lots of unproven information about all kinds of clandestine Communist activities.

You will specifically testify to the following:

1. While you were an operating agent for the Russians, you received several phone calls from a man who identified himself as "Julius." However, you never met him personally and cannot identify his voice.

2. You remember one occasion when you drove with an unidentified Soviet agent to a street near Knickerbocker Village in New York City. He told you to wait in the car while he picked up "some material from a contact, an engineer." He never mentioned the person's exact name.

3. Later that week you received a phone call in your New York apartment from a person named "Julius." You transmitted his coded message to another Soviet agent.

309

EVELYN COX

WITNESS FOR THE PROSECUTION

You are the Rosenbergs' former African-American part-time maid. You worked for the defendants after Mrs. Rosenberg had her second child. You are being asked to testify about the unusual console table in the Rosenbergs' Knickerbocker Village apartment.

You will testify to the following:

1. You remember an unusual console table in the Rosenbergs' living room. It seemed to be the best piece of furniture in their modest apartment.

2. You heard Ethel Rosenberg comment that it was "a gift from a friend."

3. One day you noticed that it had been put away in a closet. You were curious and asked Mrs. Rossenberg why. She only said that it was "too large for the living room." This seemed "odd" but you said nothing.

4. You will admit that you always found the Rosenbergs to be very pleasant people. You never heard anything related to spying or espionage.

 -

BEN SCHNEIDER

WITNESS FOR THE PROSECUTION

You are a New York City photographer. Your store is located at 99 Park Row in Knickerbocker Village, near the Rosenbergs' apartment. Your testimony will directly refute Julius Rosenberg's statements that he never visited a photographer in 1949-50, prior to his arrest.

You will testify to the following:

1. You will claim that you "specialize" in passport photography. But, you will have to admit that you don't have a sign on the outside of your shop indicating that passport photos are a specialty.

2. You remember Julius and Ethel Rosenberg and their two children coming to your Foley Square store on a Saturday. You think it was in either May or June of 1950. It stands out in your memory because of two things. First, it was a Saturday and business for passports is usually slow on that day. Second, the Rosenbergs' kids were very poorly behaved.

3. They ordered three dozen passport photos at a cost of nine dollars. You thought this was quite a large amount and asked Mr. Rosenberg why he needed so many. He said that he needed several travel documents for a trip to France. He said he was going there to "settle an estate."

EXHIBITS

"Ridiculous, a baby drawing, it doesn't tell you anything."

—Victor Weisskopf, professor of physics at MIT commenting on A-bomb sketch by David Greenglass

THE TRUMAN LOYALTY ORDER
March 22, 1947
(Federal Register, Vol. 12, p. 135, edited version)

PART I sec. 1   There shall be a loyalty investigation of every person entering the civilian employment of any department or agency of the Executive Branch of the Federal Government.

PART V sec. 1   The standard for the refusal of employment or the removal from employment in an executive department or agency on grounds relating to loyalty shall be that, on evidence, reasonable grounds exist for the belief that the person involved is disloyal to the government of the United States.

PART V sec. 2   Activities and associations of an applicant or employee which may be considered in connection with the determination of disloyalty may include one or more of the following:

A. Sabotage, espionage, or attempts or preparations therefore, knowingly associating with spies or saboteurs;

B. Treason or sedition or advocacy thereof;

C. Intentional unauthorized disclosure to any person, under any circumstances which may indicate disloyalty to the U.S., or documents or information of a confidential or non-public character obtained by the person making the disclosure as a result of his employment by the Government of the U.S.

D. Membership in, affiliation with or sympathetic association with any foreign or domestic organization, association, movement, group or combination of persons, designated by the Attorney-General as totalitarian, Fascist, Communist, or subversive, or as having adopted a policy of violence to deny other persons their rights under the Constitution of the United States, or as seeking to alter the form of Government of the U.S. by unconstitutional means.

A diagram of a portion of the atomic bomb drawn by Dr. Klaus Fuchs showing the array of spherical components of the bomb. It reveals how its high-explosive outer layers are arranged to generate a spherically symmetric, inwardly converging detonation wave, which in turn causes rapid compression of the uranium tamper and the plutonium within it. It contains specific calculations—deleted by the FBI—which show the progressively decreasing radius of the core. When it was shown to an expert, he said: "It's the real thing."

David Greenglass allegedly drew a similar diagram for Julius Rosenberg.

EXHIBIT C

ESPIONAGE CONSPIRACY

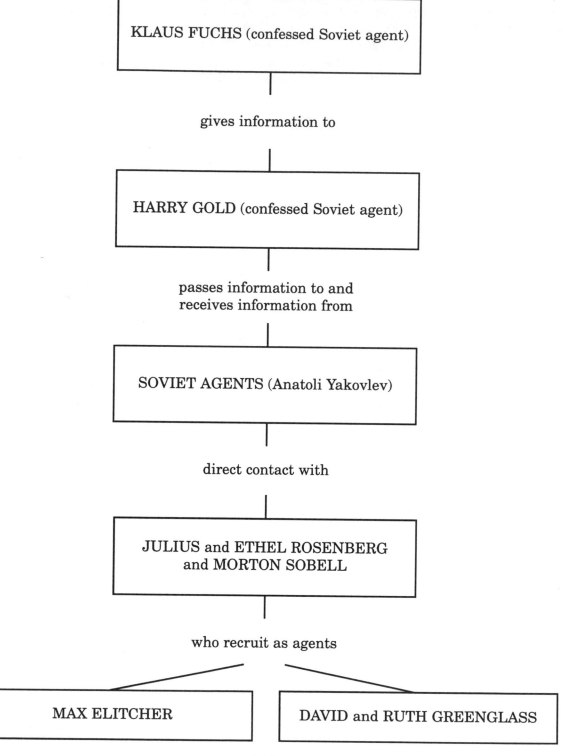

KLAUS FUCHS (confessed Soviet agent)

gives information to

HARRY GOLD (confessed Soviet agent)

passes information to and
receives information from

SOVIET AGENTS (Anatoli Yakovlev)

direct contact with

JULIUS and ETHEL ROSENBERG
and MORTON SOBELL

who recruit as agents

MAX ELITCHER

DAVID and RUTH GREENGLASS

McCARRAN INTERNAL SECURITY ACT
September 23, 1950
(Public Law 831, 81st Congress, edited portion)

<u>AN ACT</u>

To protect the United States against certain un-American and subversive activities by requiring registration of Communist organizations, and for other purposes.

Sec. 2 As a result of evidence adduced before various committees of the Senate and House of Representatives, the Congress hereby finds that—

(1) There exists a world Communist movement which, in its origins, its development, and its present practice, is a world-wide revolutionary movement whose purpose it is, by treachery, deceit, infiltration into other groups (governmental and otherwise), espionage, sabotage, terrorism, and any other means deemed necessary to establish a Communist totalitarian dictatorship in the countries throughout the world through the medium of a world-wide Communist organization . . .

(4) The direction and control of the world Communist movement is vested in and exercised by the Communist dictatorship of a foreign country.

(5) The Communist movement in the United States is an organization numbering thousands of adherents, rigidly and ruthlessly disciplined. Awaiting and seeking to advance a moment when the United States may be so far extended by foreign engagements, so far divided in counsel, or so far in industrial or financial straits, that overthrow of the Government of the United States by force and violence may seem possible of achievement . . .

THE ATOMIC ENERGY COMMISSION
August 1, 1946
(Public Law 585, 79th Congress, 2nd Session)

<u>AN ACT</u>

For the development and control of atomic energy

Section 10 (3) Whoever, with intent to injure the United States or with intent to secure an advantage to any foreign nation, acquires or attempts or conspires to acquire any document, writing, sketch, photograph, plan, model, instrument, appliance, note or information involving or incorporating restricted data shall, upon conviction thereof, be punished by death or imprisonment for life (but life may be imposed only in recommendation of the jury and only in cases where the offense was committed with intent to injure the United States); or by a fine of not more than $20,000 or imprisonment for not more than twenty years, or both.

No: 65841

HILTON HOTEL
Albuquerque, New Mexico

RECEIVED
JUN 4 12:36 pm '45

Hilton Hotel
Alburguerque

NAME _____ Harry Golb _____

RESERVATION DATE _6-3-45_ ROOM _1001_

TIME OF CHECK IN _1 50_ CLERK _9A_

EXPECTED LENGTH OF STAY _until 8 P.M_

318

ADDITIONAL INFORMATION

"Ethel! Don't be scared if some clown tells you we may be taken to the death house tonight! Everything will be alright—they can't do that."

—Julius Rosenberg

"There is no question that if Julius Rosenberg would furnish the details of his extensive espionage activities, it would be possible to proceed against other individuals."

—J. Edgar Hoover

MASTER ROLE SHEET

NAME	ROLE	STUDENT NAME
Irving R. Kaufman	Judge	_____
Irving Saypol	Prosecuting Attorney	_____
Roy Cohn	Prosecuting Attorney	_____
Myles Lane	Prosecuting Attorney	_____
Rosenbergs' Defense Attorneys		
Emmanuel Bloch	Defense Attorney	_____
Alexander Bloch	Defense Attorney	_____
Gloria Agrin	Defense Attorney	_____
Sobell's Defense Attorneys		
Edward Kuntz	Defense Attorney	_____
Harold Phillips	Defense Attorney	_____
Julius Rosenberg	Defendant	_____
Ethel Rosenberg	Defendant	_____
Morton Sobell	Defendant	_____
Harry Gold	Prosecution Witness	_____
David Greenglass	Prosecution Witness	_____
Dr. Walter Koski	Prosecution Witness	_____
Ruth Greenglass	Prosecution Witness	_____
Max Elitcher	Prosecution Witness	_____
Elizabeth Bentley	Prosecution Witness	_____
Ben Schneider	Prosecution Witness	_____
	Court Clerk	_____
	Court Bailiff	_____
	Newspaper Reporter	_____
	Newspaper Reporter	_____

MASTER ROLE SHEET, continued

NAME	ROLE	STUDENT NAME
	The Jury[*]	
	Juror One	_____
	Juror Two	_____
	Juror Three	_____
	Juror Four	_____
	Juror Five	_____
	Juror Six	_____
	Juror Seven	_____
	Juror Eight	_____
	Juror Nine	_____
	Juror Ten	_____
	Juror Eleven	_____
	Juror Twelve	_____

[*]The jury included ten white males (three auditors, two accountants, one estimator, one sales manager, one caterer, one restaurant owner, one retired civil servant), one African-American electrician, and one housewife.

TRIAL PROCEDURE

1. Judge Kaufman enters the court and "all rise."

2. Judge Kaufman "charges" the jury with their obligation to hear the evidence and render a verdict.

3. The defendants rise and the clerk reads the charges. They enter a plea of "guilty" or "not guilty" to the charges.

4. Prosecution gives its opening remarks.

5. Defense gives its opening remarks.

6. Presentation of prosecution witnesses: direct testimony and then cross-examination.

7. Presentation of defense witnesses: direct testimony and then cross-examination.

8. Rebuttal witnesses or recall of witnesses (*optional*).

9. Prosecution gives its closing remarks.

10. Defense gives its closing remarks.

11. Judge Kaufman reminds the jury of their obligations to render a fair verdict based on the evidence.

12. Jury deliberation.

13. Jury renders a verdict: "guilty" or "not guilty."

14. If the defendants are found "not guilty," they are declared "free to go." If the defendants are found "guilty," Judge Kaufman may sentence them to one of the following punishments:

Death in the electric chair.

Life in prison.

30 years in prison with no parole.

SUGGESTED COURTROOM SET-UP

CLERK AND BAILIFF	JUDGE	WITNESS STAND

DEFENSE ATTORNEY(S) AND DEFENDANTS	PROSECUTION ATTORNEY(S)	JURY

WITNESSES AND SPECTATORS

LEGAL TERMS

CONSPIRACY A combination of two or more persons to commit a criminal or unlawful act, or to commit a lawful act by criminal or unlawful means; or a combination of two or more persons by concerted action to accomplish an unlawful purpose or some purpose not in itself unlawful by unlawful means. It is essential that there be two or more conspirators; one cannot conspire with himself or herself.

CONSPIRATOR One involved in a conspiracy; one who acts with another, or others, in furtherance of an unlawful transaction. It is not necessary that all of the conspirators either meet together or agree simultaneously. It is not necessary that each member of a conspiracy know the exact part that every other participant is playing; nor is it necessary in order to be bound by the acts of his or her associates that each member of a conspiracy shall know all the other participants therein; nor is it requisite that simultaneous action be had for those who come on later, and cooperate in the common effort to obtain the unlawful results, to become parties thereto and assume responsibility for all that has been done before.

ESPIONAGE The practice of spying.

FIFTH AMENDMENT The amendment to the U.S. Constitution, part of the Bill of Rights, that establishes certain protections for citizens from actions of the government by providing that (a) a person shall not be required to answer for a capital or other infamous crime unless an indictment or presentment is first issued by a grand jury; (b) no person will be placed in double jeopardy; (c) no person may be required to testify against himself; (d) that neither life, liberty nor property may be taken without due process of law; and (e) private property may not be taken for public use, without payment of just compensation.

SPY One who secretly tries to obtain information for his or her own country in the territory of an enemy country.

TREASON The crime of adhering to the enemy and rendering the enemy aid and comfort. Under the U.S. Constitution, treason may only consist of levying war against the United States or adhering to its enemies and giving them aid and comfort, and a person may only be convicted of treason upon the testimony of two witnesses to the same overt act or on a confession in open court.

SUBPOENA

YOU are hereby commanded to appear in the *UNITED STATES FEDERAL COURT*, sitting for the *SOUTHERN DISTRICT* of *NEW YORK*, on the date and time specified below.

Please appear on _____ at _____.
           (date)   (time)

Oyez, Oyez!

WHEREAS, The Federal Court for the Southern District of the State of New York *SUMMONS YOU,* _____, to the trial of the United States v. Julius Rosenberg, Ethel Rosenberg, and Morton Sobell, on the charges of *ESPIONAGE* and *CONSPIRACY TO COMMIT ESPIONAGE;*

and, *WHEREAS,* in the United States of America, such charges may be brought only in the presence of, and given into the judgment of, *A JURY OF PEERS,*

YOU are herewith *DIRECTED* and *ORDERED* to *PRESENT YOURSELF* to the attorneys practicing in the case instant for the purpose of *IMPANELMENT* as a member of the sitting *JURY.*

Failure to appear will result in one or all of the following: serious academic suffering, total grounding, or detention.

This *SUBPOENA* must be brought with you to the Federal Court for the Southern District of the State of New York, currently sitting in Room _____.

APPROVED by the *HONORABLE JUDGE KAUFMAN*, Presiding Judge.

SIGNED and *SEALED* this day _____.

_____
(clerk of the court)

JURY EVALUATION SHEET

Prosecution Witnesses

NAME	TOLD THE TRUTH	MOSTLY TOLD THE TRUTH	LIED
Max Elitcher	❑	❑	❑
Harry Gold	❑	❑	❑
David Greenglass	❑	❑	❑
Ruth Greenglass	❑	❑	❑
Dr. Koski	❑	❑	❑
Elizabeth Bentley	❑	❑	❑
Evelyn Cox	❑	❑	❑
Ben Schnieder	❑	❑	❑

Defense Witnesses

NAME	TOLD THE TRUTH	MOSTLY TOLD THE TRUTH	LIED
Morton Sobell	❑	❑	❑
Julius Rosenberg	❑	❑	❑
Ethel Rosenberg	❑	❑	❑

JURY EVALUATION SHEET, continued

The most convincing evidence against the defendants was: _____

_____

_____

The most convincing evidence for the defendants was: _____

_____

_____

I believe Morton Sobell is (guilty, not guilty) because: _____

_____

_____

I believe Julius Rosenberg is (guilty, not guilty) because: _____

_____

_____

I believe Ethel Rosenberg is (guilty, not guilty) because:_____

_____

_____

CHRONOLOGY

September 1949 —The Soviet Union explodes its first atomic bomb.

February 2, 1950 —Klaus Fuchs, a British physicist, is arrested in England. Fuchs admits passing atom bomb information to an American agent working for the Soviet Union. A week later Senator Joe McCarthy makes a speech in Wheeling, West Virginia, beginning the "McCarthy Era."

May 23, 1950 —Harry Gold, a chemist from Philadelphia, is arrested by the FBI and charged with espionage. Gold admits that he was the agent who received the atom bomb secrets from Fuchs near the end of World War II.

June 16, 1950 —David Greenglass, a former Army sergeant stationed at the atom-bomb facility at Los Alamos, is arrested. He is charged with passing secret information about the atomic-bomb project to Soviet agents through the confessed spy Harry Gold.

July 17, 1950 —Julius Rosenberg is arrested. The head of the FBI, J. Edgar Hoover, alleges that Rosenberg is another link in the Soviet espionage network operating in the United States.

August 11, 1950 —Ethel Rosenberg is arrested and charged, along with her husband, with espionage and conspiracy to commit espionage.

August 18, 1950 —Morton Sobell is arrested in Laredo, Texas, just over the border from Mexico. He is charged with espionage. He claims he was kidnapped by the Mexican secret police.

March 6, 1951 —The trial of Julius and Ethel Rosenberg and Morton Sobell begins in New York with Judge Irving Kaufman presiding. The charge is "espionage" and "conspiracy to commit espionage during wartime."

March 29, 1951 —All three defendants are found guilty.

April 5, 1951 —Judge Kaufman sentences the Rosenbergs to death and Sobell to thirty years in prison.

June 19, 1953 —After many appeals, Julius and Ethel Rosenberg are executed in the electric chair.

AFTERMATH

On April 5, 1951 Judge Kaufman sentenced Julius and Ethel Rosenberg to die in the electric chair. He sentenced Morton Sobell to thirty years in prison with a recommendation of no parole. He described their crimes as "worse than murder" since these conspirators had put the A-bomb in Russian hands, leading to Communist aggression in Korea, with its thousands of American casualties.

The next day he sentenced David Greenglass to fifteen years in prison. He was released from jail in 1960 after serving less than two-thirds of his sentence.

Julius and Ethel Rosenberg were executed in the electric chair on June 19, 1953. They maintained their innocence to the end.

Despite Judge Kaufman's recommendation, Morton Sobell was eventually paroled in 1964. He wrote a book, *On Doing Time*, in which he proclaimed his (and the Rosenbergs') innocence.

Harry Gold was released from prison in 1965. He was awarded the "Order of the Red Star" by the Soviet Union.

DISCUSSION QUESTIONS

1. Did the Rosenbergs and Sobell receive a fair trial? Why or why not?

2. What was the most convincing evidence against the defendants? What was the least believable evidence?

3. The Rosenbergs and Sobell were accused of conspiracy to commit espionage. Do you think there is evidence to support the theory that there was a conspiracy by the FBI and other government agencies "to get" the Rosenbergs and Sobell?

4. How were the lives of the Rosenbergs and their chief accusers interconnected? Explain.

5. What role, if any, did the fear of worldwide communism and the Soviet Union play in this trial?

6. Do you think the threat of long prison sentences or the death penalty motivated the Rosenbergs' accusers? Explain.

7. Most scientists today dismiss the information provided by confessed Soviet spies like David Greenglass and Klaus Fuchs as nearly useless in the construction of an atomic bomb. Does that make the death penalty for the Rosenbergs seem unjust? Why or why not? Do you think they would have received such a harsh penalty today? Why or why not?

8. Do you think the prosecution of the Rosenbergs and the efforts to make them reveal names of other agents amounted to a "witch hunt" similar to what happened at Salem in 1692? Explain the similarities and differences.

BIBLIOGRAPHY

Commager, Henry Steele (ed.). *Documents of American History, Vol II.* NY: Appleton-Century-Crofts, 1968.

Fineberg, S. Andhil. *The Rosenberg Case: Fact and Fiction.* NY: Oceana Publications, 1953.

Goldstein, Alvin H. *The Unquiet Death of Julius and Ethel Rosenberg.* NY: Lawrence Hill and Co., 1975.

Herken, Gregg. *The Winning Weapon: The Atomic Bomb in the Cold War.* NY: Alfred Knopf, 1980.

Hyde, H. Montgomery. *The Atom Bomb Spies.* NY: Ballantine Books, 1980.

Lamphere, Robert. *The FBI-KGB War.* NY: Berkley Books, 1986.

Meeropol, Robert and Michael. *We Are Your Sons.* NY: Ballantine Books, 1975.

Philipson, Ilene. *Ethel Rosenberg: Beyond the Myths.* NY: Franklin Watts, 1988.

Root, Jonathan. *The Betrayers: The Rosenberg Case—A Reappraisal of an American Crisis.* NY: Coward-McCann Inc., 1963.

Schneir, Walter and Miriam. *Invitation to an Inquest.* Baltimore: Penguin Books, 1973.

Sharlitt, Joseph H. *Fatal Error: The Miscarriage of Justice that Sealed the Rosenberg's Fate.* NY: Charles Schribner's Sons, 1989.

Sobell, Morton. *On Doing Time.* NY: Charles Scribner & Sons, 1973.

Wexley, John. *The Judgement of Julius and Ethel Rosenberg.* NY: Cameron and Kahn, 1955.